INTOXIC

Southern France

*Uncorking the Magic in the French Riviera,
Provence, Languedoc, Dordogne, and Bordeaux*

PJ ADAMS

Intoxicating Southern France: Uncorking the Magic in the French Riviera, Provence, Languedoc, Dordogne, and Bordeaux

For information: www.meanderingtrailmedia.com

Editor: Andrea Glass
Developmental Editor: Shaun Griffen
Interior Design: Rachal Cox

Manufactured in the United States of America
The Library of Congress has catalogued the paperback edition as follows:

Adams, P. J., 1952-

Intoxicating Southern France : uncorking the magic in the French Riviera, Provence, Languedoc, Dordogne, and Bordeaux / P J Adams. -- Rancho Mission Viejo, CA : Meandering Trail Media/PJ Adams Books, [2015]

pages ; cm.

ISBN: 13-digit: 978-0-9895162-2-8 ; 10-digit: 0-9895162-2-9 ; 978-0-9895162-3-5 (ebook)

Summary: PJ Adams, who uncorked the magic of Paris in "Intoxicating Paris" is back with another quirky journey. She explores the magic of the French Riviera and Provence, then takes us through the wilds of the Languedoc, across medieval Dordogne, to the renowned vineyards of Bordeaux. Fabulous food, fine wine, formidable history, fantastic fortresses, and fascinating friends tell the story of this exhilarating journey through Southern France.
—Publisher.

1. France, Southern—Guidebooks
3. Provence (France)--Guidebooks.
5. Dordogne (France)—Guidebooks.
7. France, Southern—Description and travel.
9. Provence (France)—Description and travel.
11. Dordogne (France)—Description and travel.
13. Americans—France, Southern—Guidebooks.

2. Riviera (France)—Guidebooks.
4. Languedoc (France)—Guidebooks.
6. Bordeaux (Aquitaine, France)—Guidebooks.
8. Riviera (France)—Description and travel.
10. Languedoc (France)—Description and travel.
12. Bordeaux (Aquitaine, France) Description and travel.
14. France, Southern—Social life and customs.

I. Title.

For Ashley, John, and France lovers everywhere

Contents

Introduction

Sipping chilled champagne in Monaco as we gaze across the rippling Mediterranean. Picking lavender from the sunny fields of Provence. Surveying a sea of vines from the turrets of fortified Carcassonne. Striding the Roman arena in Nîmes. Spelunking the deep caverns of Lascaux and Pech Merle. Ascending in a Rocamadour hot-air balloon over the medieval castles along the Dordogne. Savoring a legendary *cassoulet* in Toulouse-Lautrec's Albi. Descending into a 300-year-old Medoc wine cellar, then toasting with goblets of legendary Bordeaux *grands crus*.

These are some of the delights we'll explore in *Intoxicating Southern France*—a coast-to-coast journey through the regions of Southern France. We'll begin first on the French Riviera, home to sunny beaches, famous resorts, the dazzling Cannes Film Festival, and royal Monaco where gambling is king and starlet Grace Kelly became a princess.

We'll move on to lovely Provence and the lavender-scented hill towns of Gordes and Ménerbes where some of the most charming people in France call their home. From there we'll head to Van Gogh's much-loved Arles, then on to medieval Les-Baux-de-Provence and the vast Camargue—home to feisty black bulls and wild white horses.

Next, we'll meander through the grand Languedoc where Roman might lives on in the Pont du Gard and Nîmes's Roman amphitheater, then on to lovely Albi where Toulouse-Lautrec was reared, and crag-perched Cordes-sur-Ciel, a medieval village in the sky.

From there we'll enter mythical Périgord where kings have prayed for miracles in Rocamadour and where the winding Dordogne River splits the land between warring 14th century Castelnaud and Beynac. We'll descend into ancient caves to see art etched by primitive man. And we'll float down the river on a barge and later dine on Sarlat's famous *foie gras* and black Cahors wine.

Finally, we'll travel west to Saint-Émilion, ancient wine hamlet and purveyor of famous vintages. Then we'll enter the noble grape kingdom that is Bordeaux. We'll explore this vast wine domain that's home to Lafite and Margaux—and some of the finest wines on the planet. We'll tour some of the *grands crus* estates, learning from wine pros how the great Bordeaux vintages are made and taste the fruits of their labors.

This book is about the history, food, culture, art, architecture, wine, lifestyle, and people who live in this fabled part of France. Above all, it's a guide to the delights of Southern France for those who journey here—or dream of doing so one day.

This book was 10 years in the making. But this is not because it took a decade to pen these pages. It took 10 years to visit the vast acreage explored herein. The Southern region of France from coast to coast is well over 500 miles if you were simply to drive straight through. But to meander through the five regions of this book was a journey of at least 1,000 miles—and many months experiencing the tiny villages, bustling cities, rolling hillsides, famous fortifications, ancient arenas, vast vineyards, delightful cuisine, unforgettable wine, and charming people of Southern France.

This book is dedicated to the courageous souls who travel—who leave the comfort of home and bed behind to experience life as others live it. This book is dedicated to those who love climbing to the top of an ancient fortress and seeing what medieval man must have seen. To those willing to drop into an underground cave or climb into a hot-air balloon to get a new perspective. To those happy to place themselves in the hands of a passionate French chef whose great joy in life is to create a cornucopia of tastes made by his or her own hand. And finally to those able to share the exhilaration of a people who are so proud of their wine, or their farm, or their *faience*, or their cheeses that they clasp you to their breast when they realize you understand their reason for living.

I hope you enjoy this quirky journey through Southern France. And, in some small way, perhaps you can join me there within these pages—or plan for your own adventure. *Bon voyage!*

Part One:
The French Riviera

"The chauffeur, a Russian czar of the period of Ivan the Terrible, was a self-appointed guide, and the resplendent names—Cannes, Nice, Monte Carlo—began to glow through their torpid camouflage, whispering of old kings come here to dine or die, of rajahs tossing Buddhas' eyes to English ballerinas, of Russian princes turning the weeks into Baltic twilights in the lost caviar days...It was pleasant to drive back to the hotel in the late afternoon, above a sea as mysteriously colored as the agates and cornelians of childhood, green as green milk, blue as laundry water, wine dark."

—F. Scott Fitzgerald, *Tender is the Night*

The French Riviera is the breathtakingly beautiful southeastern coastline of France. Also called the Côte d'Azur, this iridescent blue coast is lapped by the Mediterranean and bordered by the lush terrain of Italy just miles away. It sparkles with life. Known for dazzling people, mesmerizing light, languid beaches, splendid yachts, Provençal traditions, and a volatile history, the French Riviera remains a place of glamour and verve.

The French Riviera is a well-known uber-tourism and art mecca. It's heralded in song, literature, film, photography, and artistic masterpieces. But it's also the coastline of Provence, where solid peasant food, earthy values, and local traditions ground a savvy, irrepressible people who've survived a variety of invasions but adapted to make the most of their coveted locale. Yes, the yachts sail into Port Hercule in Monaco harbor. But if you look out in the bay, you'll also see ordinary fishermen catching their supper in the ultramarine waters of the Mediterranean. The French Riviera is a charming blend of age-old refinement and contemporary panache.

When I travel here, wending along the azure coastline with my convertible's top down, I can almost hear the strains of Henri Betti's *C'est Si Bon (It's So Good)*, which was written in Nice, ringing in my ears:

"C'est si bon, de partir n'importe ou,

Bras dessus bras dessous, En chantant des chansons,
C'est si bon, De se dire des mots doux
De petit rien du tout, mais qui en disent long."
(It's so good, just wandering around,
Arm in arm, arm in arm, and singing songs.
It's so good, to whisper sweet words,
Little nothings, but little nothings that can be
Said again and again.)

The French Riviera is pure magic. And it has had its share of visitors over the centuries who came for this magic—and fell in love for a lifetime: Romans, Germans, Russians, artists, cultural icons, millionaires, middle class tourists, film producers, and even a lithesome starlet called Grace who married into royalty on the Riviera. Picasso painted and sculpted on these lovely shores. Bardot put Saint-Tropez on the map with her nubile look and iridescent beauty. Disney found images for his enchanted castles in the bewitching hills. Somerset Maugham wrote many of his novels on Cap Ferret, as Hemingway and Fitzgerald drew inspiration and partied nearby. The Rolling Stones recorded here. And Bono visits his magnificent villa in Èze-sur-Mer on this sunny coastline.

Technically, this sun-kissed territory stretches from the border of Italy near Menton all the way down through Monaco, Villefranche-sur-Mer, Nice, Cannes and south through Saint-Tropez and Hyères. From the coastline of the Côte d'Azur it backs up to lovely hills with ancient towns like Èze, Grasse, and Saint-Paul-de-Vence where medieval history remains despite the pressures of glitzy global tourism.

The French Riviera is traditionally part of Provence, however. Provence—that honeyed land of practical virtues and delectable one-pot peasant cuisine. But the Riviera has two things that set it apart from the rest of down-to-earth Provence: a seductive seaside and a constant influx of wealth. As such I am separating the French Riviera (Part One) from inland Provence (Part Two) in these pages. They really are two worlds apart, bound by land but separated by an ocean of eye-popping opulence and high-def stardom.

History & Landscape

The Côte d'Azur was first settled by Celto-Ligurians of Northwestern Italy. Later the Greeks began trading on the coast in the 7th century B.C. Colonizing Romans followed, although the bulk of them ventured further into Southeastern France setting up large colonies in Arles and Marseille. With the rise of Christianity in the Roman Empire, Saints Nazaire and Celse brought the new religion to what would become the French Riviera. The oldest Christian structure on the Riviera is Fréjus Cathedral built in the 5th century south of Cannes.

Invading Visigoths, Burgundians, and Ostrogoths followed the demise of the Roman Empire. Later Saracens and Normans invaded the coast in the 9th century bringing further disorder and destruction. Finally, the rise of the Kingdom of Provence, ruled by the Catalan Bosonides (879-1112) brought some stability to the area. But with the emergence of the House of Grimaldi in the 13th century, calm came to the coast. Though the Grimaldis were actually expelled nobles from Genoa, Italy, they nevertheless took possession of Monaco, the largest city on the Côte d'Azur. They've overseen a remarkable regime that continues today under the rule of Prince Albert II.

The House of Savoy took control of Nice and the surrounding region in 1388. The rest of Provence became part of France in 1486, but Nice and its environs, save Monaco, remained separated from Provence until it was united under Napoleon III in 1860.

From the 1500s to the mid-1750s, the coast was mostly known as an impoverished area producing flowers for the perfume industry and as a fishing and olive-growing enclave. Curious tourists began trickling into the area as early as 1750, however. They were intent on escaping bad weather and "consumption" (tuberculosis), which was sweeping the colder countries. In 1763, British author Tobias Smollett visited Nice and later wrote *Travels Through France and Italy*. In his widely-read book, Smollett described the warm climate and sunny seashore. Around the same time, Scottish physician John Brown famously advocated fresh air and sunshine as a cure for consumption and other ills.

From then on, visitors flooded into the area. Britons, Germans,

Italians, and Russians all came for the mild winters at Nice and Cannes from November to May. Many of them arrived in horse-drawn carriages after a 24-hour trek across icy mountains. The long-awaited railway did not extend to the Riviera until the 1860s, however, much to the consternation of the well heeled who sometimes came for months or years at a time.

When the railway was finally built around 1862, a new era was born. An English doctor named James Henry Bennett who lived in Menton (next to Monaco) wrote a book called *Winter and Spring on the Shores of the Mediterranean*. Like Smollett a century before him, Bennett extolled the virtues of the coast for consumptive cure. The number of winter visitors then ballooned to more than 150,000 a year. The very romantic, less medicinal descriptions of the area in Stéphen Liégeard's book *La Côte d'Azur* published in 1887 was such a resounding success that it became the accepted title of the area thereafter. The stubborn English took to calling it "the French Riviera," however. Both names apply.

Soon, summer days on the French Riviera became popular as well. During the late 19th century, several fabulous resorts developed in Menton, Cap-Martin, Cap-d'Ail, Cap d'Antibes, Beaulieu, and Cap Ferrat. In the 1930s, a huge influx of American artists and moneyed tourists in the summer months suddenly made the French Riviera a popular destination year round. These adventurous Americans loved swimming in the sea and lounging on the rocky beaches.

This is one of the reasons that designer Coco Chanel launched the "beach pajama," the *de rigueur* uniform for chic beachniks when switching out of bikinis or swimming trunks. The warm weather and fantastic ambience attracted many famous artists and writers; they took advantage of the light and abundant drama bubbling along the shoreline.

But not only were the rich and daring drawn to the Côte d'Azur. French paid holidays were introduced at this time. Regular workers, morphing into a substantial middle class, traveled to the southern coast to grab their place on the sand. Mass tourism was born.

These days, the modern French Riviera is famed for beach-chic days and paparazzi-worthy nights. High-priced resorts sit side by side with

beach shacks. Purveyors of *haute cuisine* serve up the latest creation while street *cafés* shovel five-euro *pomme frites* and fresh sardines onto your plate. Everywhere rich people and wannabes lap up the sun and the limelight.

Behind the beachfront, however, particularly in the winding streets of Nice or up in the hills around Grasse and Vence, simple Provençal life lives on. Here, street vendors sell mushrooms the size of your shoe or scoop succulent green olives into paper cartons for you. And there's not a paparazzo in sight. There are gorgeous views of the blue coast to admire as you wander along the simple shoreline, despite the fact that you're not floating on a mega yacht in the harbor. You can sit for free on a Cannes park bench, watching a game of *boules* played by locals dressed in simple shorts and fisherman's caps, as you sip a plain Coca-Cola. Cost? Two euros.

There's something for everyone along this coastline lying between the Mediterranean Sea and the Alpine summits that's blessed with 300 days of sunshine per year. And despite the hype, you don't actually have to empty your 401K to lay your head here. Alongside the *haute* resorts, you'll find inviting bungalows and reasonably-priced B&Bs. And it's not all surf and sand fun. Ancient hill towns are artistic havens, as well as medieval hamlets that offer picturesque stays and reasonably priced bistros.

Èze, the enchanting hilltop village perched 1,280 feet above Monaco, is one of these medieval wonders, for example. In Èze, the Riviera glamour drops away and ancient France comes alive. Grasse, the hilltop town famous for its perfume factories and Fragonard, is an olfactory delight. Here, the flower-rich fields of the Riviera hills yield fabulous perfumes that are sold worldwide. And then there's Saint-Paul-de-Vence, one of many fortified towns with windy streets and chic art shops where many famous artisans have lived and died.

Dolce far niente, the Italian phrase for "the joy of doing nothing," captures the atmosphere of this ultramarine coast. Interestingly, Italy and France struggled for centuries to dominate this *dolce*-drenched area since the countries are cheek to jowl. As a result, there's a certain Italian-French feel throughout the Riviera. It all makes for a lovely blend of Italian passion and French panache.

People & Lifestyle

"Uummm, C'est bon.
Je cherche un millionnaire, avec des grands Cadillac car
Mink coats, des bijoux, Jusqu'au cou, tu sais?
C'est bon, cette petit sensation
Ou peut-tre quelqu'un, avec un petit yacht, no?"
(Uummm - It's good. I'm looking for a millionaire
With big Cadillac cars, mink coats, jewels
As big as your fist, you know?
It's good. This little feeling
Perhaps someone with a little yacht, no?)

The French Riviera has many faces. Brigitte Bardot first donned a bikini on the sandy beaches of Saint-Tropez. Millionaires come to bank and sometimes gamble their wealth in Monaco. Movie stars and their producers arrive to hawk their latest flicks in Cannes. And up and down the rocky coast, the "beautiful people" tarry to see and be seen like this *Nice Carnaval* reveler pictured.

But there's also the daily

Carnaval de Nice by Paul Shawcross
Copyright © 2014 Paul Shawcross

profile of the resident locals. From a seaside perch such as your hotel or the beach promenade, you can see local fishing boats bobbing along in the water catching anchovies, bass, and sea bream. Near them are stately yachts tossing champagne corks into the sea. You can watch budding artists painting canvasses filled with cerulean skies and crescent beaches. At the same time you see teens, their book bags slung over their shoulders, as they ride their motor scooters to school. And despite the beach chic, business people, real estate developers, pharmaceutical pros, biotech experts, and high-tech consortiums also have a major presence on the charming Côte d'Azur.

The French Riviera actually has a fascinating demography behind that sand and surf persona. The total population of the Riviera is about two million. It's the only region in France with residents from more than 163 countries. About 12% of the population is of foreign origin according to the Côte d'Azur Convention Bureau. Most of this 12% speaks English; hence the main language outside of French is English. But you'll also see Russian on the menus since this is the seaside-locale-of-choice for many wealthy Russians. And of course Italians vacation here—and the French often pop over to Italy.

The French Riviera is a "melting pot of innovation." Its Sophia-Antipolis high-technology park has more than 130 laboratories and companies, plus 10 international schools (the highest concentration in Europe) and a major public university. More than 1000 information technology companies call the French Riviera home. Among them are France Telecom R&D, Asco Systems, Texas Instruments, IBM, and Thales Alenia Space.

With 71 miles of coastline and beaches, 18 golf courses, 14 ski resorts, 3,000+ restaurants, and 30,000 hotel rooms, the tourism industry is a billion-dollar business. Major international hotel chains are represented, including Intercontinental and Relais & Châteaux. And there are apartments and *gîtes* (houses) for rent throughout the region.

There's a wealth of things to do on this sparkling coast for visitors beyond just tanning on the beach. Along with water sports, boating, river rafting, kayaking, and mountain biking, in the Riviera towns there are 130 museums, two operas, several theaters, and a plethora of art galleries. Excursions run the gamut for locales up and down the coast from Saint-Tropez to Monaco, as well as Italy.

The French Riviera is also a shopper's paradise. Most every luxury brand has a niche somewhere along the coast. But local shops situated away beyond the luxury streets display beautiful Provençal linens, *faience* (pottery), and tempting home goods. For nightlife, you can bop 'til you drop. The French Riviera has all-night dance clubs like Le Quai in Saint-Tropez, a cork's throw from the port. In Nice, you can pop into High Club or Checkpoint Pub. Quieter late night venues include Jam, Fred's Bar, and La Havane in Nice. In Cannes, Le Pastis or the Palm Beach Casino offer quiet after-dinner drinks and lovely music.

Up the coast, visitors who grow bored with sunning, shopping, or slurping, can indulge their gambling fantasies in Monaco—that tax haven and casino destination for high rollers and high seas enthusiasts with spectacular yachts. This .78 square miles of land is officially known as the Principality of Monaco. The population of roughly 36,371 includes many who "live" in Monaco a portion of the year for tax purposes. Though Monaco is a sovereign city-state, France defends the state and helps to spend her gambling, hotel, and business proceeds. Workers generally drive in from Italy or elsewhere on the Riviera. Few can afford to actually *live* here. Watching the wealthy and the common working people interact is a sport in and of itself in my opinion.

But probably the most-loved activity on the French Riviera—whether you're rich, poor, working, retired, famous, or infamous—is enjoying the sand, warm sea, and incomparable sun. Topless or not.

Food, Wine, & Shopping

Food

The Mediterranean cuisine of the French Riviera is a

wonderful combination of Italian, French, and Provençale flavors. Since so many cultures influence this area, it's no wonder that you can find *socca*, squid pasta, *paella*, fish soup, Parma ham, *foie gras*, *salade niçoise*, *ratatouille*, and steak tartare on the same menu! The French Riviera effortlessly blends hardy Provençale flavors with the olive and tomato tastes of the Mediterranean.

Ratatouille, a favorite "peasant" food is made here with olive oil, ripe tomatoes, garlic, onions, *courgettes* (zucchini), *aubergines* (eggplant), bell peppers, carrots, marjoram, and a mix of green herbs like *herbes de Provence*. It's often served as a side dish, but a robust French *ratatouille* can be the main course when accompanied by pasta, rice, or hearty bread.

Fish is fabulous on the Riviera—fresh off the boat. I've enjoyed delectable lobster and sea bass that's divine. Another Riviera favorite of mine is the *pissaladière*, an onion tart covered with anchovy fillets and black olives. *Socca*, the crêpe made with chickpea flour, water, and olive oil, then cooked in a wood-fired oven until the edges turn black, can be found anywhere—but often in Nice. I often buy one and eat as I wander. I see other people eating a *socca* and slurping back a glass of ice-cold local rosé. These two together are often called "the taste of Nice."

Salade niçoise is another of my favorite culinary creations. The flavorful lettuce, fresh tuna, ripe tomatoes, green peppers, hard boiled eggs, black olives, and celery (and sometimes artichoke hearts and broad beans) all mixed with oil to taste and a bit of lemon make a lovely meal day or night. Sometimes I enjoy wonderful *pan-bagnat*, a favorite with vegetarians—or just anyone who loves the flavors. This round sandwich is made with crunchy round bread filled with *salade niçoise* and spring onions.

Banga càuda, a vegetable fondue, is fun-in-a-pot as you dip raw vegetables into a pot of hot oil, garlic, and anchovies. And of course I adore classic *soupe au pistou*, French vegetable soup with basil, sometimes topped with deep fried *courgettes* (zucchini) flowers. *Les Beignets de Fleurs de Courgettes* (zucchini blossom fritters) makes for a crunchy treat. The tasty flowers go great with a crisp white wine or chilled rosé. To go with wine and a *beignet*, I sometimes sample some of the famous Riviera cheeses like soft *Mont d'Or* or aged *Comté*.

Gnocchi, the soft dumpling dish, is popular too. It's made with durum semolina (the Italian way) or potato flour. Other local delicacies include *tripe à la niçoise, raviolis niçoise, stockfish* (dried cod base cooked in white wine and vegetables, then served with black olives), *porquetta* (stuffed suckling pig), and of course *aioli*, the famous garlic mayonnaise that's slathered on almost everything.

This area of the Mediterranean is *charcuterie* heaven. Fine sausages and meats show up on most menus. My clever friend, Chef Pascal Bessett, who was raised on the French Riviera and now lives in California, has taken cured meats and *salamis* to a new level. His company, Angel's Salumi & Truffles, uses Southern France meats like duck and wild boar and combines them with flavors such as white and black truffles to create heavenly gourmet *charcuterie* and butters. Chef Bessett's products are packaged and shipped from California in the U.S., but the ingredients originate in France. Many of these products are nitrate free. He also offers some unusual churned butters built on French traditions from Périgord (Dordogne) and elsewhere. Among his products are raspberry butter, wild blueberry butter, white truffle oil, porcini butter, black truffle peelings, black truffle caviar, wild boar prosciutto, and black and white truffle *salami*. You can get more information at www.angelsalumi.com.

Nice's old town by the harbor is perhaps the best place to taste this uniquely French/Mediterranean cuisine. Pizza-like pastries topped with fried onions and anchovies or fresh tomatoes and crisp local black olives are readily available. Another snack specific to Nice is stuffed vegetables, typically peppers with rice and mince.

Naturally, the French Riviera shares a favorite with Italy: gelato. *Arlequin* is one of the most famous ice cream stores in Nice—so come with your sweet tooth. Many popular French Riviera desserts start with seasonal fruit. *Pompe aux pommes du Perigord* uses apples and almonds in flaky pastry, French *crêpes* are rolled around fresh berries, melon chunks, or fruit fillings, and *le clafouti*, is made from newly ripe cherries plopped into a delectable cake. Tarts are common here and I especially enjoy *tarte à la rhubarbe* for its sweet/sour flavor.

Since the French Riviera is inundated by well-traveled visitors, French Riviera restaurants have joined the other three-quarters of France's 110,000 restaurants by offering hamburgers. Yes, that

American favorite is slowly taking over the world. According to a 2014 study by Paris-based restaurant researcher Giraconseil, the burger is now beating traditional *steak-frites* and *baguette* sandwiches. The burger represents nearly half of all sandwiches sold in France today. Burger trucks also serve curbside fare—and you can even have your burgers delivered on motorbike. However, the French still eat burgers with a knife and fork!

Wine

The Riviera produces some excellent rosés, as well as whites and a few nice reds. You might be surprised to learn that there are hundreds of private vineyards around the Côte d'Azur. Varieties grown include Cinsault, Grenache, Syrah, Sémillon, Merlot, and Chardonnay. Cannes has even become host to *Le Mondial du Rosé*, an International tasting competition of the world's best rosé wines.

Many of the wines served in fine dining French Riviera venues hail either from inland Provence or the major wine-growing regions of France: Burgundy, Bordeaux, Languedoc, Loire, and Châteauneuf-du-Pape. As Italy is so close, you'll also find Chiantis and fine Italian wines on the menu. But everywhere there will be local rosés; they're almost always the house wines since rosé goes perfectly with hot weather!

Toulon, a large military harbor on the Mediterranean coastline at the southern tip of the Riviera, is famed for Bandol wines. These famous wines are made from Mourvèdre grapes with Grenache and Cinsault juice added. Red Bandol wine is characterized by its dark color and rich flavors of black fruits, vanilla, cinnamon, and leather. The white wines of Bandol are composed primarily of Clairette Blanche, Bourboulenc, and Ugni Blanc. The rosés of Bandol are characterized by spicy, earthy flavors that can resemble the Rhône rosés from Tavel AoC (*Appellation d'origine Contrôlée*), with some having strawberry notes. By the way, AoC is the esteemed designation of the world's finest first-class wines. (I'll say much more about this in the Languedoc and Bordeaux sections.)

Pastis, that anise-based *liqueur* famously paired with the game of *boules*, is plentiful here. But my guess would be the most frequent liquid poured in the French Riviera is champagne. For my money, Veuve Clicquot or Taittinger will fill the bill nicely. (Quirky note: Veuve Clicquot seldom gives you a hangover. I have no idea why, but it seems to be true.)

Shopping

Shopping on the French Riviera is literally a mixed bag. You'll have lots to choose from: large shopping malls, street markets, hand-made goods, designer consortiums, flea markets, and food markets. Shopping malls are sprinkled throughout the region, and the marketplaces of Nice, Cannes, and other towns offer up fresh produce nearly every day in open-air markets.

Along the waterfronts, you'll find the high-end shops like Prada and Jean Paul Gaultier. But along the winding back streets, I've discovered that an entire world of shopping opens up. Goods range from traditional Provençal linens, crockery, and home goods to expensive antiques, perfumes, and artwork. You'll be able to shop some of the notable designers in Galeries Lafayette, but you'll also find reasonably priced boutiques like Etam or rocker-edged Zadig & Voltaire.

In my opinion, Nice has the greatest variety of shopping options.

The outdoor market at Cours Saleya gives you the opportunity to buy fresh flowers, fruits, vegetables, cheeses, wines, and clothing from open bins, baskets, and stalls—and mingle with the locals. When you tire, you can stop at one of the sidewalk *cafés* for coffee or a pick-me-up. At night, the Cours Saleya area transforms into nighttime fun where you can dine, club, or *flâneur.*

But sometimes I prefer Nice's Cap 3000, the largest shopping mall in the region; it has 100+ shops, restaurants, banks, and department stores. In downtown Nice, I enjoy Etoile, a four-story mall with a variety of shops and *cafés* under one roof. Along Rue Masséna, I've strolled the pedestrianized promenade running parallel to the beach and found swim gear, nightclub togs, and designer fashions. When I want fast and trendy, I go to Centre Commercial Nice Lingostière, which is Nice's answer to a sprawl mall.

Personally, I really like Cannes for shopping. Along the Croisette, shoppers can access upscale shops like Gucci, Dior, and Louis Vuitton. But a block or two from the Croisette toward the center of town is one of my favorite shopping streets: Rue d'Antibes. From one end to the other (8-12 blocks), it has every shop imaginable including French favorites like Vanessa Bruno and Maje. I bought a sleek black velvet zipper jacket in Cannes along Rue d'Antibes that I still wear to this day.

When I have time, I make my way to Rue Meynadier in Cannes for its gourmet food shops. Cannes is also home to one of France's most renowned antique shows, Salon des Antiquaires de Cannes, held twice a year in July and December. Most of these stores will ship anywhere in the world.

Forville Market is Cannes' version of a flea market, but you can also load up on fresh fish, fruits and vegetables, furniture, books, antiques, and "treasures" of all kinds. It's particularly fun for people watching—especially the high-heeled lasses trolling for offbeat swag.

Seaside towns like Saint-Tropez and Antibes have their specialties as well as their open-street markets. In the old quarter of Saint-Tropez, you'll even find the designer storefronts facing the open-air stalls. After you buy your Louis Vuitton bags in Saint-Tropez, you can head to Place des Lices Market and stuff them with pottery, plants, artwork, scarves, handcrafted jewelry, and more.

Be sure to pick up a pair of *Sandales Tropezienne* at Rondini on Saint Tropez's Rue G. Clemenceau. This Spartan-like sandal hit the big time when Brigitte Bardot was widely photographed wearing a pair in her blonde-bombshell movies of the 50s and 60s. By the way, Bardot instigated a few other fashion trends: the Bardot neckline (a wide-open neckline that also exposes both shoulders), the bikini, the *choucroute* ("sauerkraut" or beehive hairstyle), and gingham (checked) dresses nipped in at the waist. (Quirky note: John Lennon and Paul McCartney reportedly idolized Bardot. They were planning a film with her similar to *A Hard Day's Night*, but it never happened. They loved her look; it's probably no coincidence that both Lennon's and George Harrison's wives at the time lightened their locks and fuzzed them up *à la* Bardot.)

In the hillside town of Grasse, there are various perfumers who'll give personal access to their newly-poured creations. Parfumerie Galimard is one of the oldest in the area where you can also make a custom scent to take home with you as a gift or for yourself. (I made my own perfume concoction at the Fragonard Factory; I still have a few drops left in my tiny golden bottle. Every time I smell the elegant aroma it takes me back to the Riviera.)

There are several olive oil producers in Grasse like Huilerie Sainte Anne that guide you through the process of olive oil production; you can sample some of the shop's wares and buy a few bottles to take home with you. In Grasse, there's Centre Commercial Leclerc, a small commercial center anchored by a LeClerc supermarket and several smaller shops. Èze is another picturesque hillside town where I've discovered some superb olive oil shops, as well as tapestry and pottery consortiums. Many of them will ship your treasures home for you.

Monaco is a mecca for high-end shopping—no surprise there— but there are a few bargains to be had, particularly in the winding streets west of the harbor. I've wandered into some quirky boutiques that sell Monaco paraphernalia, trinkets for the home, and unusual jewelry. Of course, the Monaco seaside shops are wall-to-wall *haute couture*—and if your credit card has no limit you'll love picking up a Chanel bag or a Gucci belt. If shoppers run out of boutiques, they can head to *Le Métropole*, one of Monaco's upmarket shopping plazas with more than 80 different shops and food venues. The smaller Centre Commercial de Fontvieille has shops selling everything from wrist cuffs to musical instruments. If you run out of toothpaste, there's also a *Carrefour*, the equivalent of Walmart.

Culture & Art

"The Riviera has been a magnet for writers [and creatives] for 700 years. Early in the fourteenth century, the exiled Florentine poet Dante passed through, and wrote of its vertiginous mountain roads in his *Inferno*. Since then, generations of literary migrants of every nationality and genre, have followed."

—Ted Jones, *The French Riviera: A Literary Guide for Travelers*

This tiny strip of coastline backed by mountains dotted with pine forests and medieval hill towns, inspires many with its luminescent light, sun-soaked days, and twinkling night skies. If you visit the Côte d'Azur for creative inspiration, you'll be in stellar company. Many of the world's most creative people visited regularly, retired to, or died in the French Riviera— such is its allure as an inspirational heaven on earth. Sculptor César Baldaccini's *Thumb* (shown) reminds us that the hand of genius is ever creating here.

Robert Louis Stevenson, novelist, poet, and travel writer, was a British visitor who came for his health. In 1882, he rented a villa called La Solitude at Hyères, where he wrote much of *A Child's Garden of Verses*. Auguste Renoir, Henri Matisse, and Pablo Picasso made much of the Riviera light. Henry James set part of his novel *The Ambassadors* here.

The French Riviera is and always has been attractive to artists and creatives of all types, but it rose to new heights in the 1920s. American society hosts Gerald and Sara Murphy, who were bored with Paris, popped into the Hôtel du Cap-Eden-Roc one fateful season upon the advice of Gerald's Yale friend, Cole Porter. Before their appearance, wealthy French vacationers would never have dreamt of staying over on the Riviera in the summer.

But the Murphys loved Antibes so much they convinced the Hôtel du Cap to keep on a skeleton crew one summer to accommodate them. Soon they were living on the Riviera most of the year, and they entertained a steady stream of the rich and famous. Friends like F. Scott Fitzgerald (fresh off his success with *The Great Gatsby*) and Ernest Hemingway arrived by the dozens—effectively popularizing the French Riviera as a newly minted all-year resort. Other revelers included John Dos Passos, Jean Cocteau, Dorothy Parker, and Robert Benchley.

Soon other literati arrived to bask in the sun and create in serenity. Jules Verne wrote *Around the World in 80 Days* here. Guy de Maupassant penned *Mont-Oriol* while enjoying the delights of the Riviera. Graham Greene wrote numerous works onsite and Fitzgerald wrote his masterpiece, *Tender is the Night* based on his experiences on the Riviera. Fitzgerald reportedly depicted the Murphys as Dick and Nicole Diver in *Tender is the Night;* the Hôtel du Cap was thinly veiled as the Hôtel des Etrangers.

The Murphys also surrounded themselves with famous or soon-to-be famous artists. The Murphys even kept some of them afloat financially while they labored over their bodies of work. Regular guests included Pablo Picasso and Henri Matisse. Subsequent years brought other celebrants to this glittering waterhole, including Marlene Dietrich, the Duke and Duchess of Windsor, and Charles de Gaulle. Of course photography was a boon pastime along the dazzling coast—and there was much to record.

Other wealthy arrivals who vacationed, bought homes, or simply came for the inspiration include W.B. Yeats, H.G. Wells, Gertrude Stein, Tennessee Williams, Anaïs Nin, Ring Lardner, James Joyce, and Lawrence Durrell. Yves Montand, Simone Signoret, Walt Disney, and David Niven all visited or bought homes along the Riviera.

French novelist and performer Sidonie-Gabrielle Colette adored Saint-Tropez particularly. Among her most famous works are *Chéri* and *Gigi*. *Gigi* was so popular, it was about to become a much-anticipated Broadway musical, but the producers were having a hard time casting the leading role. During a visit to Monaco, Colette happened to be crossing the lobby of the Hôtel de Paris and saw a young performer in the lobby. This unknown had a bit part in a film called *Monte Carlo Baby*. "There's my Gigi!" Colette cried out. Her name? Audrey Hepburn.

Movie star Grace Kelly also made a notable film or two and visited the Riviera to promote one of her films at the Cannes Film Festival. She met a certain Prince Rainer—and she ultimately married him and became a princess. Today, Bono, Bill Gates, Ringo Starr, and many, many others continue to enjoy their high-profile life in this French paradise.

While a noted film and photography darling, the French Riviera is also known for its serious art houses and museums. There are dozens of fine galleries where you can see internationally renowned works. Among them are museums or installations dedicated to Picasso (Antibes), Chagall (Nice), and Matisse (Nice). More contemporary pieces can be found in Nice's modern art gallery, MAMAC, which is located roughly half way between the old and new town. For longer stays, it's worthwhile making a stop at Saint-Paul-de-Vence, an artist's haven with a dazzling reputation.

Navigating the Area

Although there are no formal boundaries, the French Riviera is basically the tiny corner of Southeast France that hugs the steep coastline from the Italian border in the east to Saint-Tropez and Hyères. But there are two segments to the Riviera: the coastal real estate and the backcountry hill towns where you'll find Èze and Saint-Paul-de-Vence. As such, there are various ways to tour them.

One of the quirks of visiting the resort towns perched on the edge of the coast is that they're living with 19th century infrastructure in a Wi-Fi world. This makes for spectacular scenery in somewhat cramped quarters. The roads are narrow along the Mediterranean. Parking is sometimes a challenge. And the traffic is a continuous stream moving between Saint-Tropez, Cannes, Antibes, Nice, Monaco, and the Italian border.

There are several ways to see the Riviera. First, if you come strictly for gambling, you'll of course stay in Monaco itself. If you have megabucks, a helicopter can ferry you to various places in and out of your palatial accommodations or resort. Or if you have a rental car, you can zip in and out of Monaco to points north and south.

Second, if you come to stay primarily in one of the resort cities like Nice, Cannes, or Antibes, you'll probably park at one of the resorts and use shuttles, taxis, or drivers to ferry you out for seeing the sights and dining. The alternative is to drive your own car—but sit back and relax, because it may be slow going due to traffic. Of course, if you arrive in Cannes for your next film premiere, you'll probably stay at the plush Carlton Hotel and "walk" the few block or so to the Film Festival building as I have (although I'm certain Nicole Kidman has a driver to ferry her from the Carlton's carpet to the Film Festival's grand staircase).

You can fly into the French Riviera via the international Nice airport from the rest of Europe or New York. Or you can drive in from Italy or Spain. And you can sail in on a ship from various ports. Trains will also transport you into the area with style.

If you fly, you'll land at the Nice Côte d'Azur Airport. This is France's third busiest airport after Paris-Charles de Gaulle Airport and Paris-Orly. The Nice Airport sits on a bit of partially reclaimed coastal land at the western end of the Promenade des Anglais. It's also one of the teeniest international airports I've ever seen, managing 10 million visitors a year from 30 countries. As of this writing, you can fly into Nice directly from New York, London, Paris, Rome, and many other cities.

What the Nice airport lacks in size, it makes up for in charm. Led by Air France and EasyJet, there are more than 50 airlines that account for up to 600 flights a day. After you find your luggage, car rental companies are located within yards of the front entrance. (More on renting cars in the section on Nice.) Taxis stand at the ready with Jean-Paul Belmondo look-alikes at the wheel. Most of these taxi drivers are unbelievably tan and friendly. Many wear open white shirts, and gold necklaces dangle down into their curly chest hair. If you're with your husband, they'll keep their eyes on the road. If you're a single woman or a mother with her pretty 20-something daughter, they'll give you smoldering looks in the rearview mirror.

If you own your own jet, you can fly into Cannes Mandelieu Airport and skip the tourist hubbub. You can also take the high-speed TGV train into Nice, which I find very efficient and pleasant—although you'll be hauling around your luggage unless you have a helper or a strapping companion with you. It's only five and a half hours from Paris to Nice via train, by the way.

Of course if you drive in, there are any number of routes that will get you to the Riviera from Paris, Lyon, Barcelona, or Rome. The A8 superhighway is very efficient, although it sits slightly inland from the Côte d'Azur congestion. The good news is it's a feat of multi-lane efficiency. But have a bag of euro coins ready since you'll be feeding the tollbooths regularly as you travel along. (Note: There's nothing a French truck driver hates worse than a tourist driver fumbling for change in front of him. So be ready with your coins, or you might see a colorful French hand gesture in your rearview mirror.)

The French Riviera is also a major yachting and cruising location with several discreet marinas along its coast. The Côte d'Azur Economic Development Agency reports that it hosts more than half of the entire world's super yacht fleet, with approximately 90% of all super yachts visiting the region's coast at least once in the ship's lifespan. If you're so lucky as to arrive via private yacht, you'll undoubtedly have your choice of slips. But if you arrive by large cruise ship, you'll hop off for a few-hour stopover in one of the Riviera ports. Wear good shoes—and be prepared for anything, since you'll find the best shopping and dining further back from the touristy concessions right at the pier.

If you lack a yacht or a limo, the hop-on-hop-off buses along the Riviera are actually pretty efficient and fun to ride. They give you a no-frills tour of the coast, which is a great introduction to the area. These buses can also ferry you to some of the museums. I've used them often—and love the wind on my face as we roll along.

The beach scene is worth a visit, even if all you do is stroll along

Nice's Promenade Des Anglais or Cannes's Croisette. But be aware: they attract thousands of visitors a year unless you go off-season (my preference). The Nice beach isn't great for swimming since its baseball size rocks make it hard to get to and from the water. Cannes glamorous beaches have more sand, and the sea is very accessible.

Should you have a car or can hop on a municipal bus (each town has a bus station), then plan a day trip over to Monaco to see the area around the casino and harbor. There are excellent stops along the way. See the outrageous Villa Ephrussi de Rothschild in Cap Ferret by the way; it's a treat. Return by the upper roads behind Monaco through Èze, and stop for lunch at the famous Château de la Chèvre D'Or. Another very pretty drive is along the coast to Saint-Tropez. Just don't attempt this on a weekend in season as it can take four or more hours one way. Off-season during the week, you should be able to do it in half the time.

The coastline along the French Riviera offers plenty of opportunity for excursions by boat. Tours of celebrity homes are popular. Other options include trips from Cannes to the Lérins Islands, which I've found refreshing. These islands include Île de Sainte-Marguerite (where the fabled "Man in the Iron Mask" was incarcerated) and Île Saint-Honorat (where monks brew the alcoholic lemon liqueur Limoncello). High-speed ferries can also whisk travelers from Nice to Calvi and Bastia in Corsica.

If you decide to stay in this beautiful part of the world for a few days or weeks, there are a few practicalities of life on the French Riviera you may wish to consider. First, you may want to have your own car so you can come and go as you please. But since parking is such a premium, you may want to pick accommodations with adequate parking as a first priority.

Second, you'll find many vantage points from which to

see the fabulous yachts and cruise ships docking along the coastline. If you arrive on a cruise ship, you'll disembark to wander around the Riviera, which is fairly accessible for a day or two. And you'll see some unforgettable scenery.

Third, be ready for some of the best seafood anywhere in the world. With the local fisherman catching fresh seafood daily, plus the tasty blend of Provençal and Italian cooking, most every meal will be a delight. Wine is plentiful, and you can enjoy Provençal specialties or drink (or bathe in) champagne since celebrating is part of the intoxicating lifestyle here. I often visit my local market or *épicerie* and pick up goodies to go in my in-room refrigerator (I always ask for one).

That way, you can create your own breakfast or other meal and enjoy it on your own deck (I usually try to get one of those too). You don't have to dine out for every meal. Eating in can be just as fun.

Fourth, you don't have to be wealthy to visit the Riviera, despite the hype. You can stay in some of the more reasonably priced hotels and B&Bs and merely *visit* the more tony hotels. Having breakfast, a drink, or a reasonably-priced lunch can feel just as luxurious. You can also enjoy wandering the streets in the back areas of Nice, Cannes, and elsewhere on a few euros a day and have a great time. There are agreeable little parks and plenty of French corner bars with a few seats on the pavement from which to watch the Riviera world go by.

Fifth, pack sturdy walking shoes, despite your yearning to wear flip-flops or kitten heels. The cobblestone walkways and pebbly beaches are tricky. A good hat or a visor is a must. And you may be glad to have an umbrella for changes in the weather. Remember that the *mistral,* that wicked wind that sweeps down from the Alps like a winged razor blade, also blows along the coast; if you get caught out in it, you may be practically swept down the street like a paper bag as I was in Cannes one winter.

Smart travelers may be especially interested in the *Côte d'Azur Card,* which offers discounts on more than 100 sights from perfume making to dining and boat rides. For those of you with smart phones, I highly recommend Paul Shawcross's app, *Nice and Beyond.* A professional U.K. photographer and travel writer, Paul has created this terrific app that offers colorful detail on the French Riviera that you can read "on the hoof" or in your room before you venture out for the day. It's quick, easy, and accessible. Paul's other apps are *Provençal Roaming* and *Dordogne Explorations*. I consulted all three apps as I wrote *Intoxicating Southern France*.

Finally, August is the toughest month to visit the French Riviera. August is when the French stream into the area for their annual vacations by the shore. Americans should try July or September or any other time of year in my opinion—although you will take your chances with the weather. At least you'll get a table for dinner! May is Film Festival month, so good luck getting a hotel room anywhere near Cannes. But you may meet a celebrity at a *café* or over a barrel of olives in May, so the inconvenience may be worth the trouble.

Favorites

Cannes, Antibes, Nice, Cap Ferret, Èze, Saint-Paul-de-Vence, Monaco. These are some of my favorite places on the Riviera to feel the sun on my face, the Mediterranean at my toes, and the champagne fizz on my tongue as the yachts glide by and the enchantments begin. Journey with me as we stroll the glamorous Cannes Croisette and splendid Antibes, and as we mingle with rich Russians and flirtatious Parisians along the way. Wander with me through the bustling Nice Cours Saleya marketplace for hot *socca* fresh from the grill while elegance oozes from the grand estates on Cap Ferret. Climb up the steep hillsides together in Èze and Saint-Paul-de-Vence, and breathe the atmosphere of *artistes*

extraordinaire. And finally, saunter with me through Monaco's famed principality, and sample the life that millionaires—and royals—live. Your pleasures await.

Cannes

Cannes (shown) is often called the "Queen of the French

Riviera." The first time I saw it, I fell in love with the seaside architecture, walkable streets, and beach-chic vibe. Early on, however, Cannes was just a sleepy little fishing village founded in the second century B.C. by a Ligurian tribe struggling to stay alive. It remained an area of invasion by assorted factions, among them the Romans, Saracens, and various religious groups. In 1830, it was "invaded" yet again by vacationing British aristocrats like Lord Henry Brougham, designer of the one-horse coach and one of the founders of the *Edinburgh Review.*

Brougham was on his way to Italy when a cholera epidemic sidelined him in Cannes. Experiencing the benign climate, glistening sea, and cobalt skies, Brougham fell in love with Cannes. He quickly bought land and built Château Eleanor-Louise. He loved his elegant *château* (mansion) so much, he returned each winter for 34 years. Most of the British aristocracy followed him. This marked the beginning of the town's affluent history. Luxury residences cropped up all over the hills, and visitors today can wander past some of these *Belle Époque* luxury estates in the Quartier de la Californie area of Cannes.

Brougham, who was former Lord Chancellor of England, was accustomed to making public improvements. And Cannes was no exception. Brougham went to his friend King Louis-Philippe, the last king of France, who ruled from 1830-1848. He convinced Louis to spend two million francs on a harbor wall so that a decent, strollable seaside promenade could be born.

In 1871, a cement boulevard similar to the Promenade des Anglais in Nice was finally laid. It was christened "The Promenade de la Croisette." In 1961, it was redone to make it accessible to automobiles and buses, as well as to create a wide, walking boulevard for strolling tourists, cyclists, and beach stands. Despite efforts to hold back the sea, it's still sometimes awash in waves during a storm. (I had full experience of this one blustery September where my meander along the Croisette turned into a struggle to stay upright.)

In 1946, Cannes hosted its first *Festival International du Film de Cannes.* This movie extravaganza had originally been planned for debut in 1939 as an alternative to the *Venice Film Festival.* (The *Venice Film Festival* was notoriously run at the time by a bunch of "Italian Fascists" according to the French). However, Hitler's march across Europe disrupted the quest for cinematic glory. In fact, star guests Mae West, Tyrone Power, and George Raft had just arrived by sea; they had to turn around and promptly return home when war broke out.

It wasn't until the armistice was signed that the festival was launched again. Jean-Paul Sartre was one of the stars on that debut red carpet in 1946. As a quirky note, the architects for the original film festival building (on which the JW Marriott now stands) had apparently forgotten something very important. They'd overlooked the fact that a film must be projected through a window from the projection room. Thus, while the glitterati of the time sat fuming in their finery, carpenters rushed in to quickly cut a hole in the projection booth wall so the first film could be projected onto the screen.

From such humble beginnings, the *Festival de Cannes* is now a world-class event. The 2012 festival touted the fact that films from more than 40 countries were hosted. Internet users can now follow the event not only in French and English, but also in Spanish, Portuguese, Chinese, Japanese, Arabic, and Russian. Touted as a juried film festival, the underlying purpose of the festival is to find distribution for the current films, backing for new films, and "face time" for performers and directors showcasing themselves for new projects.

Of course *couture* plays a huge part in the festival these days. Big name designers often show up in tandem with their "stars" displaying their current designs. Today's tickets for the screenings run anywhere from $5,000 and upwards to $20,000. At festival time, every hotel room within 50 miles of Cannes is booked—and the traffic is nightmarish.

In recent years, *Cannes Film Festival* staffers have become sensitive to the fact that mostly only professionals were allowed to screen and review the current slate of films. The public wanted in on some of the magic too. Meeting the call of the lowly filmgoer, the festival now has a public viewing venue called the *Cinéma de la Plage* (Cinema on the Beach). This is an outdoor cinema that previews a different film each night of the festival to the public. Though these films are typically not part of the primary competition, they are often Cannes Classic films. It's quite enjoyable watching the films on the beach across from the Majestic Hotel. You can even take a picnic and sit on beach chairs or blankets downing your own Provençal wine and goodies. You only need to stand in line to grab a spot, since no tickets are required.

Other opportunities for tourists include the *Critics' Week Films* and the *Director's Fortnight* screenings, which do require tickets. If you want to attend any of these events, you can check with the ticket booth near the JW Marriott, your local concierge, or the Cannes tourism office. Details about the festival can be found at www.festival-cannes.com.

Interestingly, the second time I visited Cannes, my 22-year-old daughter and I stayed at the handy Noga Hilton (now the JW Marriott). As previously mentioned, this site was the original location of the film festival. When my daughter and I exited the hotel the first morning, the boardwalk stretched out before us to the sea a bit like a runway at Atlantic City. In fact, this was the same boardwalk trod by the glamorous film community more than 60 years ago. (On this particular September day, our bikinis were back in our hotel room since it was pouring rain; we were reduced to traipsing up and down the Croisette in raincoats hefting wind-whipped umbrellas. Unglamorous indeed.)

Today's home for the film festival has moved to the south end of the Croisette. Built in 1982, the Palais des Festivals et des Congrès now operates not only as the venue for the *Cannes Film Festival* every May, but it hosts a multitude of other glamorous events and artistic festivals in multiple auditoriums throughout the year. If you get bored with movie magic, there's also a casino, gaming rooms, and a nightclub. Wandering around the grounds off-season, you can see movie star handprints in the cement by such luminaries as Catherine Deneuve.

If you're not part of the film scene, you can still enjoy shopping, dining, and seeing the main attractions in Cannes, which include some of the most famous hotels in France. The glamorous InterContinental Carlton Cannes Hôtel was built in 1911 from plans by Charles Delmas. It has 355 fabulous rooms and suites with prices starting at a few hundred euros a night to several thousand, depending on the time of year. The suites are named after famous people like Cary Grant. One of the hotel's catch phrases is: "Not just a hotel but a palace which tells a story of elegance and pleasure…" (Note: the website is in French, English, and Russian.)

The Carlton's façade is a registered historical monument. I go there every time I'm in town. It's instantly recognizable from a number of films including *To Catch a Thief* with Cary Grant and Grace Kelly, *French Kiss* with Meg Ryan, and the Elton John music video *I'm Still Standing*. It's also the place where Grace Kelly posed with Prince Rainer III of Monaco in 1955 during the *Cannes Film Festival*. It must have been an electrifying shoot. A year later they were married. Several scandalous jewelry heists have taken place at the Carlton despite the obvious security in and around the property.

The hotel's twin domes were reportedly modeled after a certain part of the anatomy of World War I courtesan Caroline Otero. The 11th floor formal dining room is also named after her. One can only surmise how vast her influence was to have garnered such attention.

The massive Carlton Restaurant on the ground floor is beautifully ornate. It has colonnades, a spectacular painted ceiling, artfully framed bay windows, and stunning carved cornices that are always reflected in the immaculate stone floor waxed daily to perfection. I've had lunch there a couple of memorable times. But even a pair of salads and ice teas will run you the price of dinner elsewhere. One September, I sat at the very table where Meg Ryan's film boyfriend in *French Kiss*, played by Timothy Hutton, sits with his French sweetie having breakfast. They're gazing handsomely out the sunny bay windows at the Bay of Cannes. I hoped for the same ambience. Unfortunately, it was pouring rain and my damp-from-walking companion and I watched as the wind whipped the deck chairs across the patio in hurricane fashion. But the salads were superb. The service was impeccable. And the old-world charm the Carlton exudes in every corner is well worth the price.

Another famous Cannes hotel is the Hôtel Majestic Barrière. A few steps from the Carlton, the Barrière is known for its fabulous views, glamorous suites, and penthouse luxury. Film festival stars particularly enjoy this hotel by all reports. The third notable hotel on the Croisette is the Grand Hyatt Cannes Hôtel Martinez. The Hôtel Martinez was opened in 1929 by the noble Italian Martinez family. It features art deco *décor* and considers itself the flagship hotel on the Riviera.

During World War II, the Martinez was taken over by various entities: the French army, the Italian army, the German army, and later the U.S. Air Force. The hotel became part of the Hyatt chain in 2012. It has 400 rooms and suites, a noted piano bar, a private beach, a heated pool, and three restaurants, one of which, La Palme d'Or, has two Michelin stars. I haven't eaten there, but having a drink there is a treat. The penthouse suite, by the way, reportedly goes for $37,000 per night.

The fourth major hotel in Cannes is the JW Marriott Cannes (formerly the Noga Hilton). My stay at the Marriott gave me complete access to the Croisette and beach, as well as the other famous hotels mentioned above, but without the astronomical price tag. Built in 1992 as a five-star hotel by a Genevan hotel empire, this hotel was renamed the Palais Stéphanie in 2007. Then it was renamed again in 2011 when Marriott acquired it.

The JW Marriott is located conveniently between the Carlton, Martinez, and the Majestic. It has a variety of rooms, modest to expensive, with views facing the streets or the beach. It seems to cater to the business crowd during off-season. It also has a casino and a fabulous terrace restaurant with spectacular views of the bay. The Marriott's slice of the Cannes beach is just a few steps from the entrance. With its handsome umbrellas, lounge chairs, and snappy beach service, it's a delight. Even an American tourist can feel like royalty here.

My daughter and I had gone to Cannes expecting spectacular September weather for lolling around on the beach. As such, we'd purchased new swimsuits: a skimpy polka dot bikini for my daughter and a more modest, but shapely, one-piece for me. As the weather in France is unpredictable, I shouldn't have been surprised when it rained almost every day we were there. Sadly, the polka dot bikini only saw the light of day once. But we consoled ourselves with the wonderful dining, abundant shopping, and gossiping with the locals who were more than happy to tell tales of movie star antics, as well as coach us on our French.

Speaking of bikinis, Brigitte Bardot didn't appear in any of the

Cannes Film Festival flicks in 1953. But she arrived as a nubile 18-year-old starlet, and she hit the beach in a "shockingly brief" bikini. During that week, she was photographed all over Cannes beaches in her scandalous attire. "Bardot flaunted spontaneity and informality via her girlish barefoot gait, long, loose hair, and unfussy, mostly skimpy attire," says Columbia film producer Edward Baron Turk. "She invented a new image of the French starlet: anti-snobbish, non-intimidating."

Just as quickly as she'd appeared, Bardot retired and vanished 20 years later in 1973. She's one of those French women who lives life *her* way. She enjoyed filmmaking, movie star life, and multiple relationships—until they all lost their charm for her. Now she's a feisty 80-year-old vocal advocate for her animal rights organization, which she runs from her estate La Madrague in Saint-Tropez. From her enclave shrouded in bamboo and pines she shares with businessman husband Bernard d'Ormale, she regularly pens notes on her famous blue paper to the powerful regarding animal causes. Among them is Paul Watson, co-founder of Greenpeace, who combats whale hunters. (One of his boats carries Bardot's name.) Another is Vladimir Putin, who Bardot has thanked for protecting the wolves of Russia. This is a woman with a brain to go with her legendary body.

The Russian connection is a fascinating one. When I first traveled to Cannes, I was surprised to discover that most of the menus on the French Riviera are written not only in French and English, but Russian. When I arrived in Cannes, I dimly noticed there were several couples around me deep in conversation in a language that sounded a lot like Russian. I don't speak it, so at first I wasn't sure. Then these people would suddenly turn to their servers or hotel staff and speak perfect French.

One morning, my daughter and I were having breakfast in our hotel's main restaurant on the sunny terrace overlooking the shimmering sea. There was a rather heavyset Russian foursome (two men and two women) sitting opposite us and down one table to my left. I noticed the women were stealing glances at us throughout the meal. They seemed very interested in our jewelry (which was not over the top) and our apparel. I queried the concierge, and he explained that yes, many Russian families come to the Riviera.

Over the course of the alternately rainy week, we passed these same Russian couples regularly on our way to and from the lobby. One morning, when the sun had finally appeared again, we sat out on the terrace again for breakfast. One of these Russian couples sat down at the table next to us. The man smiled broadly and stopped speaking Russian to his companion. Then, he leaned over to me and said in perfect English, "Good morning. Are you enjoying the fine weather?"

I replied, "Yes we are. Thank you for asking."

"You are very welcome," he said and returned to eating his *brioche*.

I looked down at my smoked salmon plate and picked up my fork. But as I slathered cream cheese on my bagel and laid some salmon delicately on top, I had the vague feeling that I'd somehow slipped into a James Bond movie.

After doing at little research, I shouldn't have been surprised that the Côte d'Azur is a favorite vacation locale for Russian citizens. In fact, Eugène Tipet, the French Consul in Moscow around 1850, bought a large piece of land in Cannes where he soon built the Villa Alexandra. After marrying, Tipet successfully encouraged many members of the Tsarist aristocracy to visit Cannes and buy property there too. It's been a favorite destination for wealthy Russians ever since. The beautiful Russian Orthodox Church in Nice is a testament to the Russian fondness for the Riviera.

The locals whispered to me that the French Riviera is where some wealthy Russians dispose of their wealth in unusual ways. They reportedly enjoy staying in the most expensive suites. Sometimes they order $10,000-a-bottle wines in a restaurant, then sip one glass and leave the rest on the table. I was also told about a certain Russian billionaire with a villa on Beaulieu-sur-Mer (between Nice and Monaco). This billionaire grew unhappy with the train noise. He approached the local town magistrates and offered 100 million euros (about 130 million dollars) to move the trains elsewhere. The locals didn't bite. But I can definitely confirm that it feels like you're sharing the Riviera with Russian powerbrokers. I can also confirm they've been very cordial to me.

There are plenty of dining opportunities in Cannes, from *haute cuisine* to homey Provençal fare. Since Cannes is relatively small, there are also some wonderful eateries back up the quaint streets away from the main Croisette. I had a delightful experience at Le Mesclun, for example. Le Mesclun is a cozy Mediterranean restaurant on Rue Saint Antoine. It features *foie gras*, lemon-olive chutney, lobster fricassee with champagne cream, and *Crêpes Suzette*. Since one of the waiters was related to the concierge at our hotel, he'd been warned in advance that I, and my attractive blonde daughter (who seemed to garner a lot of Bardot-ish attention as we wandered around the French Riviera), would be dining that night.

Once we arrived, the handsome young waiter seemed delighted to serve us. He proceeded to shower us with complimentary dishes, additional wines, and several desserts. All the while, he and his compatriots kept standing in the door to the kitchen giggling and eyeing my daughter's every move. (I felt like I was companioning Princess Stephanie that evening; no one appreciates a pretty American girl more than a Frenchman—especially in Cannes!)

Other eateries I can recommend outside the aforementioned hotels include Il Convivo (Italian) and the two-Michelin starred La Palme d'Or. For sheer fun, don't miss one of the bayside *cafés* along La Pantiéro and Quai Saint-Pierre south of the Palais des Festivals; the fresh fish is amazing, the prices are nominal, and the people watching is fantastic. If you want a memorable Michelin-starred experience, you might venture about eight kilometers into the hills directly above Cannes to Mougins. Mougins is home to Moulin de Mougins, a famed restaurant and small inn where master chef Alain Ducasse learned Provençal cooking under founder Roger Vergé. Vergé, now retired, is considered one of the great chefs of all time.

If you tire of shopping, eating, and lolling about on the beach hoping to be discovered, you might try the 15-minute boat ride from the Gare Maritime port of Cannes to the Lérins islands nearby. It's an easy walk from the Palais des Festival to this small port. Shuttle boats go over several times a day to Lérins' two small islands, Sainte-Marguerite and Sainte-Honorat. For a nominal fee, you can hop on one of the boats without reservations. You'll be rewarded by fabulous views of Cannes from the sea. The ferry will drop you off at the tiny pier, and you can explore the captivating islands at your leisure.

Sainte-Marguerite, the first island, is most famous since it allegedly housed the mysterious Man in the Iron Mask depicted in Alexandre Dumas's novel. The identity of this masked man was never known. But he must have been of noble birth (or Louis XIV's secret twin) since he was always served on silver and was perpetually clothed in fine linen. The second island, Sainte-Honorat, has monasterial remains and beautifully secluded paths that wind through forests of pine and eucalyptus. Along the coastline, you'll find a relaxed cluster of beach "dives" where you can get an inexpensive lunch and get to know the friendly French natives.

Ultimately, Cannes is one of those must-see places in Southern France. Its reputation precedes it to some degree, but I always find it an elegant locale to enjoy the best the Riviera has to offer. There are a variety of hotels and apartments to fit your travel needs. Restaurants and entertainment abound for every taste. Shopping is local and suited to any pocketbook. You can play golf or tennis, ballroom dance, and play *boules* in Cannes. And the sandy beach, compared to Nice's rocky one, makes frolicking in the sea delightful. Be sure you bring your bikini though. You never know who might be watching.

Cap d'Antibes

"I sat on the mole...to look at Antibes in the setting sun.
I have never seen anything so spectacular or so beautiful."
—Guy de Maupassant

On the coast between Cannes and Nice lies the discreet town of Cap d'Antibes. Situated at the eastern end of the Bay of Cannes, Cap d'Antibes is the exclusive enclave of the immensely wealthy, particularly

American tycoons. As journalist Ted Jones observes: "Cap d'Antibes reaches out into the Mediterranean like a basking dolphin, with old Antibes as its tail...and its nose the Fabled Eden Roc Hotel—host to the fabulously rich."

Antibes was named some 2,300 years ago by the Greeks who dubbed it "anti polis" (the city opposite), because it sat across the bay from their original colony at Nice. It sits slightly off the main auto route, so you'll have a traffic jam to wade through to get to the end of the cap if you visit. The peninsula of Cap d'Antibes is rather beautiful. But it's bordered on either side by some of the worst areas of congestion in the Riviera.

Beach shacks abut fabulous homes and small hotels, creating a sort of beachy rabbit warren of architecture. Offshore, yachts large and small bob in the water. Antibes is a yachting haven. And if you moor your boat near Antibes, you'll be in good company. Jules Verne wrote his scenario for *Around the World in 80 Days* from the deck of his yacht here. Or you might decide to secure an apartment like Graham Greene who spent his last 24 years in an Antibes apartment where he penned his last several novels.

Gerald and Sara Murphy, the wealthy socialites who lured their army of American and British friends, artists, and literary geniuses to this sunny spot, were the ones who really put Antibes on the social map. Droll John Dos Passos, radical American novelist, and friend of Fitzgerald and Hemingway, put it this way: "The upper-class French and British would not be seen dead on the Riviera in summer...but for Americans the temperature was ideal, the water delicious, and Antibes was the sort of little virgin port we dreamed of discovering."

When the Murphys first arrived on the Riviera, lying on the beach merely to enjoy the sun was unthinkable. The Murphys, with their extended parties and picnics, introduced sunbathing on the beach as a trendy activity. Along with the Murphys and their entourage came music, particularly jazz. Juan-les-Pins, Antibes's beach satellite, became a gathering place for musicians as a result. Since then, musicians fly in for the high-profile July jazz festival that features the world's jazz luminaries. Since 1960, it's been called *Fest Jazz à Juan Festival* and jazz greats like Ray Charles, Miles Davis, Ella Fitzgerald, and Louis Armstrong have appeared at one time or another.

The jewel on the peninsula is of course the glittering Hôtel du Cap Eden-Roc. Even now, the Hôtel du Cap Eden-Roc's exclusive clientele are as famous for their money as for the headlines they make. My most vivid memory of the Hôtel du Cap Eden-Roc a few years ago, was watching my husband fork over piles of euros for two glasses of champagne. At the time, the hotel was a cash-only enterprise. Diners had to come with wads of cash, and hotel guests who booked rooms had to wire funds ahead. In 2006, the resort finally capitulated to modern enterprise and began to take plastic.

The Hôtel du Cap-Eden-Roc is, however, a stunning place. It was built in 1870 in Napoleon III style. It's festooned with gilded chandeliers, delicate furniture, and has the best views of the Mediterranean on the Riviera. The grounds and pool area are literally built on the Rock of the peninsula, so it comes by the name naturally. The grounds are similar to the Hôtel Du Cap-Ferret (detailed later) in that pine trees are nestled among tropical gardens and yards of perfumed flowers moistened by spray from the Mediterranean.

If you opt to stay at the Hôtel du Cap-Eden-Roc, you won't be disappointed. The hotel has two Michelin starred restaurants, three bars and lounges, and its own brand of chocolate. Basic room rates in 2014 started at $1,100 per night. Note: Don't try to wander around in your bathrobe and slippers OR bikini sans wrap however. Hotel security will reportedly send you back to your room for more acceptable togs. (These are the *real* fashion police.) The other downside of all this fabulous exclusivity is that the lobby may be littered not only with glitterati, but their bodyguards as well. Clint Eastwood, Madonna, and Bruce Willis have all been spotted here.

As for the rest of Antibes, Pablo Picasso found great inspiration in Antibes; he rented a small studio in Château Grimaldi. It's now been turned into the Musée Picasso. It's filled with a stellar collection of Picasso paintings and ceramics. If you choose to wander through old Antibes, there's much to see and perhaps paint, including the old Fort Carré or the marina of Port Vauban with its mega yachts and glamorous visitors.

Cap d'Antibes is an enthralling, if privileged haven along the

Riviera. Victor Hugo particularly loved it. He set the beginning of *Les Misérables* where Valjean steals the bishop's silver candlesticks in the nearby market town of Dignes. Hugo's tribute reads: "Here everything shines, everything sings. Sunshine, women, and love are all resplendent here."

Nice

"And the colours of Nice! I wish I could take them down and send them to you."

—Friedrich Nietzsche

In contrast to staid Antibes, *Nice La Belle* (Nice the beautiful) is much more homey. Nice is the fifth largest city in France and the second most visited city after Paris. Just down the road from exclusive Antibes, Nice is bursting with neighborhood life. It's also crammed with colorful architecture that makes for lively meanders through the town. You'll find essential Nice roving the market stalls of the Cour Saleya (pictured), the most animated street market on the coast.

Nice Cours Saleya by Paul Shawcross
Copyright © 2014 Paul Shawcross

Nice is the capital city of the Côte d'Azur. It's sometimes called the "Heart of the Riviera." Nice was first settled nearly 400,000 years ago by prehistoric man. Then Greeks discovered it around 350 B.C. and dubbed it Nikea, from the goddess of victory, Nike. Romans later built spas in Nice, and ruins can still be found in Cimiez. The Italians dubbed her Nizza. Still later, France's Louis XIV wrested temporary control from the Italians and had the medieval fortifications blown up. Finally, Nice passed into French hands in 1860 under the Treaty of Turin.

But it was ultimately the visiting aristocrat Brits (and Russians) who civilized Nice for modern times. Even the Promenade des Anglais, the waterfront walkway, was named after the Brits whose enterprising efforts brought modern infrastructure (and cash) to the mushrooming area. This is an example of one of the reasons my British spouse calls his English countrymen "the shock troops of European travel." The Brits are fond of discovering new places and "civilizing them." Some people have other terms for this sort of "meddling," but you get my drift.

Finally, the railway came to the French Riviera and Nice in its completed form in 1864. The easier access brought even more tourists and a visit by Russian Emperor Alexander II and his Empress. This royal visit signaled the start of the Russian incursion. Russian aristocrats seeking sunshine and relaxation built villas and set up house during winter months. By 1900, there were two Russian libraries in Nice, a Russian sanatorium in Menton, and a Russian zoological society in Villefranche-sur-Mer. In Nice proper, Nicholas II built a gleaming gold and turquoise Russian orthodox church that looked like it was straight out of Moscow. Anton Chekhov, the great Russian playwright, was a welcome intellectual; members of the Leo Tolstoy family also came to live or visit.

But the Brits increased their numbers once Queen Victoria came to town. There's a lovely monument to her in the tony hills above Nice called Cimiez (where the uber-wealthy live). Henri Matisse, Marc Chagall, Auguste Renoir, and most of the world's wealthy found their way to Nice seeking the warm Mediterranean climate. Hans Christian Anderson and German philosopher Friedrich Nietzsche used to winter in Nice. Louisa May Alcott set part of *Little Women* on Nice's promenade.

With the arrival of better transportation and the railway, Nice finally became fully accessible. Many rich families built grand villas at the foot of the volcanic outcrop that shapes Nice. They hobnobbed with visiting royals, breathed the healing sea air, and whiled away the hours at the casinos. Later Nice was devastated for several years by World War II occupation and the heavy Allied bombing that preceded the Allied landing in Provence. Finally liberated in 1944, the city began rebuilding. Tourism returned to fuel the town's urban renewal—which shows no sign of abating today.

Modern Nice is a hubbub of activity fueled by having the third busiest airport in France, the country's second largest hotel capacity, and a massive street market held most days a week. (Airport note: If you fly into the French Riviera via the Nice Airport, be ready for an onslaught of fellow travelers who all want a rental car. I once waited nearly three hours to obtain my vehicle, during which time many of us hunkered down on the ground, picnicking on airplane food leftovers while we waited. Advice: fly in at an off time if you can so you don't get stuck in the rental car rush hour.)

When at last you can make your way to the center of Nice, you may wonder if you're in Italy or France. This is because Nice has passed so often between Italian and French influence, it looks like a cross between Florence and Marseilles. But this is part of its charm. Where Monaco has a casino money gleam to it, and Cannes has its movie star profile, Nice is a hunkered down hub, grounding the rest of the French Riviera populace.

Nice is sometimes also referred to as "the belly of the French Riviera." Her glamour has paled a bit in the shadow of glitzy Cannes and royal Monaco. However, my daughter insists Nice is "where it's happening," and the rest of the French Riviera for her is "a bit of a bore."

Nice La Belle is a tapestry of colorful, windy streets filled with shops, galleries, *tabacs*, bars, restaurants, and residences nestled among and in the medieval buildings. Often, you'll see *Belle Époque* lighting or modern neon signs topped by someone's laundry off the balcony above. The open market spills out into other areas like the Palais de Justice where there's a book and print market (usually Saturdays). I've often wandered toward the seafront to see the old port from here and then headed on to the colorful Opéra. Along the way, the aroma of food, flowers, and spices is everywhere.

You can practically eat your way around the world on the streets of Nice. Eateries offer Indian, African, Arabic, Italian, and Provençale flavors. In addition to dishes previously mentioned, Nice is famous for *bouillabaisse* (seafood soup), *quiche*, fig *tarte*, lavendar *sorbet*, plus anything featuring olive oil, truffles, *pistou tapenade*, or sausage.

I discovered that my daughter's instincts about Nice as a hot spot for cool were pretty accurate. Nice has a wealth of all-night discos and many lively bars that either stay open late, open early, or both. When I visit the Cours Saleya open-air market first thing in the morning, I watch bright-eyed farmers feverishly piling up their produce, while bleary-eyed 20-something clubbers, who've been out all night, stagger by in search of espresso and aspirin. My daughter finds it a hilarious contrast.

One of the things the locals tell me is that many of the "natives" go out clubbing at night during the week. Then they exit the clubs, grab some breakfast, and report to work in the same clothes they wore the day before. Apparently it's *très chic* to show up at your desk in your disco duds smelling of beer and cigarettes. Since I've not partaken of the Nice club experience myself, one can only wonder what happens on the weekends.

Like New York, Nice probably never sleeps. Live music venues range from concerts to pubs like Wayne's, De Klomp, and Thor. You can also consult the friendly local tourist office for more information on local happenings. Better yet, stop any young adult on the street, and they'll know exactly where to send you for a howling night of alcohol-fueled fun. Nice is also the home of the *Nice Jazz Festival*, begun in 1948. In 2011, it had more than 30,000 spectators! It used to be held in February, but it's moved to July, the traditional celebration month all over France.

Mirada, Café L'Escalinada, Tire Bouchon, and Le Bistrot d'Antoine are some of my favorite *cafés* close to old downtown. The Nice Casino has some flashy dining options. I once dined at a place called Brasserie Flo on Rue Sacha Guitry. Within walking distance of my small hotel, Flo was once a cabaret. We found ourselves eating therefore from a balcony table with full view of the stage where the cooking was taking place like some choreographed play. As a typical French *brasserie*, Flo featured a modestly priced menu with oysters, steak tartare, grilled meats, and seafood. It was here that I first ordered a cheese course that included what I thought was a modest *brie*. When the platter arrived, my companion and I were so overwhelmed by the stench, we thought we were going to be ill. We tried a bite or two, but we had to have the platter taken away. The waiter burst out laughing when he saw our faces. I believe Brasserie Flo has since closed down, but there are many similar affordable venues around Nice. Just watch out for the *fromage*!

A highlight for me in Nice is walking the glamorous Promenade des Anglais. You can stroll this wonderful sea-front boulevard any time day or night. It's a treat to smell the sea air, watch the glamorous sun-bathers, and ogle the cyclists and rollerbladers showing off. Along the way, the rich aromas of lavender, salt, fish, olive oil, and wine waft by. Nowadays, don't be surprised if you meet tour groups on Segways coming at you along the Promenade. Try one yourself if you want that Segway view of the French Riviera. Even more fun, you can rent a *vélo-bleu* (bike) since there are numerous bike stations in Nice.

My husband and I were once walking along the sun-drenched Promenade one morning, looking for someone to take our picture. I spotted a smiling, blond-haired woman in her 60s coming toward us. I caught her eye and asked her in French if she would take our picture. She threw up her hands and said in pure American English, "Oh, no. I don't speak any French. I'm from California." I laughed and told her we were from California as well; we discovered her house was five miles from ours! She happily took our photo, then commented, "They say all roads lead to Rome…but maybe now it's Nice!" By the way, Copacabana in Rio, the Malecón in Havana, and Venice Beach in Los Angeles are all said to have copied the template of "La Prom."

When I'm ready for serious retail in Nice, I make a beeline for Avenue Jean Médecin. This is the primary shopping street; it's non-stop boutiques as well as familiar chain stores. There are also some artistic sites worth a visit when you've spent your euros. I love the 1880-built Musée des Beaux-Arts museum, as well as the stunning Marc Chagall museum featuring his biblical-themed work. Of course you won't want to miss the extraordinary museum dedicated to Henri Matisse.

A visit to the luxurious Hotel Negresco, the pink and white wedding cake luxury accommodation on the Promenade des Anglais, is a heady experience even if you only stop by for an *apéritif*. Rich Baccarat chandeliers, expensive carpets, opulent lobby furniture, and a dazzling Gustave-Eiffel-designed glass and metal dome set the tone for visitors who enjoy opulence.

The suites at the Negresco feature an eclectic style of *décor* from Louis XIV to Napoleon III to oriental motifs. The consumption venues are memorable too, whether you desire a meal at Le Chantecler (the two Michelin starred restaurant dubbed Nice's finest), La Rotonde Brasserie with its family-oriented carousel theme, or simply pop in for potent refreshment at the stunning Le Relais Bar. Le Relais has some extravagant *Les Creations* drinks like the 27-euro ($33.50) Royal Negresco concocted from Kirsch, raspberry syrup, champagne, and gold glitter. If you've wanted to imbibe gold, here's your chance.

Many famed celebs still prefer the earthy ambience of Nice to any other place on the Riviera. Luminaries like Elton John, Bill Gates, Paul Allen, and Tina Turner all reportedly prefer Nice. But beware of too much showiness. American dancer and bohemian Isadora Duncan left San Francisco for Europe when she was quite young, but she died spectacularly in Nice. She delighted all of Europe with her exotic, barefoot dancing; she was often wrapped in a toga or flowing scarves. She decided to buy a car and learn to drive while living in the French Riviera. She was about to be taken out for a spin in an Amilcar sports car (not a Bugatti as is sometimes reported). But first, she flipped a long scarf around her neck. Then she got in on the passenger side. As the driver accelerated, her scarf billowed out behind her in the Riviera sea breeze. Unfortunately, the scarf got caught in the rear wheel well, strangling her instantly. (Gertrude Stein, always ready with some acid wit, commented on Duncan's death: "Affectations can be dangerous.")

But if you really want to show off everything you've got come what may, be in Nice for Carnaval. Every year in the weeks before Lent, *Nice Carnaval* erupts in the streets. This is the gigantic extravaganza that competes with Brazil and Venice's Carnivals for out-of-this-world fun. For 15 days every February, Nice goes wild with flower parades, light extravaganzas, dancing costumed characters, and music venues practically on every corner. There's also dancing in the streets—not to mention the drinking, noshing, and other pastimes that go on all night long. If you want to celebrate with the best of them, *Nice Carnaval* is your ticket.

Cap Ferret

"The Cap Ferret peninsula dangles like an earring into the Mediterranean between the bays of Villefranche and Beaulieu, its clasp the tiny sub-peninsula of St-Hospice, the jewel the coconut-ice Ephrussi Palace perched along its skyline."

—Ted Jones, *The French Riviera*

A spit of land between Villefranche and Beaulieu divides the coastline between Nice and Monaco. It's some of the most expensive real estate on the French Riviera. Its name is Cap Ferret.

Cap Ferret (shown) is almost an island, save for the tiny isthmus that connects the peninsula to the narrow coastline between. As you can see in this photo the peninsula spreads out to the sea while a tiny offshoot fans left where Saint-Jean, Cap Ferret's only town, sits quietly by the Baie des Fourmis (Bay of Ants).

The port of Saint-Jean overlooks the coastal panorama that stretches from hillside Èze, along the Corniches, all the way to Monaco up on the Rock, and then on to the Italian Riviera. Saint-Jean used to be a lazy harvester of figs, olives, and fish. Today, the tiny town is a popular tourism destination with busy pleasure boats, hotels, and restaurants.

Cap Ferret's golden age occurred in the late 1800s when King Leopold II of Belgium built a summer retreat on the peninsula. Then, he proceeded to buy up bits of land all around him. Banker Baron de Rothschild followed suit. The wealthy and famous came in discreet numbers thereafter, including Somerset Maugham who bought his Villa Mauresque in 1926.

British Secret Intelligence officer, playwright, novelist, and short story writer, Maugham was reputedly the highest paid author during the 1930s. He spent 40 years on his beloved Cap Ferret, save for World War II when his villa was occupied by Italian troops, and later German officers who basically pillaged the place. Ultimately restored by Maugham, Villa Mauresque nurtured some of Maugham's greatest works including *The Razor's Edge*. While he wrote in his fortress-like study atop his house, his gaggle of glamorous guests cavorted below or ventured out to the Riviera. Maugham usually appeared in the evening for cocktails and dinner.

Noel Coward visited Maugham. Evelyn Waugh, H.G. Wells, Rudyard Kipling, T.S. Eliot, D.H. Lawrence, and Raymond Chandler spent time at the villa. An enthusiastic writer called Ian Fleming came to soak up Maugham's stories about the Secret Service; these later became inspiration for Fleming's James Bond spy escapades. Other Cap Ferret lovers were Winston Churchill, the Duke and Duchess of Windsor, Cecil Beaton, Arthur Rubinstein, Matisse and Picasso, and Lord Kenneth Clarke. (Picasso definitely got around.)

Nearby, Jean Cocteau, multi-talented French author, painter, and filmmaker lived at his Etruscan-style Villa Santo-Sospir at 14 Rue Jean Cocteau. Princess Grace came to visit, Nijinsky talked dance, Stravinsky discussed his latest composition, and Orson Welles and Marlene Dietrich planned their next films. Other fans of the Cap include Elizabeth Taylor, Gregory Peck, Charles de Gaulle, and Jean-Paul Belmondo. In modern day, I've learned that Microsoft founders Bill Gates and Paul Allen (may) own estates there (Brad Pitt and Angelina Jolie have been spotted), but I couldn't identify their abodes, specifically since things are very hush hush on Cap Ferret.

My husband and I had the fortunate experience of staying on extraordinary Cap Ferret in the port town of Saint-Jean one late summer. We enjoyed an affordable and blissful stay at the Hôtel Brise Marine. The Brise Marine is a modest villa property nestled among the multi-million dollar estates. The villa is a pretty ochre-and-turquoise trimmed hotel with an overgrown garden. It's within a block or two of downtown Saint-Jean. Saint-Jean is basically a tiny seaside village with a few shops, some *cafés*, a grocery, an 11th-century church, and a pink town hall with frescos by Cap Ferret resident Jean Cocteau. At night, we could see the lights of Monaco twinkling through the open windows of our room.

One afternoon, we decided to amble around the magical Cap Ferret peninsula. Cap Ferret is considered the upmarket end of the French Riviera (other than Antibes). The quiet touches of old money are everywhere. The main paved road, a former goat path, is walker friendly. But you'll occasionally be interrupted by a limo or a Rolls Royce ferrying guests to their multi-million dollar villas or the *crème de la crème* resort at the end of the path, the Grand Hôtel du Cap Ferret.

The preferred walking route is clockwise so that the sun follows you; this is exactly what we did. We had a heavenly time admiring the colorful villas, tropical gardens, and umbrella pines backlit by golden sunshine. It has a similar vibe as the 17-mile drive in Carmel, California, although Cap Ferret is even more private. The ultra-quiet buzz of uber-wealth saturates the place.

There are more than 14 kilometers (8 miles) of public walking trails on Cap Ferret. They tuck in and out of the scenic pines, and rhododendrons and jasmine perfume the air, especially in summer. As we wandered along, we got stellar views of Monaco *and* Nice, as well as cruise ships and yachts bobbing in the harbor.

Along the way, we paused near ironclad gates of spectacular mansions like Villa Socoglio, formerly owned by David Niven. One scene from the *Pink Panther* was filmed on Cap Ferret by pal Blake Edwards. Niven also wrote his memoirs *The Moon's a Balloon* and *Bring on the Empty Horses* at his Cap Ferret villa. Down the way, the Villa Nell Côte is famous too. It's where the Rolling Stones recorded *Exile on Main Street* in the 1970s.

About 30 minutes into our walk, we came to the tip of Cap Ferret. Here sits the most opulent venue on the peninsula, the Grand Hôtel du Cap Ferret. Nestled amid park-like grounds, with a spectacular infinity pool offering Hawaii-beach resort ambience, the Grand Hôtel du Cap Ferret is elegance personified. Its obvious *cachet* keeps it one of the top 10 hotel destinations in the world.

A young writer named Murray Burnett visited the Hôtel du Cap in the early 1940s. He sat in the lounge watching an African-American pianist playing on a glamorous piano. Afterward, he felt inspired to write a little play called *Everybody Comes to Rick's*. He later sold it to Warner Brothers. It became the movie *Casablanca*.

In later years, Aristotle Onassis visited the very romantic Hôtel du Cap as did Frank Sinatra, Paul McCartney, George Bush, and Bill Clinton. But you don't have to own the Time Warner building in order to stay in this mega-watt resort. You just have to be willing to shell out the nightly $600-$5,000 fee. (There's a two-night minimum, depending on the season). If you have buckets of cash, you can enjoy the 6,000-square-foot Villa Rose-Pierre next door, which is managed by the hotel. It's available for a scant $36,000+ per week.

I had the opportunity to lunch at the hotel's terrace restaurant, which overlooks the sun-kissed grounds and the sparkling Mediterranean beyond. The clothed tables were set with fine French china and expensive glassware against a backdrop of French Riviera scenery. It was like something out of a film set. My husband and I ordered a pared-down lunch in order to save some of our budget for a high-end dinner engagement we had later that evening. Nevertheless, our modest *foie gras* and salad, plus half carafes of wine and some Evian water (no coffee or dessert) still ran us about $200. But it was one of my favorite dining experiences of all time.

If you have a bottomless budget, you might want to try a full-blown luncheon or dinner at La Véranda. Or you might want to step into the Grand Hôtel's bar and settle in under the Murano chandeliers for a mojito or high tea. If you're feeling especially generous, you can request the *sommelier* to uncork one of his vintage bottles of Château d'Yquem (dating from 1854) or some Château Lafite Rothschild (dating from 1799).

After lunch, the walk back along the other side of the Cap was equally impressive. The artist Matisse was so mesmerized by the light on Cap Ferret he wrote: "This is the place where light plays the first part. Colour comes afterwards." I agree that the Cap has a glow that's indescribable. We could see yachts and cruise ships sailing into the Bay of Villefranche-sur-Mer as we ambled down one of the coastline paths. And, as we strolled, it almost felt like we were passing through a painting created by Matisse himself.

My week on Cap Ferret was memorable in a number of other

ways. First, the Saint-Jean spit of land where I stayed at the Brise Marine offers a unique experience of affordable comfort where visitors can wander down to the local bakery for daily baguettes or simple foods for picnics. There are also restaurants within walking distance at the Porte de Saint-Jean that are delicious and affordable (under $100 for dinner). Americans will find the Brise Marine rooms rather small, however; if you can secure a room with a terrace you'll be rewarded with a fabulous view and extended space.

Second, there's fantastic proximity to the rest of the coastline from Saint-Jean. We strolled up the coast on the east side a mile or two to handy Beaulieu-sur-Mer for shopping and meals. And we meandered back toward Villefranche-sur-Mer along the neck of the peninsula, passing the fabulous Villa Ephrussi on the way.

Third, the Brise Marine is happily within walking distance of the bathing-suit optional Paloma Beach just down the hill. Here, the locals sunbathe, splash in the waves, and fish. True to the French stereotype, most of the women are topless.

One sunny afternoon, we strolled down to Paloma Beach, took out our towels and our basket of goodies, and spread everything out on the beach. Then, we lay back to enjoy the view. From the tiny beach where we were sunbathing, we looked over the waterway and saw cars and busses rushing along the Corniche roadway between Nice and Monaco. But we weren't prepared for what happened next.

Suddenly a plane roared in and dipped down as if it was going to crash into the bay. Leveling out over the water, its belly magically opened up, and, as the plane slid over the water, it scooped up several tons of water before closing up and climbing again. It then headed off over the hills. Very soon, a second plane and then another and another flew in and did the same thing.

We discovered later that they were probably Canadairs, the French/Canadian flying amphibious aircraft designed to fight fires in France. These flying fire engines are the main defense against the raging fires that move through Provence and the Côte d'Azur in minutes, especially during the *mistral*, when winds can reach up to 80 miles an hour. These particular planes were probably dropping water on some fire in the hills beyond our view. It was a spectacular process to see in the flesh. Chilling, but fascinating.

As we trekked back to our hotel late in the afternoon, we had one more remarkable experience. We spied a lithe, near-nude matron, fishing off her private pier. There she was, fishing pole in hand, reeling in fish, and wearing nothing but her bikini bottoms. She seemed unperturbed that her breasts were occasionally interfering with her flipping fish into her bucket.

Finally, we had an unexpected companion during our week's stay on Cap Ferret. She watched us from the balcony wearing her jet-black furs like Bulgari mink. She was an elegant sort of female, with all the coquettish charm of one who knows what she wants and where she can get it. Each morning, my husband would amble down the road to the tiny shops in Saint-Jean. There he'd buy a baguette, some *pâte*, a few cheeses, some French butter, and a couple of pots of French jam. Then, he'd saunter back up the hill to our room. Out on the balcony, we'd spread out our breakfast feast. And as we ate, we'd see our unexpected companion, watching us stealthily with her green eyes flashing as the lights of Monaco blinked behind her in the distance.

I learned later that her name was Minette. (Talk about a French coquette.) She was the evident queen of the Brise Marine—and went wherever she wanted. She was, of course, the house feline. How appropriate, I thought. Here in the land of *To Catch a Thief*, where Cary Grant's character, "the Cat," shows up metaphorically as a black feline who climbs Riviera rooftops and robs the wealthy socialites of their jewels.

I pondered. Was this a new breed of cat burglar come to pay me a call on my own Cap Ferret balcony? Or was it Cary Grant reincarnated as a come-hither feline to see what he could get?

I'll never know the truth. But I can definitely tell you Minette was not nearly as interested in my jewels as she was my *pâte*. We ended up feeding her every morning for week. We even had to put her out at night, because she had a very bad habit of languishing on the bed whenever we got ready to go to sleep. There's nothing like a forward femme fatale!

Cats aside, one of my other favorite experiences on Cap Ferret was visiting the Villa Ephrussi-de-Rothschild. This Italianate villa was built in the early 1900s by Béatrice de Rothschild, (born Baroness of Rothschild) and her rich banker husband, Maurice Ephrussi. Ultimately, the Baroness separated from the dastardly Ephrussi. He was an inveterate gambler and philanderer; he infected the Baroness with a disease, most likely syphilis, that kept her from having children.

Though she already owned a Monaco estate, she fell in love with Cap Ferret. A very shrewd lady, the Baroness bought 18 acres of prime land on the Cap before stunned King Leopold II of Belgium could get his hands on it. When her father died, the Baroness inherited his vast fortune. She quickly built her large, shocking pink Renaissance villa on the acreage. She must have loved Italy, because it's very similar to the grand residences of Florence. The rest of the land was made into a series of contiguous gardens in the shape of a ship, with the "deck" decorated with waterfalls and pools. A Temple of Love crowns the prow. The sea lays on either side of the land. Therefore, the entire estate forms a spectacular vantage point for much of the Riviera.

The Baroness had her seven gardens tended feverishly by 30 sailor-clad, red-bereted gardeners. She'd stand on her house's upper deck and bellow orders to them through a megaphone as if she were a ship's captain. The seven gardens are still immaculate. They're shaped around different themes: Spanish, Florentine, lapidary, Japanese, exotic, Provençal, and rosary. The Baroness also installed a zoo filled with exotic birds and animals like flamingos, monkeys, mongooses, and gazelles.

She was also an avid art collector. Even today you can see some of her priceless treasures, which include a whist table owned by Marie-Antoinette. Sometimes the Baroness would dress up as her royal idol, and receive her guests looking like the beheaded queen. Her furniture is 18th century French. And the entire villa looks like a mini Versailles.

Upon her death, she bequeathed Villa Ephrussi to the Academy of Fine Arts of the French Institute. They now run it as a public museum. The opulent site often serves as the backdrop for advertising for Fragonard, Louis XVI furniture, and Sèvres porcelain. On the day I visited, a French film crew was filming a Kellogg's cereal commercial in the middle of the living room. The actors wore sultan and harem costumes. Tony the Tiger figured prominently. It was hilarious. I can only wonder what the regal Baroness would have thought of a cartoon tiger cavorting around her mini-Versailles.

Above all, Cap Ferret is a secluded, elegant enclave of the French Riviera where ultra-wealthy vistas make it well worth a visit. Of all the coastal environs, it may come closest to capturing the sun-soaked Riviera ambience of old.

Èze

If you're traveling on one of the Corniches or roadways cutting into the hillsides between Nice and Monaco, you'll undoubtedly see the turnoff to Èze. Èze (pictured) is the bewitching medieval hilltop town overlooking Monaco and Cap Ferret. There are three Corniches: the Basse Corniche or N98, which is the heavily-traveled roadway that hugs the coastline and passes through all the resort towns; the Moyenne Corniche or N7, the wider middle road that cuts through the mountains; and the Grande Corniche or D2564, which follows the route of the ancient Roman Aurelian Way.

Many travelers take a tour bus to reach Èze. As Èze is only 30 minutes from Monaco or Nice it's also fairly easy to reach by car. The stunning views from the ancient streets ringed with hot pink bougainvillea and succulents are completely otherworldly. They speak of an ancient time before the glitz and glamour of the Riviera glossed over the centuries of Côte d'Azur history evident in Èze. This tiny village was once occupied by Romans, Moors, and Italians. Visitors can see evidence of the House of Savoy who built up the town in 1388, creating a fortified stronghold that's like an "eagle's nest" since it sits 1,400 feet above sea level.

Today's Èze is affectionately known as a "museum village."

Donkeys still haul groceries up the steep lanes. It's famous particularly for its Jardin Botanique d'Èze, the Chapelle de la Sainte Croix that dates back to 1306, and Notre Dame de l'Assomption church built in 1764.

The tiny town's stone alleys and vaulted passageways are stuffed with art galleries, hotels, restaurants, and chic shops. Many honeymooners sojourn here. Château Eza, a hotel converted from a château on the Rue de la Pise, has particularly palatial rooms with superb views. A variety of restaurants perch on the edge of the cliff side, but I love Michelin-rated La Chèvre d'Or, which serves a stellar luncheon. For the budget minded, there are pizza and sandwich places as well.

Èze was a favorite of Walt Disney who, I suspect, incorporated some of its visual elements into the Disney parks. Frederic Nietzsche, German philologist, philosopher, cultural critic, poet, and composer, especially loved Èze. Nietzsche used to walk up to Èze several times a week from his villa in Nice (about 7 miles). He found it soothing to his rather depressive nature. "The richness of the light on a tortured, sometimes suicidal, soul like me is almost miraculous. Like a plant, I grow in the sunshine." Later, this beloved path was renamed Sentier Friedrich Nietzsche. You can walk the same winding footpath today, although you'll need good shoes and determination since it's quite steep.

I had a heartfelt experience in Èze that has stayed with me to this day. I wandered into the inviting medieval church called Notre Dame de l'Assomption. Its ochre-colored walls and statuesque clock tower, which can be seen for miles, attracted me. Stepping inside, I saw the most beautiful chapel of ornate gold and marble filled with modest pews. After a time, I stepped over to the guest book. Flipping back through the pages, I saw that many people had visited this special place of spiritual unity just after 911 (September 11, 2001). As most know, this was when planes flew into the World Trade Center in New York, killing thousands. I read prayers and thoughts of compassion for the 911 tragedy from visitors from all over the world: China, Italy, Croatia, Canada, Germany, Australia, Japan, Mexico, Brazil, and on and on. All were praying for healing in this tiny chapel on the French Riviera hillside. In that moment, the glitz of the Côte d'Azur disappeared into a deep-felt moment of worldwide compassion. Who knew prayers for America would appear in such an unlikely place? I signed the book, thanking all who had remembered us and wrote how much my visit to Èze had meant to me. This is just one of the memories that keeps me traveling and writing about new and wonderful places where a common humanity connects us all.

Below hill-perched Èze is Èze-sur-Mer, the on-the-coast sister to the village above. Rockers Bono and the Edge bought a 3.8 million euro luxury mansion here that has 20 rooms. It has its own private beach plus a private island. The paparazzi regularly snap Bono strolling around or sailing on his boat while entertaining visitors like Robert de Niro, George Clooney, and Penelope Cruz.

Saint-Paul-de-Vence

Saint-Paul-de-Vence is one of the oldest medieval towns on the French Riviera. Situated in the Alpes-Maritimes away from the coast, it's still easily reachable by car or bus. Like Èze, it sits on a fortified spur of rock. But Saint-Paul-de-Vence has a medieval *rue grande* that now is overstuffed with touristy art galleries, eateries, and souvenir shops. When the sun goes down, however, and the tourist busses head off down the hill, the grand avenue reclaims much of its medieval charm.

An old military stronghold in the 16th century, Saint-Paul-de-Vence became a home over the years to artists, writers, poets, and actors who relished an artist colony-type atmosphere. In the 1960s, actors Yves Montand and Simone Signoret lived there. Other Saint-Paul-de-Vence lovers were artist Marc Chagall, American writer James Baldwin, and British actor Donald Pleasance. Former Rolling Stones bassist Bill Wyman reportedly has a home in Saint-Paul.

James Baldwin, the African-American novelist (*Go Tell It on the Mountain*), playwright (*The Amen Corner*), and activist wrote about living in France and Saint-Paul: "I think exile (in France and elsewhere) saved my life, for it inexorably confirmed something which Americans appear to have great difficulty accepting. Which, simply, is this: a man is not a man until he is able and willing to accept his own vision of the world, no matter how radically that vision departs from that of others…What

Europe gives an American…is the sanction to become oneself."

Traveling up to dramatic Saint-Paul-de-Vence is fairly easy; parking and traversing the tiny medieval town popular with tour groups is another matter. If you can get yourself there in early morning or late afternoon, you'll enjoy a Carmel, California-like atmosphere. The streets are meticulously refurbished and host art studios and adorable teashops.

Saint-Paul-de-Vence has some premiere art galleries and museums with fine pedigrees. The Fondation Maeght, built by Paris art dealers Aimé and Marguerite Maeght, is one of Europe's finest museums of modern art. Scattered among the terraced gardens dotted with pine trees there are also mobiles, sculptures, and mosaics by Miró, Giacometti, and Hepworth.

One of the most famous sites in Saint-Paul-de-Vence is La Colombe d'Or (the Golden Dove). It began in the 1920s as Chez Robinson, a modest bar with an open-air terrace where people would dine, drink, and dance on weekends. Soon, it attracted a famous clientele and expanded to a large hotel (13 rooms and 12 suites) with a pool and a 70-seat restaurant plus an expansive garden terrace to accommodate the stars, artists, writers, and film elite who gathered. Patrons included Picasso, Modigliani, Colette, Cocteau, Miró, Braque and Chagall—some of whom paid for their rooms or meals in artwork, which can still be seen today. F. Scott Fitzgerald and wife Zelda had a legendary fight there over dancer Isadora Duncan. Zelda threw herself down the stone stairs in anger. Yves Montand married Simone Signoret on the terrace. Sartre came, as did Greta Garbo, Sophia Loren, Burt Lancaster, and Catherine Deneuve.

Both Èze and Saint-Paul-De-Vence have maximized their tourism value. Èze just seems to me to have maintained more of its medieval purity. But both are well worth a visit.

Monaco

"Monaco: the snobbiest place on earth. It makes L.A. look like North Korea."

—Jeremy Clarkson, *Top Gear*

Monaco. Land of millions and millionaires, princes and princesses, yachts and high rises.

Monaco is a term used generically for the whole principality of Monaco (shown). Monaco is essentially a prominent escarpment at the base of the Maritime Alps that slopes down to the French Riviera. As a prime chunk of Côte d'Azur real estate however, Monaco had been fought over for centuries. It became a colony of Genoa in 1215. Then it came under the rule of the House of Grimaldi in 1297 when swordsman Francesco Grimaldi ("the cunning one") dressed as a monk, got inside the castle gates, and killed the guards. He then let his colleagues in to capture the fortress on the Rock. You can still see the statue of the sword carrying "monk" in front of the palace.

In 1419, the Grimaldis purchased the land officially from the crown of Aragon. The princes of Monaco became "vassals" of the French kings but remained independent rulers. The Grimaldis were turfed out temporarily during the French Revolution. But they returned to rule Monaco again as a principality in 1815. They've continued ever since.

Monaco became completely detached from France in 1861, but it struggled financially. Monaco came into its own in the 1870s, however, when financier François Blanc set up a casino named after the prince, Charles III. It was called Monte Carlo. Blanc was a clever man with a fine financial mind. He'd already lent France 4.8 million francs to finish building its famous Paris Opera Garnier. In return, he got architect Charles Garnier to design the Monte Carlo casino *and* convinced France to build a railway to ship gamblers in by the trainload.

The partnership was so successful that the flourishing principality abolished taxes for nationals and anyone meeting the strict residency status of six months per year. Taxes were also abolished or reduced for companies based in or trading in Monaco. World War I and II caused some blips in the Monaco calm since it was occupied in rapid succession by Fascists and later the German Wehrmacht. After WWII, Grimaldi Prince Louis II returned to rule until his death in 1949 when Prince Rainier took over.

Prince Rainier III famously married starlet Grace Kelly in 1956. The couple had three children, the last being a boy, Albert. The principality of Monaco is now governed under a constitutional monarchy headed by Prince Albert II, 56, who succeeded to the throne upon the death of Rainier in 2005.

Late breaking news: Prince Albert and his bride Princess Charlene happily announced the birth of twins at the end of 2014. Babies Gabriella and Jacques arrived within minutes of each other, with the little girl born first and her brother following two minutes later. Despite being the younger, it will be Prince Jacques who succeeds his father on the throne, thanks to Monaco's continued embrace of Salic law. Salic law states that male heirs always take precedence over their older sisters. The babies were delivered at Princess Grace Hospital, which is named after their late grandmother.

Monaco remains one of the smallest countries in the world at about 499 acres (.78 square miles). Interestingly, Monaco has a territorial "golden parachute." Though bordered by Italy and France, Monaco enjoys the privilege of having France as its military protector, but maintains the freedom of an independent nation.

Economic development mushroomed once the Monte Carlo Casino became such a monumental success. The whole gambling enterprise came about as a result of a loophole, however. Because Monaco was an independent nation, it could establish itself as a gambling empire. This was particularly important since prohibition was in vogue in Germany, Italy, and France at the time. Its first casino opened in 1863; it retained its monopoly on roulette until 1933.

With no state income tax and very low business taxes, Monaco understandably has a very dense population of more than 37,000 residents. The official language is French, but Monégasque, Italian, and English are widely spoken and understood. According to the *CIA World Factbook*, Monaco has the world's lowest poverty rate and the highest number of millionaires and billionaires per capita. Monaco also has the world's most expensive real estate market at approximately $58,300 per square meters (10.7 square feet).

You can see why it's a well-loved tax haven. The major objection to living in Monaco, however, is that there's very little land. Therefore, all the residential builders have to build up. Thus, you may have your fabulous Monaco retreat, but it will be in a massive high rise. Most don't seem to mind.

Monaco is a must-see destination. But if you're driving to Monaco from either Èze or Nice, you'll encounter traffic along the narrow, sometimes dangerous Corniches that lead into Monaco. Princess Grace was driving with Princess Stephanie on September 13, 1982 on the RN53, a treacherous part of one of these roads connecting the Grande Corniche and the middle Moyenne Corniche. She apparently suffered a stroke. Her vehicle went over the side of the road. Princess Stephanie survived but Princess Grace did not. Today, many people stop to see where this tragic accident occurred. Be aware: there's a sharp drop below if you too decide to stop here.

As you pass along the Corniche into Monaco proper, you'll come around the hillside. Suddenly the splendid palace of the principality of Monaco sits like a crown on the top of the Rock. This alabaster palace with handsome red roofs sits magnificently on a mammoth outcrop while down below lies a sparkling blue harbor filled with large and small white yachts. The whole scene is breathtaking.

Below the Rock sits the tiny town of Monaco. It's nestled among apartment high rises that lead up to a palatial garden square, which is anchored by Monte Carlo. The streets are inordinately clean, especially compared with the rest of France. There are plenty of policemen standing around in white hats and gloves. Petty crime is almost unheard of (no wonder). Large crime from one-armed bandits and roulette tables is another matter, however.

The general world populace was probably blissfully unaware of Monaco until Alfred Hitchcock decided to make a little movie in 1954 called *To Catch a Thief* with Cary Grant and Grace Kelly. This romantic thriller about a cat burglar was filmed all over Nice, Cannes, and Monaco. This included the part of the Corniche where Kelly races along the road, then stops for an impromptu picnic with Grant. In the film you can see the Monaco Palace behind them as they romance over chicken and beer. Little did Kelly know she was going to spend the rest of her life in that palace.

Kelly was asked to come to the Cannes film festival in May 1955. During the festivities, Kelly got to meet and take photographs with Prince Rainier. Rainier was enchanted by her. Within a year, most of the world's best photographers converged on tiny Monaco to witness the royal wedding of Prince Rainier and Grace Kelly of Philadelphia.

The tiny city that Princess Grace was to make her home is roughly divided into three parts: the "old city" and Palace on the rocky promontory extending into the Mediterranean known as Le Rocher, the "Rock of Monaco"; Monte Carlo, the principal resort, residential and town area ("La Condamine"); and Port Hercules, the southwestern area that includes the port.

Because exotic Monaco is so small, visitors can easily park in the underground parking structure near the casino and see the whole area on foot within a couple of hours. If you're with a tour company, the buses will most likely unload you on the Rock near the palace. After seeing the palace (and perhaps the changing of the guard), you can easily wander around the shops, restaurants, and gardens, and then take a leisurely stroll down to the town and port area. Then you can meander your way up the hill to the Place du Casino.

For first time visitors, the Palace is a wonderland of 15th century frescoes, 18th century architecture, and artifacts from centuries of royal collecting. Limited palace tours are available, depending on whether the royal family is resident or not. Most travelers come for the grand changing of the guard. A white-uniformed band accompanies this regal ceremony, and it takes place outside the palace precisely at 11:55 a.m. daily.

On my second visit to Monaco, I was without a rental car and landed at the royal palace via group van. My daughter and I were therefore at the whim of our driver who unloaded several of us near the palace in torrential rain. The driver then got called out to pick up another group down in Nice; he didn't return for nearly five hours. This is far too much time to spend on the Rock in my opinion; the medieval streets are interesting but not worth a several-hour sojourn. During this particular trip, we'd already seen the palace and the changing of the guard. Since it was pouring rain, my daughter and I therefore took refuge in the only real restaurant nearby aside from pizza eateries. It's called Castleroc.

Both a bar and restaurant, Castleroc has a fabulous location and some notable cuisine. It's famed for traditional Monegasque cooking that blends Italian and French flavors. Diners can also find stockfish, one of Monaco's national dishes made from dried cod and vegetables, grilled fish offered in rustic style with grilled vegetables, and sublime scallops. The prices are high since it's a prime tourist location. But on a day of rain-drenched skies, it made an elegant spot for lunch while we watched the rain gently slide down the palace walls and waited for our van.

For some reason, the restaurant was fairly empty, despite the clumps of wet tourists milling around the Palace seeking cover. Our dapper servers were quite attentive; with flair they presented gold embossed menus and happily pointed out the day's special of fresh sea bass. I scanned the room. Most of the diners were ordering coffees and simple dishes. I turned back to the menu and thought to myself: "If we're in the land of nobility, why not be treated like royals?" I ordered the sea bass and champagne.

The waiter clapped his hands and scuttled away. Soon, he was back with chilled glasses and a bottle of ice-cold Veuve Clicquot. As we sipped, a series of elegant *amuse bouches* appeared before us: salmon *mousse,* scallops, and vegetable puree. Soon after, a massive sea bass simmering in butter and lemon slices was rolled across to us on a grand trolley. Next, two servers hand-carved large portions for us. Then they slide the plump slices onto warm china where a heavenly pile of roasted potatoes and caviar-topped asparagus spears joined them on each plate. The servers set warm pots of lovely hollandaise next to the vegetables and presented our meals to us. The whole restaurant watched as we ate our way through all this delicious fare.

Throughout the meal, we were chatting in English but practicing our French. Over a shared dessert of *tarte Tatin,* we puzzled over some French weather terms. I noticed an older French couple at the table next to us eyeing us and smiling. Several times, the gentlemen nodded at me. I nodded back. Soon, he slid over to say hello in English.

This aristocratic little gentleman, who had to be 75 at least, explained that he and his wife were visiting Monaco on a vacation from Paris where they lived. He had a white, upturned mustache and a full head of white hair. He reminded me of Charlie Chaplain's little tramp—if he'd been a white-haired senior citizen. His wife was also in her 70s; she was beautifully attired in a jewel-blue silk dress and matching scarf. The man explained in English that he had been a language professor before he retired. He said he was very happy to coach us on some French terms if we liked while we enjoyed our after-lunch coffees and waited for the rain to stop.

For the next hour, he kindly taught us all kinds of French weather terms like *pluie* for rain, *parapluie* for umbrella, and more. We had a merry time laughing at our terrible accents and garbled pronunciations. His wife smiled gaily throughout, but she rarely said anything (I suspect her English was limited). But she seemed to really enjoy seeing her husband back in his element as a tutor. Finally, the rain stopped and it was time to depart. We thanked them both profusely, and he handed me his card. He said that the next time we were in Paris we should pay them a call. In retrospect, it was one of my earliest experiences with French strangers who were extraordinarily kind and helpful. Since then, I've experienced these sympathetic encounters over and over. It's one of the reasons I so enjoy France.

Wandering outside, the skies opened up and began to pour again, unfortunately, as soon as we entered the street. We made a dash to one of the other main attractions on the Rock: Monaco Cathedral. This cathedral is where Princess Grace and Prince Rainer were married. It's also where they're entombed under the marble floor near the altar. Since it's open to the public, anyone can file around the altar to see the floor plaques indicating the resting place of the royals. Princess Grace's area was festooned with flowers and cards. Her pavement slab is inscribed in gold with this statement, *"Gratia Patricia Principis Rainierii III Uxor."* It's a very dignified resting place for a much-admired royal princess.

Another tourist favorite nearby is the Oceanographic Museum. The Oceanographic Museum, a great favorite of Prince Rainier, is an aquarium and underwater research center. A few steps down the street are art galleries, shops, and the *Musée de la Cire Historial des Princes de Monaco*, a wax museum devoted to Grimaldi royalty. Here, visitors can enjoy life-sized wax figures of the royals in full regalia.

Heading down Avenue de la Porte Nueve, which is a very pleasant walk from or to the palace, you quickly find yourself at the picturesque harbor. Looking out over the flat stretch of promenade facing the harbor toward the Mediterranean called La Condamine, you'll see mega-yachts bobbing in the sunshine. As you wander through the tiny town or amble along the harbor, you'll have a variety of photo ops as well as stellar shopping and eating venues. Many of the *bistros* offer reasonably priced fare served under curbside umbrella tables, which, in the sunshine, is delightful. (Yes, you can dine for under $50 in Monaco if you aren't too picky.)

In fair weather, I really enjoy wandering around the Monaco streets near the port. This tiny space is teeming with Monégasque everyday life intersecting with visiting millionaires hopping off their yachts. Since Monaco is so close to Italy, the cuisine is a mash-up of French, Provençal, and Italian cooking. There's usually something for every food taste on the menu. You'll also find French and Italian wine in abundance.

The harbor area has an excellent daily food market at La Condamine. Locals wake up to the fresh aromas and abundance of a typical French street market (with Italian influences). Carts are piled high with fruits, cheeses, fresh breads, and flowers. Afterward, you can wander past the harbor up the hill toward the casino and turn your attention toward luxury. Lanvin, Hermès, Céline, Gucci, Cartier, Chanel, and Prada will be happy to take your euros at their gleaming storefronts. Or you can meander through the alleys and byways of the old town or shopping centers like Métropole (facing the casino gardens) and Fontvieille where merchants offer souvenirs, ready-to-wear, leather goods, home *décor*, and art. You can also drive off in a new Maserati or Lamborghini, since high-end car dealerships abound in Monaco.

If you're ready to do some gambling, there are various opportunities, from formal games to slot machines. Of course the most famous venue is the Casino de Monte Carlo. Built in the *Belle*

Époque style, it has a variety of gambling options. Other venues include the Casino Café de Paris, the Sun Casino, and various other gambling niches inside the resorts, hotels, and meeting places.

Like Las Vegas in the U.S., the French have capitalized on the idea that you may want to slip a coin into a slot machine anytime, day or night. As you prepare to "donate" your money on the "altar" of craps tables and roulette wheels, I'd suggest you take note of the Monaco coat of arms. It's a pair of monks in soldier boots, brandishing swords. Moral: beware of bandits masquerading as holy men.

For those who'd rather spend their funds on dining, spa experiences, or palatial hotel rooms, Monaco has much to choose from. One of the most famous is the Hôtel de Paris, which is steps away from the Casino. The Hôtel de Paris, also built in the *Belle Époque* period, has a stunning marble-floored lobby with handsome chandeliers, fabulous flower arrangements, and an air of French elegance that rivals those of Paris hotels. It's frequented by the Rockefellers, the Rothschilds, the Vanderbilts, as well as visiting royals and politicians and such famed guests as Winston Churchill and James Bond film stars.

The Hôtel de Paris is just one of the properties of Monte-Carlo SBM that first brought gambling to Monaco in 1863. Quirky note: SBM stands for La Societé des Bains de Mer—in English "The Sea Bathing Company." This innocuous sounding mega-consortium now runs the casino, the Hôtel de Paris, and several other properties like the Monte Carlo Bay Hotel & Resort.

The Hôtel de Paris, as the premiere property, however, is like no other. The resort is a vast complex housing gourmet dining venues, spa facilities, gambling, fabulous rooms and suites, and beach activities. The dining here is phenomenal. Le Louis XV-Alain Ducasse is the regal, Michelin-starred restaurant dedicated to "taste and fantasy." It combines French and Italian Riviera influences in such offerings as breast of squab, Mona Lisa potato *gnocchi*, and *ravioli de foie gras de canard*.

From opulent Le Grill, another restaurant in the hotel, you can see both France and Italy from the bay windows. On most evenings, the ceiling even rolls back to reveal starry skies above. (I'm assured it's closed quickly if the weather turns iffy.) If you desire a lighter option, you can try L'Hirondelle or Le Bar Américain off the lobby which both have marvelous drinks plus a local appetizer called *barbajuans* (vegetable and cheese turnover) that originates in Monaco. There's first-class live entertainment most nights; Prince Albert and his guests are known to pop in.

At the Hôtel de Paris, there's also a 600,000-bottle wine cellar hewn from the Monaco rock in 1874. The cellar's corridors are almost a mile long in total (nearly the size of Monaco). The hotel's wine museum makes for interesting viewing. At the splendid spa called the Thermes Marins Monte-Carlo, which occupies four floors, you can enjoy a variety of elegant treatments, especially seawater therapies. Its facilities include two heated seawater pools, saunas, a fitness facility, and 37 treatment rooms.

As a guest at the Hôtel de Paris, you have free entry to the casino. But before you cross through the lobby to the casino, you're supposed to go to the statue of Louis XIV and his horse. There, you're to rub his knee for luck—the horse's knee that is. You'll see there have been a few people before you; the brass is worn to a polished sheen.

Sea lovers will find a private beach club and a plethora of water sports, as well as golf and tennis. And you can bring your pet if you can't bear to leave Fifi at home. As of this writing, rooms start at about $600, but a diamond suite will run you anywhere from $9,500 to $15,000 a night. Heated floors are a highlight.

Speaking of luck at the casinos, Monaco abounds with bizarre tales of rituals espoused and adopted to increase one's success at the gaming tables. For example, one story involves a certain Reverend Taylor, pastor of Monaco's Anglican church. Used to having a modest attendance, he was stunned to see a huge congregation seated before him one morning. As he was very familiar with the machinations of Monte Carlo, he went looking for an explanation in the casino. There he learnt that one player, returning to the casino after attending mass where hymn no. 36 had been sung, had bet on this number at roulette and won. Word spread quickly. For weeks afterward, worshippers hurried from the services to the casino to bet on the number of that day's hymn. The appalled Reverend got the last laugh, however. He knew a French roulette table has only 37 numbers. From then on, he made certain only hymns numbered 38 and above were sung. The reverend's congregation returned to its normal size.

Across the square from the Hôtel de Paris is the well-known Café de Paris. The Café de Paris is one of the most popular watering holes and *brasseries* in Monaco. With its sprawling outdoor terrace perfect for people watching, and its steep prices for even an espresso, the experience is worth the price. Even if I don't dine there, I always stop in for coffee or *apéritif* since I get a ringside seat for all the Ferraris and Rolls Royces gliding by. Watching their occupants isn't too bad either.

The food is excellent at the Café de Paris, however. You may want to try their legendary *Crêpes Suzette*. They were invented here. At the end of the 19th century, the Prince of Wales loved visiting Monaco. The prince, who later became King Edward VII of England, was lunching at the Café de Paris one sunny day. Chef Henri Carpentier was preparing pancakes with Grand Marnier liquor. Suddenly, they burst into flames in the frying pan. The prince was so enthralled with the spectacle that he asked the chef what the recipe was called. Fast on his feet, the chef quickly replied that the fiery pancakes should be dubbed "princely pancakes." But in a gesture of gallantry, the prince suggested they be named after the young woman who'd joined him for lunch. *Crêpes Suzette* was born.

On another intoxicating note, Monaco is home to one of the most exciting annual events in the world: The Monaco Grand Prix. This Formula One motor race has been held every year since 1929. The Grand Prix is revered as one of the most prestigious auto races alongside the Indianapolis 500 and the 24-hour Le Mans. The 161-mile race is held on a narrow course over the tiny streets of Monaco. Drivers must navigate the tight corners, rapid elevation changes, and speed through a tunnel over and over. Each lap of 78 total is only about 2 miles. But the treacherous nature makes it one of the most dangerous courses in racing. Racing buffs know that Brazil's Ayrton Senna won the race more times than anyone else (six) until his life ended in a crash at age 34 in the 1994 San Marino Grand Prix.

If you can't jet in for this year's race, rent the Academy Award winning 1966 movie *Grand Prix* starring James Garner, Eva Marie Saint, and Yves Montand. It tells the story of the Grand Prix race with real-life racing footage of actual Formula One world champions. *Grand Prix* is a high-octane action romance—especially since Yves Montand and James

Garner ooze testosterone as they navigate Monaco and the women who love them. (Watch this flick with a glass of champagne for full effect.) By the way, for a modern foray into the Formula One racing world, catch 2013's *Rush* directed by Ron Howard. It captures even more of that high-octane testosterone on wheels—and it's actually superbly acted and beautifully photographed to boot! Some of you may also know star Chris Hemsworth was named *People Magazine's* 2014 Sexiest Man Alive. Perhaps watch this movie with a *bottle* of champagne.

The French Riviera in Sum

Overall, the French Riviera is a splendid locale to access old-world glamour and seaside charm. The cuisine is superb. The accommodations are world-class. And the lifestyle is as intoxicating as a magnum of Dom Pérignon. Most of all, the French Riviera offers unforgettable light that dazzles against the blue sea and bright shoreline. It's unmatched anywhere on the planet.

"Magic has its components, and the most important of them here [in the Riviera] is the Light. Without the Light it is fair to say that the Riviera would not exist…It still glows down, sparkling in sequined disarray upon the deceptively clear sea; still scorches the pale bodies unwisely ignoring its power along the artificial beaches. It exaggerates light and shade…and enhances color—fierce, harsh almost, brilliantly exploding color that one never suspected could exist in nature, so that pink is suddenly carmine, the soft green of the maritime pines is viridian, tiled roofs burst with orange fire, and the dust under one's foot is a rich copper. This, of course, is why Bonnard and Braque, Monet and Renoir, and all the others came here, determined to capture the Light and set it for all time on canvas."

—Dirk Bogarde, *European Travel & Life*

Indeed, until I came to this beautiful coast of France myself, and basked in the rays of this glorious sunshine, I didn't grasp why light exists as the creative heart of the Riviera. The Côte d'Azur is like a sparkling jewel in contrast to the gray skies of Paris and elsewhere.

It's not until one drives to the southern regions of France and the Riviera—as many of the northern French do in August—that one looks happily upward. Upward through a brilliant blue sky to a round yellow sun that burns into the landscape and shadows, making colors and sparkling variations like nowhere else on the planet.

The French Riviera remains an inviting seaside enclave where creativity, joy, and magic flourish. It's clearly a place everyone should visit at least once in a lifetime. And, perhaps, you too will hear the strains of *C'est Si Bon* lingering in your mind long after you've left this incomparable paradise:

"Aahhh c'est bon, c'est bon, c'est bon
Vous savez bien que j'attendrai
Quelqu'un qui pourrait m'apporter beaucoup de 'loot.'
Ce soir? Demain? La semaine prochain?
N'importe quand. Uummm, c'est bon si bon
Il sera très, crazy, no? Voilà, c'est tellement bon!"
(Aahhh it's good, it's good, it's so good.
You know I'm waiting for someone who can give me
Plenty of loot. Tonight? Tomorrow? Next Week?
Doesn't matter when. Uummm, it's so good, so good.
It will be very crazy, no? It's very good!)

Part Two: Provence

"Quand le Bon Dieu en vient à douter du monde, il se rappelle qu'il a créé la Provence." ("When the Good Lord comes to doubt about the world, he remembers that he created Provence.")

—Frédéric Mistral, Nobel Prize winner in Literature, 1904

To many Francophiles, nowhere in *l'Hexagone* says "France" like the region of Provence. It's an irrepressible area. An area shaped by its quirky people and colorful culture, as much as by its landscape, food, and history.

Provence is a land of changing geography where verdant valleys end in cliff-hanging villages. Where bulls run wild on marshy lands, and where the Luberon is ringed by ancient villages like Gordes and Ménerbes that end up on book covers and in movies. Yes, this is also a place where a river runs through it—but here it's the Rhône, hailing from the Swiss Alps and flowing freely by flourishing vineyards, Pope's palaces, and finally out to the Mediterranean sea.

Papal wine is grown in this lush land. White horses run in the Camargue. Lavender spreads like a purple carpet across the floor of the pastoral valleys. Popes have spoken to God in Avignon. And Brit author Peter Mayle has lived here—and brought the considerable charms of Provence into the living rooms of millions.

When I first came to Provence, it was a full decade after Mayle's *A Year in Provence* had brought the ways of the Provençal peasant into worldwide awareness. But the appeal of his book (plus later projects) played up the quirkiness of the Provençaux and his experiences of them. Several locals have told me they have mixed feelings about the publicity Provence has garnered. They love the influx of commerce, but they aren't thrilled about their depiction as rather insular, unsophisticated rubes.

Personally, I love this beautiful terrain and the quirky culture of these resourceful, grounded people. But I'd suggest they defy categorization. These are resilient, colorful, unconventional people with an agenda all their own. They create their own brand of cuisine for example—not quite French, not quite Spanish, but a unique blend of local ingredients that come together in dishes that don't just stick to your ribs—they stick to your soul. This is a land not just blessed with earthly abundance and historical wonders. It's a land where culture, tradition, and reliance on solid values color the way the Provençaux live, how they dress, what they do, and how they handle the tourism spotlight.

Since I've returned to Provence again and again over several years, I've met a lot of people, sipped wine with many of them, clambered inside ancient fortifications, walked where Vincent van Gogh carried his easel and paints over weathered cobblestones, rode the Rhône River, and spent the night in an iron forge. But nothing matches the laughter I've shared with these very droll people. They laugh at themselves—and they've been unabashed at sometimes laughing at me as well. In retrospect, it's refreshing.

I once stood in line for coffee at a busy *boulangerie* right next to the super-busy street *marché* on the main square of Saint-Rémy-de-Provence, for example. I was in line behind 10 or 11 elderly ladies who were doing their mid-morning shopping and had stopped for coffee. Behind me were another five or six elderly locals speaking rapid-fire French. All of them had to be at least 70 years old.

When I finally got up to the counter, the graying *madame* behind the counter started speaking to me in Provençaux French (a mix of *Occitan*, the ancient Provençal language, and French). I panicked. I had no idea what questions she was asking me. But I knew I had to answer fast. I froze when I began to hear some hissing behind me. Soon it became a roar. This was the Provençal way of signaling me to "hurry up and get out of the way."

Out from the back of the line came a young woman about 30 who sidled up next to me, smiled, and said in perfect English. "Can I help you?"

"Yes!" I cried. "The dialect is strange."

"It's *Occitan*. She wants to know what you want with your two coffees and what kind of milk you desire."

I answered quickly and soon I was turning with my snacks in hand to face this line of grumpy Provençal ladies behind me. I knew this was my moment to sink or swim in Provençal France.

Instead of slinking off, I wandered down the line and to these little ladies (that all frankly reminded me of my grandmother) I used my get-out-of-jail French phrase: *"Je suis désolé. Mon français est très mauvais. Mais je l'aime tellement Provence."* ("I'm sorry. My French is very bad, but I love being in Provence.")

These little ladies studied me for a moment; then they responded. Some with a smile and a nod. Some with a raised eyebrow and a laugh. But I could tell I was forgiven. My very bad, contrite French allowed me a moment of connection with each of these wonderful ladies. On their way out, most of them smiled at me over at my table. I felt we had made a connection, and they seemed to understand I was making an effort to accommodate their needs.

Provence is a place of proud history and traditional culture, like other areas of Southern France. But rather than the land shaping the people, I'd suggest the people significantly shape the Provence we know and love. Provence is well known as the home of the French "peasant." Where earthy values, age-old traditions, and strong resolve against interlopers has been elaborated in film, art, and literature. Some of these include the movies *Manons of Spring* and *Jean de Flourette* where both the greed and the nobility of the Provence peasant are cinematized.

The peasant is king in Provence. Popes and royals have come and gone here. But the Provençaux hold sway. And they don't brook a lot of nonsense from outsiders in my experience. Hearty peasant food from nearby farms and ranches is *de rigueur*. Flavorful cheeses from local animals and rich Châteauneuf-du-Pape wines cultivated from ancient vines taste of tradition and staying power. Dwellings are built to last against the menacing *mistral* winds. The treasured truffle is harvested in secret by only those most intimate with the land. Old papal palaces live on as reincarnated world heritage sites. And Les-Baux-de-Provence has created a vast medieval experience for modern visitors out of its ancient trebuchet and cliff-clinging fortifications.

We'll explore this resilient land of strong people and vivid places in these pages. But nothing can describe the reality of being here. Indeed, as Thomas Jefferson said on a visit to Aix-en-Provence in 1787, "I am now in the land of corn, wine, oil, and sunshine. What more can man ask of heaven?"

History & Landscape

It was Julius Caesar who christened the area "the Province." During Roman times this "Province" covered a huge chunk of Southeastern France real estate from Geneva to Toulouse. But it didn't stay stable over history; gradually it shrank to the outlines of modern

Provence. These borders now extend from the southern Rhône River's left bank in the west to the Italian border on the east. Then north to south, from the lower Rhône Valley all the way down to Marseille, Toulon, and the Camargue at the Mediterranean.

Historically, Provence has withstood a variety of settlers over the centuries. Prehistoric peoples first inhabited the region. They left their mark in cave paintings of bison, seals, and horses in the Cosquer Cave near Marseille. The land was soon overrun by waves of conquerors and later the Greeks arrived.

Founding the original trading port of Massalia (later called Marseille), the Greek colony spread rapidly, bringing a thriving trade and a robust viticulture. Greek coins are sometimes still found in Provence, and many of the vineyards and acres of olive trees are examples of Greek plantings. The Romans invaded the area from 2nd century B.C. to the 5th century. Marseille was particularly established with diplomatic relations with Rome, at least in the beginning.

The Romans delighted in this new land. But they found it chaotic, undisciplined. So they shaped the landscape with a Roman fist, laying down Roman roads, forging massive settlements, erecting monuments to themselves and their leaders, and creating pleasure centers that included theaters, baths, and villas. Their might harnessed the meandering Provençal waterways with gigantic aqueducts. They worshipped the god of grape and planted wine vines, garlic, and other crops to bring "civilized" food and drink to this feral land. Roman soldiers were even issued garlic to take with them on campaigns; the belief was that garlic inspired and gave courage, as well as added flavor to campaign rations. The Roman generals had garlic planted for the armies to use wherever they sojourned for a time. Thus, you find garlic in abundance all over Provence.

Formal Christianity came to Provence around the 3rd century. Many churches, monasteries, and bishoprics were organized to meet the spread of formal religion. As Rome's military power waned, waves of tribes overran the area including Visigoths, Burgundians, Franks, and even pirates from North Africa. From the 7th century onward, warring factions fought for control of this prized land, including three different dynasties of Counts of Provence. Naples claimed dominion over the area for nearly a century in the 1200s. Even the Roman popes decamped to Avignon for a time in the 14th century; they built a massive palace that stands today.

Provence finally became legally incorporated into the French royal domain in 1486. Many writers and historians suggest, however, that though Provence has been legally part of France for more than 500 years, it still considers itself independent from France. Even efforts to stamp out the local Romance language of the common people have not been very successful.

After the 1400s onward, Provence became involved in the Wars of Religion (Catholic, Jew, Protestant) over the next 300 years. It was overcome by the Plague between 1720-1722. But the French Revolution brought newfound freedoms to Provence, giving power to the people. Unfortunately, Napoleon tried to restore some of the powers to the old ruling families in Provence, much to the consternation of the locals. Many of the common country folk were glad when Napoleon was overthrown (and subversively thwarted him whenever he was in the area).

By the 19th century, Provence had grown into a prosperous region anchored by burgeoning cities like Marseille, Toulon, and Aix-en-Provence. It was fueled by an industrious citizenry, a robust farming network, and a manufacturing zeal that became the envy of France. Once the railroads connected Paris with Marseille around 1848, and Toulon with Nice in 1864, the area opened up to tourism, extended commerce, and gateway travel to and from Italy, North Africa, and the Orient.

In the 20th century, Provence became the center of the resistance movement during World War II. Italian and/or German soldiers occupied its eastern areas. In 1944, the allies landed in Provence two months after the invasion of Normandy in the north. Fighting was fierce; bombings left the area scarred. Post war, Provence had to rebuild hundreds of structures and bridges, particularly around the port areas. But culturally, the region blossomed. Over the next 60 years it became a mecca for people all over the world drawn to this beautiful locale brimming with fresh produce, superb wine, incomparable light, fine Mediterranean weather, and architectural wonders.

Modern Provence buzzes with life. Of all the French regions, Provence has seen the most changes in economy in the last few decades due to a major shift from agriculturalism to industrialization and adaption to large-scale tourism. Provençaux work the land and the vineyards. They labor in the new industries of petroleum and chemicals among others, or tend to tourism and commerce. Expats and Northern French set up second homes in the beautiful countryside. Artists come to capture the allure. And hordes of around-the-world visitors find their way to this lavender-scented land, wanting to experience the Provençal lifestyle for even a week.

Geographically, Provence is a land rich in contrasts. There's salty seaport Marseille and its Mediterranean coastline to the south. Aix and Sainte-Victoire entice with their thermal springs, Roman ruins, and religious history. River port Arles competes with Barcelona for Catalan earthiness. And the mystical Camargue, a nature-preserve and zoological treasure of wildlife, vegetation, native bulls, and untamed white horses spreads to the sea. Limestone hills of the Alpilles and the Montagnette cap the valleys. Bold Mont Ventoux offers panoramic views from its lofty peak and Avignon, once home to the popes, offers a window into the life of the ancient papacy. There's Orange, the northwest gateway to Provence, with its Gallo-Roman ruins and hectares of vines, and Comtat Venaissin and Carpentras, rich in Jewish heritage and brimming with orchards and vegetable fields. And finally, the Luberon, with its delightful hilltop *villages perchés* like Bonnieux, Ménerbes, and Gordes, is a delightful enclave of Provençal enchantment.

Part of what shapes this region, beside its marked geographical contrasts and colorful people, is its weather. Provence enjoys relatively mild weather throughout most of the year. Its low rainfall and exceptional light make for great paintings and photography. However, in the winter and spring the legendary *mistral* wind sweeps down from the Alps across the plains radically shifting the weather in a matter of hours. Sometimes attaining velocities of up to 115 miles per hour, the mighty *mistral* has forever bent many of the trees in Provence. Hence, most Provençal dwellings hang colorful, heavy shutters from their windows they can bang shut in an instant as this icy wind that "can blow the ears off a donkey" whips across the land.

The region is a history buff's paradise. The numerous hill towns, medieval villages, and varied domestic dwellings form an architectural roadmap of the changing social organization that shaped the region. Ridge towns like Gordes, Lacoste, Banon, and Les-Baux tell the tale of medieval settlers who found plentiful stone and clean air, and built great perches to protect their loved ones and watch for enemy invaders.

Underhill villages like Cotignac form enclaves of domesticity. But there are also conch-shell shaped villages at major crossroads like Pélissanne that provided easy access but a fortified environment. There are *bastide* estates, or *maison de maître*, which is the Provençal term for an agricultural estate belonging to a rich landlord. These compounds consist of a main residence and several outlying buildings; they're the medieval equivalent of a palatial ranch compound.

Stone Romanesque churches dot the landscape with their sky-piercing spires, ornate columns, and intricate façades. And Roman ruins are everywhere, telling the tale of a mighty empire that left its remains in bloodlust amphitheaters in Arles where Romans fought ferocious beasts and waged sea battles on an artificial sea.

But above all, this is an awe-inspiring land. Some of the most beautiful sights as you drive along the country roads are the colorful fields of vines and lavender bounded by cypress trees and reeds. The rich perfume of wine and lavender, honey and rosemary, offers a perennial bouquet of pleasant aromas. The low mountains are perpetually green with acres of cedar, pine, and scrub oak trees where rabbits, game, boar, and truffles abound—until hunting season that is, when reportedly every local with a gun and a truffle-hunting dog heads to the hills in search of culinary treasure.

The 6,265-foot "Giant of Provence," Mont Ventoux, also beckons. Mount Ventoux is a gentle limestone peak sometimes blanketed by snow or mists, which is easily accessible in about an hour and a half from multiple routes. On a clear day from the top, you can see the Alps stretching off in the distance, as well as the Alpilles, the Rhône Valley, and the Pyrénées off to the southwest. At night you can see a black carpet with sparkling lights from the towns and homes of the Provençal plain below.

And of course, northern Provence/south Rhône Valley has

hectare after hectare of sun-drenched vineyards, spreading through the valleys and up the limestone hillsides. The most well-known wine-growing area is the Southern Rhône Valley, south of Lyon toward Avignon. Here lies Châteauneuf-du-Pape one of the most famous red wine growing areas in the world. But the rest of Provence also produces some wonderful rosés, whites, and reds. Sixteen high-end *Cru*, 18 named villages, and more than 200 villages and communities provide Rhône wine of varying quality. The Châteauneuf-du-Pape wines are grown and harvested from vines first cultivated when the papacy, lovers of rich Burgundy wines, relocated to Avignon in 1308. Encouraging a rich viticulture during their 70-year tenure, these elegant wines, which are still bottled from this area, bear a certain papal nose.

Overall, Provence provides a number of opportunities to enjoy a variety of terrains, tasty foods, heavenly wines, and genealogically rich people with many stories to tell.

People & Lifestyle

The Provençal lifestyle emphasizes the art of "living well" instead of "living rich." The people of the region are known for many things: their dedication to good cuisine and wine, love of their robust market culture, and their deep commitment to long held traditions. Nearly every town and village in Provence has a *Fête Votive*, which is a festival specific to that town, rather than a national holiday. This is one of the reasons I have such a soft spot for Provence. It feels like being in another time and another place to me—but one that feels a lot like going back to home and hearth.

The cares of life drop away from me here. The rugged cuisine is served in unfussy settings by down-to-earth people who seem to want nothing more from me than to see me relax, imbibe, and savor the hours.

And maybe this is one of the reasons the Provençal populace enjoys a higher life expectancy at birth than the rest of France. They eat well, drink well, and live well. And when I'm here, I do the same.

The flip side of this insouciant lifestyle, however, is the tug of industrialization and grand-scale tourism which sometimes adds stress to the Provençal tranquility. A burgeoning population of 4.5 million, with 850,000 of those occupying the Marseille metropolis alone, adds to the mix. This may be one of the reasons tourism has changed drastically in the last decade.

When I first went to Provence in 2002, many restaurants, wineries, and hotels seemed unaccustomed to large crowds of non-French speakers. A decade on, I've never seen so many Wi-Fi *cafés* and big volume tourism. I was used to hearing Germans, Italians, Spaniards, and British accents in the past. But now I also encounter groups from Romania, Turkey, Czech Republic, and far-flung Chinese provinces. And everyone is carrying smart phones, iPads, and high-tech cameras of course.

Life has become more complex in Provence since the days of Peter Mayle's tranquil sojourn in the early 1990s. High-volume agriculture now requires a lot more time and energy. But so too do the new industries of aeronautics, electronics, nuclear power, chemicals, and light industry like packaging and high volume confections. In addition to the old occupations of shipbuilding, mineral processing (ochre, bauxite), soap making (Marseille), construction, salt works, and small-town tourism are relatively new industries.

Modern tourism has gone mainstream to some degree in Provence. Today's big-time hoteliers and service sector workers must be multi-lingual, Internet savvy, and globally experienced—but must be able to promote the local charms. Many of them often grow up in Provence but have gained experience on cruise ships and in Paris or London where they've learned high-end service techniques.

Still many of the old ways live on. Fishermen practice the old methods in Marseille. Camargue ranch hands work the land and commandeer the white horses and black bulls the old-fashioned way. And shepherds even have an honored presence in modern society as they make the transhumance (sheep migration from mountains to

pastures) through towns like
Saint-Remy that celebrate with
La Fête de la Transhumance.

Street market life still plays
a large role in Provençal culture.
It's not only a source of local
commerce but a social construct
that feeds the soul as well as the
belly. Products abound—and so
does local gossip. You find out
who's marrying or divorcing
whom while you buy your melons and mushrooms. You hear about the
French government's new trade policies as you riffle through the latest
blue and yellow Provençal linens. And you kibitz with the farmers who
are getting ready to protest the latest farming restrictions.

The one occasional drawback to the region is that locals in distant
corners of Provence are still known for a somewhat "countrified
approach" to strangers. I wonder if this so-called "peasant attitude"
rears itself when the Provençaux sense creeping commercialism or un-
due interference from "foreigners." Even suspect Parisians, who love to
buy Provençal residences and morph them into fancy vacation homes
with swimming pools and tennis courts, are treated like interlopers.

I've been told that while foreigners are still viewed askance by
some locals, they trust Parisians even less! The Provençaux resist these
Parisian sophisticates who've been trying to tell them what to do with
their land and their lives for centuries.

And I've occasionally felt the chill myself. As a first-time visitor to Provence a decade ago, my companion and I once found ourselves up in the hills behind Gordes and L'Isle-sur-la-Sorgue in a tiny
café frequented only by locals. We noticed a distinct coolness when we
wandered into this off-the-beaten-path concession looking for coffee.
Absolutely no English was spoken.

Despite the fact that we were clearly *Les Anglais,* we were
nevertheless served delicious *café crèmes* and warm *brioche* once the staff
realized we spoke a smattering of French—and seemed relatively non-
threatening (I hope). Speaking even a little French is always helpful

when building cultural bridges. And knowing some French vocabulary can help you understand what's going on around you—even if you can't hold a lengthy conversation.

This brings me to the Provençal language. Locals speak a dialect that's unique to this area. Sometimes called "French-laced-with-garlic," linguists suggest the local *Occitan* is a combination of Italian, Spanish, and French. It bends French terms and accents around unique versions of terms and colloquial expressions. (Some suggest the Provençaux simply add "la" at the end of most words.)

Even Parisians are confused at times by the dialect. I don't speak it at all. But I speak very bad French very slowly, and even the Provençaux seem to understand me mostly. But in a pinch, the point and gesture method usually works as well here as in Paris when I get into linguistic trouble.

On the other hand, I bought some linens at the Wednesday Saint-Rémy street market, and found the proprietor jovial and conversant with our mutual "Franglish." I even had a riotous dinner in Apt where our server/barman Gabriel was so convivial, he had me stand behind the bar and chat with customers. (Letting them practice English with me always seems a way to make new friends in France.)

Cuisine, of course, is an excellent venue for sharing experience. These Provençaux have a finely tuned palette and expect good food as part of the daily life. Peter Mayle famously wrote, "the Provençal has a clock in his stomach, and lunch is his sole concession to punctuality. *On mange à midi,* and not a moment later. (We eat at noon and not a moment later.)"

I have learned two important things about eating in Provence. First, if you take food seriously, the Provençaux will take YOU seriously. If you go to Provence with some education about the types of ingredients and dishes prepared there, you'll have endless openings for conversation. Second, if you commit the horrible *faux pas* of looking for something decent to eat in any village in Provence after 2 p.m. on a Sunday afternoon, the locals will consider you backward, uncultured, or insane.

Let me explain. The main meal on Sunday in France is a large repast around noon, often with many close family or friends in attendance. The afternoon is spent eating a fabulous feast with several courses and multiple wines. Then there's a doze or a game or a long conversation while digesting. Perhaps the cheese course will be served at this time—or more desserts. During this lengthy Sunday afternoon feast, there will seldom be any restaurants open anywhere in town. And if you're an ignorant tourist who waits until 2 pm to look for lunch, you'll starve to death.

On two occasions, I've practically had to eat breadcrumbs and snack bars, because my companion and I waited too late on Sunday to look for a place to dine. One of these experiences was in Apt in Provence which closes up tighter than a drum on a Sunday afternoon. We ended up finding a *supermarché* (grocery store) miles away and eating bag snacks and bottled water. No dinner followed. Every eatery was fortified shut like the German army was expected at any moment.

The other experience I had was in the Loire Valley in Northern France in a teeny village called Cinq Mars-la-Pile. Like Cinderella watching the clock nearing 2 p.m., my husband and I knew we were cutting it close for finding a late Sunday lunch venue. Finally, we ended up peering into the windows of a tiny *bistro* in the middle of town around 2:20 p.m. looking like underfed orphans. The proprietress finally took pity on us. She brought us in, cut up a couple of tomatoes, gave us some kind of mysterious cheese in a plastic bag to gnaw on, and offered us a couple of dry baguettes and some French beer. Then she went home! It was my worst meal in France through no one's fault but my own.

That night, we retired to our third floor bedroom at Messier and Madame Manier's Cinq Mars-la-Pile B&B (which didn't offer an evening meal). We could smell Madame Manier roasting chicken with potatoes for her local guests, however, who I knew were downstairs drinking champagne, because I heard the cork pop and the glasses clink. A little later, the appley goodness of a *tarte Tatin* came wafting up through the floorboards. Our stomachs growled all night—but we finally learned our lesson about sitting down to lunch BY NOON on a Sunday afternoon in France. You've now been warned.

By the way, Madame Manier *did* serve us a wonderful breakfast the next morning. It consisted of fresh *brioche* and *baguettes*, delicious cheeses and meats, coffee and *chocolate au lait,* and tasty juices including pomegranate and plum. And she and her friendly husband even sat down to join us! She was so delightful. She had so much energy despite her 70+ years. She spent nearly an hour telling me (in excellent English) how she'd been born the eldest of 15 children and had inherited this 15-room *maison* (house) when her parents passed. In America we would have called this place a mansion. Happy to practice her English with us, she was in fact very Internet-savvy and begged us to stick around for a day or two, because she enjoyed our company so much. Madame also handed me a little care package of goodies as we departed. And she warmly expressed her wish that we would come back someday to learn more about Cinq Mars-la-Pile.

I have so many of these delightful experiences with local French families, that I must emphasize that getting off the main tourist routes and into darling B&Bs where you can meet the locals is so worthwhile. Further note: The cost of our overnight visit there, with an ensuite bathroom, a sumptuous breakfast, and hours of good company, plus beautiful directions to our next sight was only $65 euros (about $80). Priceless.

But back to Provence. Daily life in Provence has a similar small town feel. When not tending to tourists or working, you'll find locals hunting, fishing, boating, hiking, horseback riding, cycling, rock climbing, canoeing, viewing museums and art gallery events, and nearly always participating in the traditional celebrations in some way. These celebrations include costumed festivals, elaborate holiday celebrations, classical operas, concerts, and dance and jazz festivals.

You may be surprised to discover that there are bullfights in Provence as well. Nîmes (covered in the Languedoc section) and Provence's Arles compete with each other with their famous *férias* (bullfights) held in their ancient Roman amphitheaters. It's here in this intersection between French and Spanish bullfight culture where the cultural proximity between France and Spain narrows. (You'll also find delicious paella being enjoyed in Southern France and superb *foie gras* being served all over Northern Spain; both are border regions where the cultures blend deliciously.)

But the Provençaux make it all work. Above all, they carefully guard their comfortable customs. And on a warm summer day, you can even find them taking time out to enjoy their *dejeuner* by the carrousel like here in Avignon (pictured) or enjoying a game of *boules*.

For the uninitiated, the object of *boules* (*pétanque)* is to throw metal *boules* (balls) closest to a small wooden *cochonnet* target ball by the end of the game. Other players can knock the opposing team's *boules* out of the way. Play is energetic (read viscous). Long stretches of graveled ground especially designed for *boules* contests can be found in most Provence villages and towns. Many homes have their own *boules* court. Long a mostly male bastion, ladies now play as well. Sipping *pastis* while playing is *de rigueur.* Cheating is expected. Arguments about who actually won are often lively.

You can purchase your own set of *boules* either in France or from online retailers like Pétanque America (www.petanqueamerica.com) where I got my set. Of course, there are knockoffs at local sports stores. And there's that rival game known in Italy as bocce ball (with larger balls). But what do those Italians know? Here's the authentic *pétanque* set with the obligatory glass of *pastis*.

The young Provençaux enjoy a variety of athletics like soccer, horse riding, and kayaking. But skateboarding is much loved here. There are usually skate parks in most towns—and often well-attended skateboard tournaments are held.

Festivals and celebrations are naturally a big part of Provence life. The calendar is packed with various *fêtes* celebrating saints, food, wine, historic events, famous people, and village life activities like weddings and funerals. At the public celebrations, you may have the pleasure of seeing locals in traditional dress.

You'll enjoy listening to fife, flute, and *tambourin,* which provide accompaniment most everywhere a party is taking place. You may also see the *farandole,* a Mediterranean dance that dates back to the Middle Ages where young men and women hold each other's hands or a handkerchief as they dance to a six-beat rhythm. The festival costumes often feature men and women in Provençal fabrics or medieval attire like this serf I ran into in Les-Baux-de-Provence.

A particularly special time of year is Christmas. This is the time

when *santons,* handmade or hand-painted clay figurines, come out to be displayed in the family *crèche.* These small, brightly-colored figures are designed for nativity scenes. *Santons* or "small saints" first appeared in Provence at the end of the 18th century when the French Revolution caused the suppression of midnight mass. Without the large-scale church pageantry, the nativity celebration was reduced in size to a miniature scene that families could create at home. A small industry developed making the figurines. In Provence, baby Jesus and Virgin Mary are surrounded in these displays by the usual Christmas characters. But Provence adds some local color. Provence figures dressed in traditional costumes for the baker, fish seller, knife grinder, cheese seller, chimney sweep, plus artists like Cézanne and van Gogh and even movie stars likes Yves Montand sometimes show up in the family scene.

Above all, locals make time to live. They take long lunches. They start their days late. But they also work later into the evening. Then they sit down to a leisurely dinner after 8 p.m.—sometimes not dining until 10 p.m. They stroll their lovely villages and linger to watch the sunsets. Altogether, there's a sense of personal peace here. And always there's time for simply savoring life.

Food, Wine, & Shopping

Food

"Shallots are for babies; Onions are for men; Garlic is for heroes."

—Anonymous

Provence has some of the most memorable cuisine on the planet. All year round this Eden-like land produces beautiful vegetables, succulent fruit, black diamonds (truffles), delectable meats and poultry, appetizing fish, aromatic breads, savory cheeses, distinctive sweets, and rich wines. And it's all enhanced by the flavors of local lavender, rosemary, thyme,  and garlic. These aromatic herbs add layers of exquisite flavors to this unforgettable food and drink. Most important however is garlic.

Garlic proliferates in Provence. You can buy it smoked, fresh, dried, in colors of violet and pink, in great bundles from a roadside stand, or in individual cloves piled high in bins at the street market. It was once thought that garlic could ward off the plague. In 1858, Louis Pasteur proved that garlic has medicinal values in its antiseptic properties. France produces more than 18,500 tons of garlic every year (but China still produces more). The average French person consumes about 1.5 pounds of *ail* per year. And French children begin eating it as toddlers.

Wheat, grapes, and olives are the core crops in Provence. But across this lush land, you'll find almonds, honey, lavender, cherries, strawberries, melons, asparagus, figs, peaches, and apricots to go along with heaps of fine meats, flavorful poultry, and bountiful fish (sardines, anchovies, mackerel, and eel).

The asparagus in Provence is particularly noteworthy since the spears are usually the size of frankfurters. They make our American asparagus look like chopsticks. French asparagus is typically served in season as a delicious starter in and of itself. Or you'll find it lying in a drizzle of hollandaise next to some succulent leg of lamb or cutlet. I have to say, one of the most extraordinary things about French cooking is their superior skill with preparing vegetables. Tender yet *al dente*, succulent but bursting with flavor, the Provençaux add subtle sauces or seasonings that make these vegetables like home-grown asparagus taste like a gourmet main course.

Much of this fabulous produce finds its way into the farmer's markets in most every town. Thus, if you buy ripe Cavaillon melons or white asparagus from the weekly markets, there's a good chance they'll have been harvested that very morning. And of course, mushrooms as large as your face are a favorite here. (Notice my flirty mushroom farmer here who was only too happy to pose for a picture.)

But we mustn't forget that "ancient of ancients," olives. It's "a taste older than meat, older than wine," said Lawrence Durrell, 20th century British author. The olive tree, originally brought to Provence by the Greeks 3,000 years ago, is one of the indomitable treasures of Provence. The Greeks revered the olive tree; to them, its harvest was a foundation for civilized life. To this day, the olive harvest is a critical event in Provençal life. And some of the world's best olive oil is harvested in the olive groves here, particularly around Les-Baux-de-Provence.

Though olive trees are found all over Provence, those along the coast reach gigantic sizes up to 65 feet. Provençal oil figures prominently in the legendary Mediterranean diet that keeps people living long lives.

A particularly olive-rich area is in the Alpilles Mountains south of Avignon. Here the olive oil is of such high quality that it was granted an *Appellation d'origine Controlee* (AoC) designation in 1997. The Alpilles' Vallée des Baux produces 25% of France's AoC oil from the fruit of almost 1,000 growers.

Artisanal cheeses are another delicacy of the region, particularly *chèvre*, goat cheese. *Banon* is one of the most well-known varieties of unpasteurized cheese made from goat's milk. It comes wrapped in distinctive chestnut leaves and is tied with raffia prior to shipping. But don't be satisfied with tasting just one. There are more than 100 varieties of goat cheese in France, most of them from areas south of the Loire Valley in Southern France.

Provence is well known for rustic cuisine. But diversity is the key to its appeal. As each season passes, the cuisine blends fresh ingredients into the seasonal dishes. Melons, asparagus, strawberries, oysters—all take their place at the center of the month's famous dishes.

Of all the French cuisine approaches, this is the one I most often imitate in my own home. I use peaches in season, as well as apricots and plums in various dishes. I too have learned to love garlic and shallots; I add them to many of my dishes. Sometimes, I even roast garlic cloves in the oven, then crack and spread the warm meat on top of crusty bread slathered in olive oil. With a glass of rosé, there's nothing like it.

And of course there are truffles. The Vaucluse region (Carpentras, east of orange and north of the Luberon) provides nearly 80% of these smelly, prized tubers in France. Called the *diamant noir* (black diamond), truffles find their way into the *crème de la crème* of French cuisine. Michelin-starred chef Christian Etienne once said, "The truffle makes you crazy; the love of this magical specialty makes everyone that comes near dizzy." Some go further and even call them the food of the gods.

Known for their nutty, distinctive flavor, truffles are so prized that they go for roughly 800 euros ($1,000) per kilo (about $500 per pound). Truffle hunting is serious business in France. And various reports say that nefarious dealers sometimes try to pass off Chinese or Italian "wannabes" as Provence or Périgord truffles.

And the search is on to find more truffles, faster. France, and other countries like China, has spent millions trying to figure out how to grow the things on an industrial scale. But it seems to be one of Mother Nature's most intractable creations; truffles resist cultivation. Instead, the tubers grow mostly where they want at the root of oak trees.

It takes a "truffle nose" to find the buried delicacy—and quirky truffle hunters abound in Provence. These tuber sleuths—mostly men accompanied by sniffing dogs who've been trained to ferret out the fungi—spend the cool days from November to March trying to locate the elusive delicacies. These days, truffle-hunting dogs are preferred to the truffle-hunting pigs of old; hungry pigs have a bad habit of gulping down the truffles instead of handing them over to humans. I'm assured it's a lot easier to wrest a truffle from the jaws of a German shepherd than a 300-pound pig.

Provence has a variety of notable specialty dishes: *aïoli*, a thick dipping sauce or mayonnaise of olive oil, egg yolks, and crushed garlic; *ratatouille*, the stew of fragrant stewed vegetables; *soupe au pistou*, made with summer vegetables, ground basil, olive oil, and additives like white beans, green beans, tomatoes, and potatoes; *tapenade* relish, made with olives, capers, and olive oil; and *gâteau des rois*, an epiphany cake that's a *brioche* ring flavored with fruit *confit*.

Provence also produces some delicious confections like white nougat (made with Provençal honey and almonds), crystallized

fruits, and the famous lozenge-shaped *calissons* biscuit made of Mediterranean almonds and fruits with no preservatives.

Even poultry is mouthwatering. Almost every market will have two or more booths where rotisserie chicken slowly turns as their succulent juices drip onto new potatoes turning crispy beneath. I can attest that they are very hard to resist.

The local street markets are also famous for their meat, poultry, sausages (pictured), and *pâtés*. Country *pâté* or *pâté de campagne* is a particular specialty in Provence. It usually contains pork liver, pork shoulder or pork belly, as well as other meats like offal (organ meat) and chicken livers, bound together with a *panade* (rice mixed with butter, stock, and egg), plus garlic, wine, and other seasonings. The whole mix is placed in a terrine and chilled.

Some of these hearty *pâtés* are made with brandy, sharp onion, figs, cherries, or other intense flavors. Served with a crusty baguette, a fresh salad, and a glass of chilled rosé, it's a meal in itself. (And usually after I eat one, I'm too full for the main course, I must admit.)

Some of the area's other famous dishes include *Daube*, a Provençal stew made with cut-up beef, wine, vegetables, garlic, and *Herbes de Provence* and *bouillabaisse*, the classic seafood stew of Marseille (which, strictly speaking, can only be made with fresh fish from the Mediterranean).

Though I'm not a chef by any means, I do like to cook some of these Provençal dishes, especially my own variations on *soupe au pistou* (vegetable soup) and *Daube* (beef stew). The traditional Provençal creation of *Daube* stew takes place over a couple of days, but you can take short cuts and prepare it in one day if you choose. The Provençaux people have, for generations, often kept a *daubière* pot especially for this dish; it's placed in the fireplace for the best results. For enthusiasts who want to try this with modern ovens (and stainless steel cook tops!) here's a basic *Daube Provençale* recipe (but there are many variations):

- Marinate half a pound of cut up beef in the best red wine you can find, along with an onion cut in four, plus a clove of garlic, a bunch of mixed herbs (or *Herbes de Provence*), and salt and pepper. Marinate for one day (or more).
- On the second day, fry some bacon in hot olive oil in a large casserole dish (like Staub or Le Creuset). Then add a chopped onion, two sliced carrots, and two crushed tomatoes. After browning all these, pour off the marinade from the beef (but save it for later). Fry up the chunks of meat in the casserole along with

the onion, carrots, and tomatoes. The meat should be seared or golden brown but not cooked through.

- Pour in a glass of good red wine and bring the whole thing to a boil. Add back in the marinade, plus two glasses of water, a clove of garlic, a bunch of mixed herbs, and the peel of a fresh orange (without the pith). Season with salt and pepper.
- After the boiling point is reached on the burner or in the oven, turn the heat down to about 325 degrees and simmer very slowly for up to five hours.

Serve on warm plates with noodles or potatoes (in their jackets). And of course, pour yourself a glass of your favorite wine and enjoy.

We often eat this dish for two or three days; every reheating makes it more delicious as the flavors settle in! If you want to add some liquid upon reheating, add in some wine with your water. Cooking note: The Provençaux suggest using a dedicated *Daube* pan as previously mentioned, but they also recommend NEVER washing it. Instead, they dry the pot over a hot flame or in the fireplace, which turns the remains into a kind of ash that can be wiped around the pot. These remnants are supposed to add additional flavor to your NEXT *Daube*.

If you want more information on southern French cuisine, get a copy of the hardcover book, *Provence, 1970: M.F.K. Fisher, Julia Child, James Beard, and the Reinvention of American Taste*. It details a multi-week marathon of cooking and conversations with M.F.K. Fisher, Julia Child, James Beard, Richard Olney, Simone Beck, and Judith Jones in Provence in the final weeks of 1970. These French trained pros shaped the future of American cuisine with their integration of *haute cuisine* practices and practical American needs in this seminal meeting. Detailed by Luke Barr, it's a fascinating study well worth a read. (But enjoy it with some good cheese and a glass of your favorite bubbly or you'll feel deprived.)

Overall restaurants tend toward hearty fare rather than *haute cuisine* in Provence. But nothing sums up the tastes of Provence like this quote by Augustus Saint-Gaudens. "What garlic is to salad, insanity is to art." Just be prepared for lots of insanity in your food when you visit Provence.

Wine

Provence as a whole has a formidable wine history. Wine growing dates back more than 2,600 years. Provence's temperate climate and limestone, granite, and volcanic soils are hardy environments for the vines; the *mistral* wind helps keep the vineyards dry and low on pests. The *mistral's* harsh winds also make the vines struggle—which vintners know contributes to great vintages. Many experts suggest the copious amounts of rosemary, juniper, thyme, and lavender in Provence also influence the character of the wines.

Provence makes the most of its verdant wine growing soil. Rosé wine accounts for about 70-80% of the Provence wine production. Other Provence reds account for 20-30%; white wines make up the remaining 5%. The most famous wine-growing region is Châteauneuf-du-Pape located just north of Avignon. Châteauneuf-du-Pape is called the "gateway to the Southern Rhône Valley," which is famous for much-loved vintages. Châteauneuf-du-Pape wines are made from a rich mix of Grenache, Syrah, and Mourvèdre grapes. The Southern Rhône Valley as a whole has more than 7,000 wine growers. Many of these are situated along jagged peaks throughout the valley or along verdant hillsides as far as the eye can see.

The largest AoC (certified wine growing area) outside Châteauneuf-du-Pape and the Rhône Valley is Côtes de Provence. The Côtes de Provence region runs all the way from Toulon to the coast of the French Riviera. It produces about 75% of all the wine coming out of Provence proper; most of it is rosé.

Provençal wine is growing in popularity. Many newcomers are popping up in Provence, nurturing old or newly planted vines. They're producing some refreshing Côtes de Provence wines. One of this new breed of wine entrepreneur is Mirabeau en Provence near Cotignac. This small, but enterprising vineyard, was started by the British Cronk family. Mirabeau produces a delightful rosé that goes well as an *apéritif*s or with summer foods. The Mirabeau red is a smooth, full-bodied wine with berry aromas. The Cronks and their three children are examples of modern entrepreneurs who left corporate life in Britain for their dream lifestyle in Provence, making wine and living the Southern France way of life. They seem to be having a wonderful time as new vintners, rearing their children in France.

Another famous pair of new vintners is Brad Pitt and Angelina Jolie who also have a Côtes de Provence rosé called Miraval from their home vineyard near Brignoles. Miraval has the world-famous Perrin Family of Château Beaucastel behind it, though my understanding is the Pitt family owns the land. It's a delightful quaffing wine for about $25, though be sure to serve it chilled. Incidentally, the movie stars recently married in Provence at a tiny local church with their children all around them. Perhaps the Pitt family also feels the tug of family values in Provence.

But other families have long histories with Provençal wines. Château la Canorgue near Bonnieux has been held by the same family for more than 200 years. The actual mansion was built on grounds where a Roman villa once stood; Roman underground water canals still cross the vineyards. When Martine and Jean-Pierre Margan took over from Martine's parents in 1974, the vineyards had been neglected for 20 years because they couldn't find a profitable way to grow the grapes. With Jean-Pierre's oenological education, he set about revitalizing the vineyard, and from 1978 onward, the château has produced some wonderful certified *agriculture biologique* vintages.

Jean-Pierre's daughter Nathalie, who also has an oenological education, is the next generation to manage the wines, which include Luberon Château la Canorgue, Luberon Rosé Château la Canorgue, and a wonderful VDP Méditerranée Blanc Canorgue Viognier. (Viognier is one of my favorite whites.) The winery is open to the public and makes a delightful stop on the way to Gordes or Bonnieux. Canorgue's other claim to fame is that it served as the winery in the movie *A Good Year. A*

Good Year is the Peter Mayle tale starring Russell Crowe and directed by Ridley Scott (who has a château nearby in Oppède). In the film Crowe's character finds love with Marion Cotillard, plus a newfound desire to make Provençal wine. (Rent it from Netflix and enjoy with a glass of Canorgue.)

The Rhône Valley and Provence have many wine cellars (*caves*) open for visits. Individual producers and vineyards also offer themed tastings, vineyard walks, cycle rides, and more. For details, check with individual producers or wine organizations like www.Rhône-wines.com, www.aoc-ventoux.fr, www.vins-luberon.fr, and www.Provencewines.com. You can also check with various wine guides or resources like *Wine Spectator* for additional details.

As for the beverages, Provence is not only famous for delectable wines, but also for another famous green concoction called *pastis*. *Pastis* is an anise-based *apéritif*. It caught on after 1915 when *absinthe* ("the green fairy") was banned due to its toxicity.

Absinthe was just one of a long line of anise-based Mediterranean liquors that included sambuca and raki. However, the French had created a rather unique product in *absinthe*. At 45-75% proof, made with the added ingredient of wormwood, *absinthe* had lethal, hallucinogenic properties that caused some people to keel over or become completely unhinged. (Rumor has it that Vincent van Gogh cut off his ear while "high" on the stuff in Arles.)

Absinthe's popularity soared through the mid-1800s when it was given to French troops as a malaria preventative. When these foreign troops returned home, they brought their dry throats with them. Drinking *absinthe* at the end of the day became such a tradition with all classes of French people, that the 5 pm hour became known as *l'heure verte* (the green hour). Soon, there were crimes and even murders associated with imbibing too much of the stuff. Ultimately, it was banned once and for all (although it's still available from places like the Czech Republic, and Britain imports it into the U.K.).

Pastis, a milder beverage based on anise, is designed to be mixed with water at a 5-to-1 ratio. It became a more healthful alternative— without the nasty wormwood. Paul Ricard, a clever entrepreneur and son of a Marseille wine dealer, crafted a fine version around 1932. He dubbed it *Le Vrai Pastis de Marseille*. It sold fabulously.

Ricard and Pernod joined forces in the 1970s; they now dominate the *pastis* market. Milder than absinthe, *pastis* still packs a wallop, however. Poured over ice, it makes a very refreshing drink (although it's definitely an acquired taste). The French reportedly drink something like 20 million glasses of it every day.

When and if you imbibe, however, go slowly. It goes down easily, but it won't hit your knees until you stand up—and sometimes fall over. It's especially favored when playing *boules*—and *pastis*-fueled "debates" over whose ball is closest to the *cochonnet* are a well-known accompaniment to a "friendly" game.

Marseilles is known for its superb selection of *pastis* and modern *absinthe*, particularly La Maison Du Pastis. Home to 75 types of *pastis*, La Maison Du Pastis grew as the brainchild of Belgian musician Frédéric Bernard. Bernard suddenly realized that the cradle of *pastis* actually had no specialty *pastis* shop. Having been to Brussels, where *connoisseur* beer emporiums are as copious as U.S. shoe stores, it's no surprise to me that an enterprising Belgian would find the *pastis*-for-any-palette niche in France!

Shopping

While you're in Provence, one of the must-dos is visiting a street *marché*. Some of these Provençal markets have been around longer than some of the buildings. The Apt market (pictured), for example, was authorized by King Rene in 1523. Roussillon hosted a fabulous market starting in 1567. The Gordes market began fairly recently—in 1774!

One of my favorite things to do is to troll around these markets, looking for gifts or goodies to take home. I particularly like the 72% olive oil soap called *Savon de Marseille*. Or Provençal linens, French clothing (like my spiffy black cotton beret with swirls), or handsome *faience* (fine pottery). I also like the aromatic spices such as *Fleur de sel De Camargue* (salt) and *Herbes de Provence*. At the wander-where-you-will markets, you can also pick up colorful Provençal furniture, antiques, old books, and paraphernalia like corkscrews and picnic gear.

Of particular note are the Provençal linens and locally-crafted *faience* with its bright motifs of yellows, blues, lavenders, and reds. A fragrant feature of the Provençal markets is lavender. This aromatic plant grows bountifully in the dry hills of Provence. Lavender was first introduced by the Romans to disinfect their baths and perfume their laundry. Today, about 16,000 hectares of Provençal land are dedicated to lavender or its less fragrant hybrid, lavandin. Much of Provence land is dedicated to thyme, rosemary, sage, savory, and vines. As you drive through Provence, you can smell the lavender everywhere. Lavender itself is used in making perfume and cosmetics; lavandin, the hybrid plant, is more often used for perfumed laundry detergent, soap, and cleaning products. France supplies about 50% of the world's lavender.

One of the most aromatic items you'll find is *Herbes de Provence*. These pretty linen bags of Provençal fabric are stuffed with an herb combination of dried marjoram, rosemary, basil, thyme, oregano, savory, and lavender. Colloquially called the "taste of Provence," these bags will add the most delicious aroma to your foods or your kitchen. Interestingly, the locals tell me that lavender is not typically used in Provençal cooking *per se*; it's been added to this concoction of *Herbes de Provence* because tourists wanted it!

When you buy these lovely little bags, I have one suggestion: avoid the plastic wrapped strips of them at the airport and train stations. I understand that many of these are actually made in China. Instead, go into the *fromageries*, standing markets, or *boucheries* throughout Provence and get the real thing. You can tell a locally grown bag of *Herbes de Provence* by the red label on the outside that certifies it's the genuine product.

You'll also find tourist paraphernalia that celebrates the *cigale* (cicada). The *cigale* is the lowly but loud creature that's the symbol of Provence. Poet and Nobel Prize winner Frédéric Mistral first christened the bug as the image of the Félibrige movement in 1854.

This movement promoted the Provençal language and traditions. Legend had it that God sent the cicada to keep the Provençaux awake (after their long, wine-fueled lunches) and to keep them from getting too lazy. (Anyone who has heard these creatures "chirp" all summer long knows this is working beautifully.)

This much-loved insect mascot emerges from the ground by the thousands at the height of the Provençal summer during mating. The males are responsible for the loud, clicking/buzzing sound that's designed to attract females. (The sounds have been recorded at up to 12 decibels.)

I admit that when I hear it, it sounds to me like a thousand super-sonic crickets stuck on hyper-drive. Interestingly, the female makes no sound. She just responds to the male's loud courting, and when male and female find each other (in all the racket, how could they miss?), their union produces 300-400 eggs. Interesting psychological note: The ancient Greek poet Xenophon praised this noisy quality in the male cicada: "Blessed are the cicadas, for they have voiceless wives." (As a couple's therapist, I'd suggest there's more than a little cynicism in that statement.)

Some people find the *cigale's* din soothing; they even take home *cigale* sound-makers so they can crank up the sounds of Provence in their own backyard. Others, like me, would rather have a root canal than hear this cacophony every day. But it doesn't keep me from visiting Provence. Today, the locals believe this insect attracts luck and happiness. And cicada lovers can buy lots of luck in the form of pottery, wall hangings, tablecloths, accessories, dishware, glassware, toys, soaps, and ceramics.

Kicking around the countryside, you may unearth a Roman coin or two—or even some stray bits of marble or pottery from the many settlers who've occupied Provence over the centuries. Antique hunters particularly enjoy the shops around Aix-en-Provence and L'Isle-sur-la-Sorgue where bits of dismantled *châteaux* such as fireplaces, staircases, iron gates, pergolas, fountains, and doors can be found at a good price.

The distinctive truffle aroma perfumes all of Provence—and it's available fresh or in oil, tinned or bottled. You'll naturally find slivers of truffle in certain French dishes. But the truffle blends especially well with olive oil to make an aromatic oil for your salad or dish.

One of my favorite truffle purchases in Provence took place in Saint-Rémy-de-Provence. I bought three precious bottles of truffle oil and carted them back home in my carry-on bag. (My husband also lugged bottles of Châteauneuf-du-Pape wine and *faience* pottery that weighed nearly 25 pounds. I'm still hearing about this years later. Note: Ship things home instead of lugging them through an airport! It may save your marriage!) Every time I open one of those truffle oil bottles, the scent of Provence fills my kitchen.

Finally, another reason to visit the street markets is to observe the locals. These Provençaux shoppers, particularly the French house-wives, have a laser eye for good quality. And they have no problem cutting the vendor off at the knees if his or her wares are mediocre. When I first visited the Apt market, it was 2002. That year, France had converted from the French franc to the euro. I was standing at a linen table alongside a pair of elderly French ladies with scarves tied around their heads. They were fingering some white lace tablecloths for purchase. When they asked the price, they looked stunned when the proprietor told them the amount. Both ladies hissed. Then, they pulled a couple of gigantic calculators out of their handbags. They each began calculating the conversion from franc to euro. They soon realized he was padding the price in the conversion. Never have I heard such an outcry when these two little ladies confronted the withering shopkeeper. They told him to offer a better price or they'd walk. He capitulated. Lesson: Don't mess with these Provençaux *grand-mères*!

Check local listings for where and when the *marchés* are held, but no matter where you are on any given day, you'll find plenty of them in Provence. My favorites are Cavaillon (Monday), Aix and Gordes (Tuesday), Saint-Rémy-de-Provence (Wednesday), Les-Baux-de-Provence and Avignon (Thursday), Bonnieux and Carpentras (Friday), Apt (Saturday), and L'Isle-sur-la-Sorgue (Sunday).

Culture & Art

"The shadows of olive trees are often mauve. They are always moving, luminous, full of gaiety and life."

—Jean Renoir

Provence has glorious light, stunning sunsets, and a history filled with fanciful myths, fierce battles, and great romances. It all makes for a ripe atmosphere for depiction in song, text, sculpture, film, and paint like *Café Terrace at Night* by van Gogh shown here.

Provence has always been a land of stories. Strewn with living history, populated by a melting pot of genetically rich people, it's hard to know where fact gives way to myth. What we do know is that the story of this region lives in the rubble of the land, as well as in the records handed down over the centuries in art, architecture, and oral tradition.

Written records came late to this region. The golden age of Provençal literature occurred during the 12th century when *Occitan* was spoken and captured in the vernacular through song and poetry. Wandering poets, later known as troubadours, touted the Court of Love in such places as Les-Baux-de-Provence during the middle ages. Even the infiltration of "infidels" could not squelch the romantic notion of Provence as a fertile land brimming with fanciful history ripe for artistic expression.

Artistic flair shows up in the oral tales of the great Roman general Gaius Marius in the 1st century B.C., who built roads connecting Apt and Aix to Rome, Spain, and the rest of Europe. It flavors the writings of Petrarch, poet, scholar, and father of humanism, who followed Pope Clement V to Avignon in the 1300s. It appears in the songs and poetry of the chivalrous knights and troubadours, and in the prophecies of Nostradamus, apothecary and clairvoyant, who was born in Saint-Rémy-de-Provence in 1503. And it vividly colors the work of Alexandre Dumas, prolific writer of fiction (*The Count of Monte Cristo*), plays, and travel articles. Dumas was so inspired by the succulent melons of Cavaillon, he had the melons delivered to him each year until he died. (He also left a portion of his book collection to the local Cavaillon library.)

An elegant symmetry is depicted in Provence's Romanesque churches, Roman architectural remains, majestic statuary, and marvelous stained glass. Artistic sensibilities underlie the frescoes and artwork of the Avignon popes, and it survives in tapestries, scrolls, pottery, coins, books, paintings, clothing, linens, and ancient armor.

By the late 1800s, Vincent van Gogh, Paul Gauguin, and Paul Cézanne (who was born in Aix-en-Provence) were driven to capture this verdant land with its luminescent light that imbued everything with an unforgettable enchantment. The eccentricity of the Provençaux, their multi-hued hills and valleys, their stalwart lifestyle, their personal passions—all were captured by these artists and others on hundreds of canvasses, drawings, and walls. Sometimes, in the case of Arles lover Vincent van Gogh, the alchemy of Provence may have driven them mad.

In February 1888, impressionist painter Vincent van Gogh (1853-1890) came to Arles. Van Gogh was a Dutchman, son of a Dutch Calvinist pastor. He showed artistic talent early on as a teen. He soon became a follower of Impressionism in his adulthood. Van Gogh was ecstatic when he discovered a "new light" in Provence. He spent two years painting scenes around Arles, Saintes-Maries-de-la-Mer, Les-Baux, and Saint-Rémy. Some of his most famous Arles paintings are worth millions: *View of Arles with Irises, The Yellow House, The Alyscamps, Starry Night over the Rhône,* and various portraits including *Portrait of an Old Provençal Peasant, L'Arlésienne,* and *Madame Ginoux.*

Van Gogh's copious output included 200 paintings and 100 drawings. You can see the modern-day site of the painter's *Café Terrace at Night* at Le Café le Nuit in the Place du Forum in Arles. Not only can you sit here where van Gogh painted, you can dine on the brasserie's specialties, which include roasted bull's tail.

Van Gogh's friend Paul Gauguin came to visit him 1888, and they quarreled, plunging van Gogh into despair and possibly madness. (Some reports suggest *absinthe* played a role in van Gogh's erratic behavior and hallucinations.) After his breakdown, he was cared for at St-Paul-de-Mausole (an asylum near Saint-Rémy-de-Provence) where he continued to paint (*Wheatfields, Cypresses, Olive Trees,* and *Self-Portrait.*) Though he ultimately committed suicide back in Paris in 1890, he left behind a wonderful legacy of work.

Paul Cézanne (1839-1906) is another of the major artists from Provence. Born the son of an Aix-en-Provence banker, Cézanne left his legal studies to take up painting as a young man. He was introduced to Impressionism by his friend and writer Emile Zola. He quickly went beyond basic Impressionism and experimented with large swaths of vivid color and simple geometric forms. He rarely left Provence after 1890 and devoted much of his attention to painting the 3,300-foot Mont Sainte-Victoire east of Aix. He painted this venerable mountain 60 or more times—and never quite captured it to his satisfaction. He collapsed, brush in hand, in front of one of his works. He was carted away on a wagon surrounded by canvasses and reportedly died surrounded by artwork. His work opened the door to Cubism. Many other artists, including Signac, Chaubaud, Braque, and Picasso followed in his footsteps. You can visit sites honoring Cézanne and his life in Aix-en-Provence.

In 1959 author Lawrence Durrell said, "Some spots are the cradle of genius. Provence is one." From the roots of its literary and cultural heritage, Provence has influenced a number of cultural greats, including Marcel Pagnol, French novelist, playwright, and filmmaker who was born near Marseille; Emile Zola; Edith Wharton, who wrote and lived in Hyères; Peter Mayle and Carol Drinkwater, British expats who live in Provence; and many more including Albert Camus and Lawrence Durrell himself.

And of course the movies came calling. Two modern French films capturing Provençal life are *Jean de Florette* and its sequel, *Manon des Sources.* The first features the popular, but eccentric, Gérard Depardieu. And of course, the world wide sensation of Mayle's *A Year in Provence,* brought not only hordes of tourists to Provence, but birthed a television program of the same name. This multi-part show starred John Thaw and Lindsay Duncan. It chronicled their hilarious adventures as a pair of Brits who buy a do-over French home in the Luberon. They must learn to cope with the locals (and they them.) Today, the area is a second home destination for many entertainment people, including American actor John Malkovich (Bonnieux) and aforementioned British director Ridley Scott (Oppède).

One of the aspects of Provence that I particularly enjoy is the high personal value placed on art. The act of creation as a life force seems to be a psychological necessity in the French psyche. What I mean by that is echoed in Lawrence Durrell's statement: "It is the people who paint, not only the artists." Most Provençaux see themselves as *artistes* of some kind or another. In Provence, where the light and sky seem so freshly minted, the act of creating masterpieces is simply a natural extension of living well. When you spend time in Provence, you'll see beauty everywhere you look. Sometimes, the symmetry of the fields or the plane trees along the lanes creates a living painting. The vendors in the markets even take pride in how artistically their goods are displayed.

Artism, if I may coin a phrase, seems to be natural right brain activity in Provence. I suspect an intrinsic belief here is that creativity not only feeds the heart but is integral to the very existence of the Provençal soul. I confess I'm even treated differently here when I talk about writing books. In France, the artist is revered—no matter how much money you've made or how famous you are.

As Lawrence Durrell wrote, "the pleasure and enrichment for an artist living in France is the feeling that the whole population is subtly engaged in the same debate with itself—namely how to turn living into something more than just existing."

Today, many of the region's artists study at the École Supérieure d'Art de Design in Luminy Marseille. Marseille's elevation to the 2013 European Capital of Culture demonstrates the importance of culture and art in the region. One of the first places serious artists go in Provence is Les-Baux-de-Provence which, among several artistic venues, has turned its disused underground quarries into an art house called Carrières de Lumières. This "Quarry of Lights" features the work of such artists as Picasso and Cézanne illuminated on the vast quarry walls.

Local artists abound in Provence like my friends at a B&B near Apt (near Bonnieux). The owner's wife has an artist's studio on the premises; visitors can watch as she works. Two quirky notes: First, her many paintings feature some very intimate portraits of—I'm surmising—her and her husband (or a couple that looked a lot like them). These canvasses made for very interesting viewing since they were intimate and sexually expressive.

Second, madame was adamant that we were not to feed her lovable black cats called Abelard and Eloise, though they were always begging under the breakfast table. Interestingly, these matching felines were named after the star-crossed 12th century Parisian lovers. Abelard and Eloise's story of love found and lost has inspired dozens of books, poems, paintings, and movies. The pair were so beloved by Josephine Bonaparte, herself entangled in a tragic love affair with Napoleon, that she had their remains transplanted to Paris's Père Lachaise cemetery 600 years after their death. However, furry Abelard and Eloise were not allowed treats from our *petite dejuenier* table; they had to make do with bugs and birds. Noble names, pedestrian fodder. Such is the conundrum that is Provence.

Finally, you'll occasionally run across that quintessential French art form in Provence, the French  postcard. When I saw this on a wall in a *brasserie* in Les-Baux, I started laughing and asked the two ladies behind the bar if I could take a picture. Afterward, they were so delighted I found the postcard titillating that they came around to the front of the bar and gave me kisses on both checks! They understood I was simpatico with their cultured nuances. It was a treasured moment.

Navigating the Area

You'll be able to reach Provence by plane, train, or car. Several "no-frills" airlines (such as Easy Jet and Ryan Air) serve Avignon, Marseille, Nice, Nîmes, and Toulon from European airports. Provence has two major airports: Marseille-Provence and Nice-Côte d'Azur.

Avignon-Caumont, Nîmes-Garons, and Toulon-Hyères also serve some international destinations. Cannes and Saint-Tropez airports mainly serve private planes.

You can also fly into Paris and take the TGV train down to Lyon and hire a car and drive down into Provence. OR you can take the train further down to Avignon, Aix, or Marseilles and then rent a car and drive up into Provence. And there are various trains that split off to take you to many other major towns in Provence.

The *département* or county called Vaucluse is a natural for car or bus touring. The beautiful villages such as Bonnieux, Isle Sur la Sorgue, Gordes, Roussillon, Aix, Avignon, Carpentras, Orange, Châteauneuf-du-Pape, Les-Baux, and Saint-Rémy are must see locales. Most visitors allow anywhere from 5-14 days to see Provence. This is not because it's such a large area. But the traffic on the narrow roads will delay your getting anywhere fast. (I've had to wait for delivery vans galore—and an occasional sheep herd or farm combine. But there's plenty to snap pictures of while you wait.)

My favorite way to see the area is by car. You'll see Provençal life as you meander along the country roads. I've driven into Provence from Nice via the fabulous superhighway (about two hours). I've also driven into Provence from the north at Lyon, sampling the Rhône Valley wines as I went. After several days seeing Provence, I then drove on to the west through the Languedoc, then up through the Dordogne, then finally west to the ocean and Bordeaux. On another trip, I drove into Provence from Nice and drove back out to Nice where I flew on to Rome.

Be aware that once you enter Provence proper, you'll have mostly two-lane roads to negotiate. However, various themed travel routes can turn these two-lane roads into an adventure. The *Flânerie Entre Les Oliviers*, for example, is a route specializing in travel through olive farms, cheese growers, wineries, and restaurants featuring those products.

Another route is the *Route des Peintres de la Lumière en Provence*, which offers an introduction to the region through the various sites painted by famous artists. Aix, Saint-Rémy and Arles all have this itinerary in map form. If you're interested in the life of writer-film-maker Marcel Pagnol, you can take a bus tour of his favorite settings. (See the Aubange tourist office.) A pretty drive is along the *Route de la*

Lavande, which takes you along the prime lavender fields. The regional parks all offer guides to visiting their area; camping and picnic locales are also highlighted. The local tourist offices throughout Provence can offer you a *Provence Pass* which will give you access to many of the most famous sites throughout the region for one price.

For those of you with smart phones or tablets, I highly recommend Paul Shawcross's app, *Provençal Roaming*. Paul's travel writer savvy helps make this a key tool for visiting the Provence region with ease. There's plenty of handy detail on places to stay, dine, and visit as you meander through Provence.

Favorites

Avignon, Châteauneuf-du-Pape, the Rhône Valley, Saint-Rémy-de-Provence, L'Isle-sur-la-Sorgue, Bonnieux, Ménerbes, Lacoste, Gordes, Les-Baux-de-Provence, Arles, the Camargue, and Aix-en-Provence. These are a few of my most-loved Provence corners. Places where I've sampled the gorgeous papal wines that fascinate wine aficionados today. Locales with some of the best open-air markets in France that tantalize with delightful lavender soaps, bright colored linens, and succulent melons. Haunts where the mighty have fallen in Roman amphitheaters but where medieval France lives on in ancient weaponry, bull-fighting arenas, and handsome serfs who pop up along the way. Vast stretches of marshland where wild white horses run and feisty black bulls cavort

along the Camargue coastline. Join me as we explore my favorite pleasures in Provence.

Avignon

Avignon is often called the "Heartbeat of Provence." Sitting at the center of the region geographically, it's also arguably been the cultural, religious, and art epicenter from the point of view of history. The huge Pope's Palace rises from the banks of the Rhône here. Around it, the captivating little city of fine old houses, bustling commercial buildings, and spectacular bridge makes it a must-visit in the region.

Already a bustling city-state in the 11th, 12th, and 13th centuries, Avignon became a medieval showplace when a Frenchman, Raymond Bertrand de Got, became head of the Catholic Church in 1305. As Clement V, he promptly moved the seat of the papacy from Rome to Avignon when the turmoil within the Catholic Church propelled the papal seat to flee to France. Here, in a cream-colored palace, the popes ruled the Catholic world from 1309 to 1377.

During those years, the papacy built and expanded the magnificent fortified palace. It brought sophisticated art and culture to the city. It also founded a wine dynasty in nearby Châteauneuf-du-Pape since the princely popes had to have noble wine to succor them. The papacy also founded a university, which became a magnet for thousands of students in the day. This in turn inspired an unprecedented building boom when the medieval population jumped from 5,000 to 40,000 during the papal reign.

The palace, lavish for the time, was enlarged over 60 years as a fortress, papal residence, and religious hub. Many of the seven popes who ruled from here were art *connoisseurs*. Their papal residences were particularly sumptuous. Avignon became known as the "Capital of Christendom." After the popes retreated to Rome, the great palace was pillaged over the centuries. During the French Revolution, the furniture, statues, and artwork became the spoils of the revolution. Around the start of the 1800s, it even became a prison and barracks; during this time the soldiers and military engineers sometimes sold the frescoes to local antique dealers.

But all was not lost. Today's magnificent, partially restored Palais des Papes still creates a medieval atmosphere of religious grandiosity. Rocher des Doms, the majestic cathedral, plus the grand mansions, pink-roofed buildings, and medieval ramparts give Avignon a truly magical ambience. As you wander through the palace you'll find yourself in a three+ acre maze of chapels, passages, prison cells, art galleries, screening rooms, and souvenir shops. The restored palace, still grand in the face of much historical indignation, is worth a visit for its citadel-like grandeur and artistically enhanced presentation. Afterward, you can wander down the local streets nearby past the carousel and street *cafés* (and Apple stores) with the palace at your back; here you'll truly know what it's like to walk between the ages.

With the magnificent papal palace as a backdrop, Avignon gained modern worldwide attention when theater director Jean Vilar founded the Avignon Festival in 1946. It continues with much acclaim to this day. With a packed program of dazzling events, the July festival stages performances all over the city in dance, theatre, and cinema. This theatrical tradition is the reason that even if you visit during other months, you'll still find splendid performing mimes and other theatrical venues as you wander around the city.

Another fascinating sight next to the palace is the Pont Saint-Bénézet. This now partial bridge spanning the Rhône between Villeneuve-lès-Avignon and Avignon was built between 1177 and 1185. This early bridge was destroyed 40 years later during the Albigensian Crusade when Louis VIII of France laid siege to Avignon. The bridge was rebuilt with 22 stone arches. It was very costly to maintain, however, as the arches tended to collapse when the raging Rhône flooded. In the middle of the 17th century, the bridge was finally abandoned. The four surviving arches are believed to have been built in around 1345 by Pope Clement VI during the Avignon papacy. The Chapel of Saint Nicholas sits on the second pier of the bridge. It was constructed in the second half of the 12th century but has since been substantially altered.

As one of the central locations in Provence, there are abundant opportunities in Avignon for fine eating and excellent wine tasting. First is Restaurant Christian Etienne, helmed by famed master chef Christian Etienne. Other dining options include trendy 83.Vernet, Fou de Fafe, Le Gout du Jour, and Le Bistro Lyonnais, although you'll find dozens of eateries in the local vicinity.

Within blocks of the palace are a variety of accommodations (but you'll most likely have to park in underground parking and drag your bags a long way over cobblestones). These include Hôtel Garlande, La Mirande Hôtel, and Kyriad Avignon. If you want larger accommodations with more modern conveniences (like parking), you might try the Hôtel d'Europe. Further afield is the spa resort Auberge de Cassagne, which is about 20 minutes from the city center.

There are some agreeable shops in and around Avignon. Since it's also a college town, you'll find both traditional Provençal goods and trendy new shops with teens in mind. Above all, take some time to enjoy the ever-present entertainment around Avignon. You can acquire an *Avignon Pass*, valid for two weeks, giving you a significant price reduction on the sites around Avignon proper, as well as Villeneuve-lès-Avignon across the river. Be sure to take a moment to enjoy the daily street performers, impromptu juggling acts, toy vendors, and mimes of all kinds on the streets.

Châteauneuf-du-Pape and the Rhône Valley

About seven miles north of Avignon, sits the opulent vineyard and enclave known as Châteauneuf-du-Pape. It was French Pope John XXII who set his eyes on this spot for a cooler summer residence when he couldn't stand the heat of Avignon summers. He therefore built a vacation castle overlooking the vineyards. By this time, the vast vineyards were producing fabulous red papal wines from vines inhabiting every hectare of land within eyeshot.

"Châteauneuf" means "new castle." A lively town sprang up around this summer pope's palace. With the departure of the papacy and during various wars afterward, the village and castle were pillaged The remaining castle structure (*donjon*) served as an observation post for German soldiers during WWII. Just before they departed in 1944, they blew up the structure, but only the northern half of the tower was destroyed. Today, the southern half of the *donjon* rises defiantly at the pinnacle of this resilient town.

The modern town of Châteauneuf-du-Pape is only about 10 square miles; it has a small population of just over 2,000 people. It still has some ancient buildings and dwellings, but mostly it's become a kind of "mini Bordeaux" or "Napa Valley," with wine consortiums running up and down the main street. Wines are for sale here at fairly reasonable prices—and I never miss an opportunity to pick up a few bottles. These are some of the finest—and best-known—wines in France.

The Châteauneuf-du-Pape AoC designation permits 13 different varieties of grapes in the red wines, but the blend must be predominantly Grenache. Modern Châteauneuf-du-Pape can be either a full-bodied, dark wine which can be cellared for up to 25 years or a more youthful and fruity vintage, ready to drink within a couple of years. As usual in France, the wine is named after the village not the grape variety.

White Châteauneuf-du-Pape is a pure delight, full of rich fruity flavors balanced out by a refreshing and defined crispness. Roussanne, Grenache Blanc, and Clairette are some of the main grapes used. There's much jargon in the appellation "decree." Article 10 of the appellation rules allows the use of a slightly bulbous Burgundy bottle, with the papal coat of arms embossed into the glass and the inscription *"Châteauneuf-du-Pape contrôlée."* As such, it's pretty easy to distinguish the wine bottles in the shops.

In 2010, there were 320 producers here, and the annual production was 13 million bottles of which 95% is red. The remainder is white: the production of rosé is not permitted. This is one of the easiest red AoC wines to acquire in the U.S. and the U.K. It's fairly reasonably priced—and delicious.

Every time I've visited Châteauneuf-du-Pape, I see huge tourist groups and cyclers enjoying the warm sunshine and stopping for a wine lunch as they wend their way through Provence. Quirky wine note: There's also an official ban on UFOs in the vicinity. In 1954, fears of ET's and UFO's were all over the news. Numerous sightings of foreign objects had been reported in Châteauneuf.

The mayor of Châteauneuf, concerned about protecting his commune and their precious wines, issued a decree banning flying saucers (*cigare volants*) from landing, taking off, or entering the airspace of his community. Anyone caught landing on his territory in a space-ship would immediately be thrown into custody! As far as I know, there's no record of anyone out of this world being incarcerated—although a few inebriated tourists have probably come close to fitting the bill. In 1954, the locals would have thought the frequent cycling clubs with their alien bike helmets were space invaders!

The D68 links Southern Rhône Valley near Châteauneuf-du-Pape to Orange in the north; it runs along never-ending vineyards. This lush Rhône Valley was the result of an epic geological clash between the Massif Central and the Alps. The cataclysm created a rift valley which was flooded by the Mediterranean. Three hundred million years ago, volcanic activity in the Massif Central produced successive layers of fluvial and calcareous marine sediments. Forty million years ago, the Alps were pushed upwards, causing the valley separating the two massifs to collapse. The Alpine Gulf created in this way was filled in by the Mediterranean which gradually deposited a base layer of hard limestone and marl (calcareous clay).

This Mediterranean tributary met the Rhône River as it cascaded down from Switzerland. Together, the French Rhône began digging itself a deeper bed as it flowed to the sea, creating silt terraces on either side of the valley and mixing diverse elements in the hillside soils: sands, clay, and flinty pebbles. Today, the valley's rich soils make perfect hosts for grape vines.

In the 5th century B.C., the Greeks arrived and saw the wine potential of this fertile soil. They busily planted vines and were rewarded with some wonderful wines. The vineyards were further developed under the Roman occupation. Julius Caesar particularly liked vineyards for security reasons: it was more difficult for invaders to hide in the short rows of grape vines. The Roman legionnaires and noblemen received land and cultivated the vines, creating wine estates.

In the 1st century, the vines planted in terraces around Vienne were an early version of the renowned Côte-Rôtie variety. In the region of Tricastin, where the Grignan-les-Adhémar appellation is produced today, a large collection of amphoras (Roman vessels) was uncovered. This is a sign of the region's wine growing vocation The so-called "wine of Vienne" was the wine of choice in Roman banquets. Even today, images of Bacchus are found on unearthed Roman pitchers, presses, and statuary, paying testament to the Roman love of wine.

In the 11th century, the powerful Templars cultivated vines in Roaix where the Côtes du Rhône vintages are grown. The Counts of Toulouse cultivated the vineyards of Sablet and Calranne. The Cornas, a powerful and coarse red wine, was much appreciated by the Emperor Charlemagne, Kings Louise XI, Charles-Quint, Louis XV, and Cardinal Richelieu. The Saint-Joseph wines, harmonious and elegant, also took pride of place on the tables of the kings of France.

Fast forward to 1929 when the Côtes du Rhône AoC was awarded. The Côtes du Rhône appellation accounts for 60% of the wine produced in the entire valley. In 1966, the Côtes du Rhône Villages AoC was awarded and includes the wine of 17 villages along the Rhône. The wine fields stretch out from the mighty river, alternating with lavender, until they spill onto terraces at the hillsides and hilltops. Because of the *mistral's* strong winds that frequently blow in for successive days of three, six, or even nine days at a stretch, dark rows of cypress tress have been planted all over the southern part of the Rhône Valley to protect both the inhabitants and the vegetation. For grape vines, this means dryer vines and less pests.

The palette and colors of the wines of the Rhône Valley are endless. The vintages are spread over the north and south depending on the appellation areas. The Hermitage offers powerful noble reds and fat whites, while its neighbor the Crozes-Hermitage, produces fruity reds and pleasing whites. The Saint-Joseph variety seduces with silky reds and elegant whites. The Condrieu reveals the splendid expression of the Viognier grape. Tavel, a rich rosé, is one of the most famous wines of the Rhône.

It's all worth a visit to this accessible, yet somewhat remote wine-growing area. You may first want to visit these smaller Rhône Valley producers, then end up for the *crème de la crème* in Châteauneuf-du-Pape. These Rhône wines are reasonably priced and delicious. While lacking the gravitas of Bordeaux wines, there's still much to enjoy here.

Saint-Rémy-de-Provence

Saint-Rémy-de-Provence is one of my favorite towns in Provence. It's known as the "Gateway to the Alpilles," the long limestone mountain range east of Arles and south of Avignon. Saint-Rémy is a tourist-friendly Provençal town with congenial homes and businesses in pale pastel colors along wonderfully cobbled streets.

This distinctive village is a magnet for tourists and locals alike, especially on Wednesday market days. It's also known as a town for gardeners. Saint-Rémy specializes in the production of flower and vegetable seeds.

Michel de Nostredame (1503-1566), who later became known as Nostradamus, is probably the most famous individual born in Saint-Rémy. Professionally, he was a doctor-apothecary; he had success in treating the plague when it ravaged Provence. But he kept the remedies to himself, and the French medical profession retaliated by expelling him from its ranks. Later, he moved to nearby Salon-de-Provence, and after penning minor writings and almanacs, he began writing his major work, *Centuries*. *Centuries* is a collection of poems and prophecies written in quatrains. These prophecies, which detailed harrowing occurrences in the distant future, received mixed reviews. They were considered either evil ramblings or inspired revelations.

One of his great admirers was Queen Catherine de' Medici, wife of King Henry II of France. She regularly had Nostradamus draft horoscopes for her and her children. He also became physician to her young son who would later become Charles IX of France. His predictions are still being studied today. He allegedly predicted the Great Fire of London, the French Revolution, Napoleon and Hitler's rise, space travel, various wars in the Middle East, and the alleged end of the world somewhere around 3797. Opinions are still divided on whether he was a seer *extraordinaire* or a raving lunatic. The Nostradamus home in Salon-de-Provence has been turned into a small museum dedicated to his life. Strolling around Saint-Rémy, however, his name is often seen on shops, street signs, walls, statues, and fountains.

Near Saint-Rémy-de-Provence are the Roman remains at Glanum. A fortified town in Roman times, it's particularly known for the remains of a mausoleum and triumphal arch (the oldest in France). Unfortunately, many of the early remains were destroyed by invaders or used in building Saint-Rémy buildings.

There are some popular B&Bs and hotels in Saint-Rémy since it's a favorite of tour groups. Hôtel Van Gogh, Hôtel l'Amandière, and La Maison du Village are great locations. As for dining in and around Saint-Rémy, there are many options to choose from. Favorites include Mistral Gourmand which is ensconced in an old house on the route to Les-Baux; it has a delightful €20 three-course lunch menu—including a glass of wine. Another favorite of mine in town is L'assiette de Marie, a romantic place for a medium-priced dinner eaten by candlelight within walking distance of the town center.

L'Isle-sur-la-Sorgue

This is a wonderful walking town built on the banks of the Sorgue River. L'Isle-sur-la-Sorgue evolved in the 12th century as a fisherman's town. Built on stilts above a marsh, water continued to play a major part in the town's evolution as it became the "Venice of Provence." By the 18th century, 70 huge waterwheels lined the canals powering the major industries of tanning, paper, and silk making. Some of the tanneries survive, but today L'Isle-sur-la-Sorgue is best known as the antique epicenter of Provence. There are a few museums and a lovely 17th century church called Notre-Dames-des-Anges that's famous for its rare clock that shows the time, date, and phases of the moon.

But antiques are the main reason most people visit—and they come in droves. Now the third largest European platform for antiques and flea markets, it's a "shop-in-person-eBay." One of the most enjoyable venues in which to troll for antiques is an old textile mill that was converted into an antique market called Le Village de Antiquaires de la Gare. Open Saturday to Monday, more than 110 traders fill the niches with gilt-framed mirrors, old leather club chairs, kitchen accessories, ancient implements, vintage linens, and ancient clothing, including stunning antique lace items and Louis XIV paraphernalia like glove buttoners. There are splendid pieces of historical furniture and *château* elements. (Whenever a *château* divests of its precious furnishings and fixtures, the parts and pieces often show up here.) Sometimes entire art deco hotel bars are here for the taking.

More than 1,500 vendors offer their wares in individual shops or along the quay. There's also a delightful Sunday morning street market. But arrive before 9 a.m., as parking after that is horrendous. The biggest draws are the antique fairs during Easter weekend and over the weekend nearest to August 15. So avoid those times unless you have a sturdy resolve to shop.

The Golden Triangle

Bonnieux, Ménerbes, Lacoste, Apt, Roussillon, L'Isle-sur-la-Sorgue, and Gordes form something of a "golden triangle" in the North Luberon area of Provence. It's occasionally referred to as the "California of Europe" due to the influx of tourists and high-priced real estate.

I freely admit when I first went there in 2002, I was vaguely hunting around for the places Peter Mayle described in *A Year in Provence*. What I didn't realize until later was how easy he'd made it to actually find his house! Mayle admitted in recent interviews that he had inadvertently pinpointed where his actual home was located in this little valley. And the result was that fans were constantly showing up in his yard—sometimes swimming in his pool! Mayle vacated the whole country for a while after his runaway success. I believe he made a beeline for New York, but then over the last decade or so, he quietly moved back to Provence, somewhere near Avignon (probably behind gated walls with an attack dog or two). By the time I first visited Provence, Mayle had long been gone. But the stories in his books come alive as you meander around these delightful villages just minutes from each other.

Bonnieux

The tiny town of Bonnieux is built on a plateau above the valley; it's one of the prettiest villages in this little triangle of French heaven. Bonnieux is surrounded by plains planted with Côtes du Luberon vines, lavender, grains, and fruit trees. The town's perched locale is accessible by car. But you'll make some of the way on foot after you park. From the car park, there are some delightful little shops, terrace *bistros*, and a small weekly market. I purchased some wonderful local dishes and linens there and found it an agreeable place for dinner or a drink. Le Fournil is one of my favorites for a delightful dinner under the stars. Le Fournil also has some unique seating, because part of the restaurant is actually cut into the rock. You can truly "dine in the cave" here.

Ménerbes

Ménerbes is another of the hilltop villages nearby that's

surrounded by magnificent countryside, with ancient aristocratic houses, now restored. There are some enchanting sites here, as well as some cute little hotels (but I prefer to stay in and around Gordes across the valley). There's a 16th century castle, and a stellar wine, truffle, and olive oil education facility called Maison de la Truffe et du Vin du Luberon.

Peter Mayle bases some of his book and its characters on the people of Ménerbes. One cultural happening here includes visits by painter Nicolas de Staël, who put the final touches to his last pieces in Ménerbes. This is also the same village that famous painter Pablo Picasso came to hide with Dora Maar.

At the base of the hilltop village is the fascinating Musée du Tire-Bouchon where I once spent a pleasant afternoon. This museum is probably unique in the world in that it features nothing but corkscrews! You can wander among the softly lit cases where a fine collection of more than 1,000 pieces from several countries are proudly on display. These range from crude corkscrews from the 17th century to intricate screws from the 18th century to fantastical modern day collector pieces, some in solid gold. There are some imaginative corkscrews here including a dog lover's design with a dog's head handle; an ancestral corkscrew featuring the family seal; a pistol corkscrew attached to a gun; corkscrews disguised as grapes and vines; boudoir corkscrews for uncorking flasks of perfume; and, this being France, erotic corkscrews featuring a variety of heavenly bodies (and body parts).

Afterward, you can step into the *caveau de dégustation*. Here, tasting wines are available from owner/film maker Yves Rousset-Rouard's Domaine de la Citadelle wine estate. A darling museum boutique offers you a wonderful collection of corkscrews for purchase, as well as tasty wines and books on Provençal vintages. (The barman whispered to me that Peter Mayle has been a regular visitor over the years. I doubt he goes anywhere near the place now, however.)

As an interesting side note to this corkscrew museum experience, I must offer this marvelous tidbit. Many wine lovers know that finding a grassy Provençal hillside upon which to lay out a picnic blanket to enjoy "a bottle of wine, a loaf of bread, and thou" is a lovely way to spend a few hours here. (Apologies to Omar Khayyám.) But nothing can dampen your picnic faster than realizing you've forgotten your corkscrew. Mirabeau Wine is here to help, however. Vintner Stephen Cronk (mentioned in the wine section) has a clever video on You Tube that shows you how to open a bottle of wine with only your shoe. Yes, your shoe.

For the uninformed, it works like this: Remove the paper or foil capsule around the top of the bottle. Then take a man's shoe (high heels don't work, ladies) and place the base of the wine bottle in the shoe's heel. Steadying the wine bottle in the shoe with your left hand and the toe of the shoe in your right hand, start smacking the heel of the shoe against a wall or tree. The cork will begin to emerge gradually. After enough of the cork appears for you to grasp it with your fingers, stop banging and pull the cork the rest of the way out manually. Voila! Your wine will be open. www.youtube.com/watch?v=PMMdN4AFtqE

Lacoste

Lacoste is another quaint hill village in the Luberon which you can see from the terraces of Bonnieux. A scant 10 minutes away, you'll find yourself making the hike up the steep Lacoste streets paved in calade stone. As you climb, you'll glimpse the old hamlet with modern day Luberon stretching out beyond it. There are some handsome houses, an elegant 17th century bell tower, and the remnants of the 42-room castle where the infamous Marquis de Sade spent part of his life.

The Marquis de Sade, christened Donatien Alphonse François de Sade, was a randy lad with a penchant for rebellion. Aristocrat, libertine, philosopher, writer (novels, short stores, plays), and sex connoisseur, he fled Paris after several sexual exploits got him into trouble with the authorities.

Holed up in the family *château* at Lacoste, he used his wealthy wife's money and refurbished the 42-room castle. He added a private chapel and a private theater where he produced his own sexually-volatile theatrical productions. The Marquis eventually was imprisoned on a variety of charges that included poisoning a prostitute, doling out aphrodisiacs to underage girls, and worse.

Many of his works (which survive today) were written in prison or at the Charenton asylum. (The word sadism and sadist are derived from his name.) He was allowed to produce some of his plays in prison as part of a revolutionary new "drama therapy" approach that some consider. a precursor to Freudian principles. (Today, we would probably consider this gentleman an impenitent sex addict with violent tendencies; treatment would be very different.)

I first saw the actual Marquis de Sade's ruined haunt in the Luberon in the sparkling light of day. I was both amused and troubled to consider the desultory activities that reportedly occurred in this rather forlorn, crumbling castle. Psychologically speaking, the whole history of Provence is littered with tales of murder and mayhem— from Grecian times through to the unflinching Roman centuries, and on through to the invading hordes and Germans who pillaged and pulverized the region. The good news is that the Provençaux have capitalized on their scandalous past and reframed these sites as intoxicating tourist opportunities. (Americans and Brits are just as good at sweeping debaucheries under the underbrush, so to speak, so who are we to judge?)

What remains of the old *château* is now owned by designer Pierre Cardin. He uses it for fashion photo shoots and *soirées*. (Perhaps the ghost of the Marquis de Sade visits the hubbub occasionally.)

Gordes

Truth be told, I would rather gaze at Lacoste from across the valley in my favorite Provence hill town, Gordes. Gordes (shown) is the quintessential poster child for *Les Plus Beaux Villages de France* (most beautiful villages of France). Perched above the Imergue Valley facing the Luberon Mountains, Gordes is generally considered one of the top three attractions in the area.

Occupied since prehistoric times, Gordes' houses of white and gray stone rise up in a spiral around the main rock where the Renaissance *château* and church were built at the highest point with splendid views of the Luberon. The steps going up and down the steep streets are called *calades*; these staircases are lined with gutters made from double rows of stone. The *calades* substitute for streets in this perched town.

There are wonderful tall houses and rampart ruins; you'll also see statues dedicated to loved-ones lost in the wars. They're a poignant reminder of the brave struggles France has had over the centuries.

The Gordes castle was originally built in 1031, but sieges and wars took their toll. It had to be rebuilt in 1525. Today it serves as the Pol Mara museum featuring the work of the Flemish painter who lived in Gordes. During World War II, Gordes was very active in the resistance; it was awarded the Croix de Guerre 1939-1945. In August 1944, a few days after the Allied invasion of Southern France, the Gordes brigade attacked a German patrol. In response, the Germans ransacked the village and many fine structures were destroyed. But the little town has rebuilt and is now a tourism mecca.

The walls of the village were built in the 16th century to protect the inhabitants from marauders who poured into the valley during the Hundred Years' War. In early October, Gordes holds its *Fête Votive* (town celebration) to celebrate its resilient endurance which includes a *boules* tournament, concerts, and meals.

On the circular streets of the town's center are a number of restaurants, art galleries, and souvenir shops. Gordes also holds summer concerts and plays on the castle grounds. Tuesday is market day in Gordes; stalls are set up on Place du Château, and sellers offer their fruits, vegetables, and Provençal goods to shoppers who come in from all over the valley.

When I first visited Gordes 10 years ago, their street market was adorably quaint, clustered in the main square. Now it's a sprawling affair that extends across multiple streets and out across the terraces to accommodate the busloads of tourists who arrive in hordes. (Go early or go late. Just don't be there between 10 am-noon if you can help it.)

Cubist painter André Lhote, Marc Chagall, and Victor Vasarely are just some of the artists who lived in or worked here for a time.

Many parts of *A Good Year* were filmed using Gordes as a backdrop. The Hôtel la Renaissance serves as the *brasserie* where the lead female character works. At the center of Gordes is a beautiful fountain that Russell Crowe drives around and around in his teeny European car.

Tourist tip: Many tourist visitors flood the town after breakfast, but by 1 pm or so, the village is far less crowded. When visiting Gordes, few tourists go beyond the main streets, so there are some great photographic opportunities for the adventurous. If you have time, you may want to visit the nearby Village des Bories, a collection of ancient stone huts or *bories* grouped around a communal bread oven. These stone huts made with flat stones and without mortar served as homes or outbuildings between 200 and 500 years ago. Their original use remains a mystery, but they're a fine example of well-preserved, ancient French dwellings.

There are several hotels in and around Gordes that cater to a visit of a few days or more. My favorite is Le Bastide de Gordes, a hotel and spa. Le Bastide has fabulous views and excellent dining. I visit every time I'm in Gordes. There are less expensive venues in Gordes too, or you can try renting a *gîte* or a villa and they come in all sizes and prices. Check out www.vrbo.com and search Google for house rentals in France–Provence–Vaucluse.

Les-Baux-de-Provence

"...the key word for the Provençal soul remains *félibre*, by which Mistral proposed to designate the poets of Provence, true descendants of the troubadours who found their spiritual sources in the Courts of Love which presided over the emergent European spirit in Les-Baux."

—Lawrence Durrell,
Provence

Within the Alpilles and set atop a rocky outcrop with ravines on both sides, lies Les-Baux-de-Provence (pictured). This ancient enclave with its ruined castle, aged houses, and old bauxite quarries is a medieval masterpiece—but it's also a favorite tour destination that makes visiting it a bit tricky. Most guidebooks suggest seeing it in spring or fall since during summer it's fairly overrun with visitors—nearly a million a year.

Les-Baux has a colorful past. It gave its name to the whitish stone aluminum ore bauxite that was first discovered here in 1821. Today,the remains of Les-Baux seem a bit lonely and surreal, but in times gone by, Les-Baux's history was one of romantic intrigue and changing fortunes.

The Celts used the site as a hill fort as far back as the 2nd century B.C. Controlled by the barony of Les-Baux during the Middle Ages, it consisted of a loose configuration of castle and towns (more than 80) grouped together under the collective title of La Baussenique; sought control of Provence for years. "Warriors all—vassals never" as Mistral described them, the Baux family claimed to be descended from Magi King Balthazar who brought gifts to the baby Jesus.

Many coveted this rich estate. The lords of Baux warred against the House of Barcelona during the 11th century for rights to Provence. They were ultimately deposed and became a simple barony, but the castle at Les-Baux was renowned for its highly ornate court and creed of chivalry.

Les-Baux was finally joined to the French crown in the 1400s, but it later rebelled against Louis XI who had the fortress dismantled. It was rebuilt, but then dismantled again by Cardinal Richelieu in 1632; he tired of the fractious barony. (The inhabitants reportedly had to pay the crown for the demolition—a gargantuan sum in the day of 100,000 *livres*.)

But modern/ancient Les-Baux lives on as a tourist mecca, artist favorite, and home to a delicious AoC wine called Les-Baux de Provence. The area is hot and dry, with 3,000 hours of sunshine a year. Therefore, the surrounding vineyards on the hillsides of the Alpilles Mountains have to struggle in this Val d'Enfer (Valley of Hell) to produce the fine red wines. This is also where some of the finest olive oil in the world hails from.

Les-Baux is pretty accessible IF you arrive about 8 am and park down below the village in public parking. Then, you can walk up the incline to the town before all the crowds arrive. Beware the narrow streets if you're staying within the old city proper, however, or you'll experience what my friends Cris and Lynn did when they tried to drive up to their hotel, Le Prince Noir. They unfortunately got their vehicle stuck between two medieval buildings! Luckily, a local helped them get their car unstuck by somehow nudging it loose. (That in and of itself is a medieval mystery.)

Le Prince Noir is the only B&B in the historic part of Les-Baux. It has three unique rooms built into a rock face. There are other properties down the hill like Relais & Chateaux's La Cabro d'Or, Fabian des Baux, and Le Mas de l'Esparou. For dining in town, you can have your pick of small eateries or enjoy the culinary delights of La Reine Jeanne, Au Prote Mages, or Bella Vista, all with stellar views. If you want the ultimate in fine dining in the area, try staying or dining at Oustau de Baumanière, a fabulous multi-mansion resort with a gourmet restaurant.

Shopping is fabulous here. It runs the gamut along the steep streets that sit at the feet of the *château* ruins. Les-Baux looks a lot more like Carmel, California than medieval France to me. Every shop is fine tuned for maximum tourist appeal. You'll find several studio-art galleries, some art installations, and welcoming *épiceries*.

Les-Baux is also child-friendly. They've created a fun questionnaire for children aged 7-12 so they can explore the old fortifications along a mystery trail where the children look for hidden clues that reveal Les-Baux's history. (I often see school groups traipsing around the ruins or studying the trebuchet or getting archery lessons from "serfs" in costumes.) This is one of the reasons I enjoy Les-Baux over all the other medieval locales in Southern France. It's huge, beautifully laid out, has clear guideposts, and allows you to really feel what it must have been like to live atop this magnificent outcrop in the Middle Ages. (But you can still get a cell signal!)

But beware of occasional dangers in Les-Baux. If you try to climb the steep castle remains at the flagpole or up the craggy steps to the apex of the castle (children are not allowed up there), the intense winds may nearly blow you off the precipice, as they did my intrepid photographer.

Arles

Arles is described as one of the most picturesque cities in the whole of Provence. It was a particular favorite of the Romans. After General Marius built a canal that joined the Rhône to the Fos Gulf, it became the crossroads/sea/river port for journeys between Italy, Spain, and the rest of France. By 49 B.C. when Julius Caesar defeated Pompey and his favorite city, Marseilles, Caesar developed Arles into the capital of the Roman Provence.

Arles became the first large military colony to be planted outside the frontiers of Italy. Claudius Tiberius Nero was the official tapped by Caesar to distribute the spoils of Provence among 6,000 Roman officers and men. It was only a matter of time before a teeming "little Rome" on the edge of the Rhône became a thriving town. The industrious Romans built shipyards, a residential district, docklands, a forum, several temples, a basilica, roman baths, and a 20,000-seat amphitheatre that's still in use today. A massive aqueduct brought pure water from the Alpilles Mountains.

At that time, the Mediterranean extended nearly 30 miles inland. The new settlement numbered nearly 100,000 people and was built to rival Marseille. During the 5th century, Arles became an active industrial center where textiles, gold, and silver goods were manufactured. Wine, pork meat, olive oil, and other commodities were also exported in massive quantities. Later, when the Romans were gone and the grand structures fell into ruin due to multiple invasions by the Franks and Saracens, Arles became a major religious center in the Middle Ages. Pilgrims journeyed here in droves. Later, the Mediterranean receded into its current location, leaving Arles marooned amidst a sandy estuary. Arles was further marginalized once train travel overtook river travel as the preferred method of getting around Provence.

Today's much smaller Arles reveals both ancient and modern faces. While the huge Roman ruins like the amphitheatre in the heart of town anchors old Arles, newer modern buildings and fresh endeavors like Parc de Ateliers demonstrate Arles's ability to look to the future. The Parc de Ateliers is a major restoration being undertaken by U.S. architect Frank Gehry, opening in 2014/15; it's a vast cultural educational and exhibition complex.

The Arles of today is less a tourist destination than a working French town. Filled with great restaurants and museums as well as bustling local commerce, Arles is still a marvelous place to view French life in action with Roman ruins as a backdrop. The Roman Arena, built in the 1st century, is the town's centerpiece. After Roman times, it was used as a fortress and, still later, was transformed into a small town of 200 houses and two chapels. After being restored in 1825 (with three of the four watchtowers remaining), it has been actively used in modern day.

Today, the arena regularly hosts plays, concerts, Provençal bull-fights (*férias*), and *courses camarguaises* (bull chases). Arles's biggest actual bullfighting and horse riding event is the *Féria de Pàques* at Easter time. Bullfighters dress in the traditional costume of Goya's time. The town goes wild during this week—with brass bands and loud music playing in the bars and on the street. People dance and celebrate long into the night. Incidentally, *Ronin*, the 1998 spy thriller starring Robert de Niro, used the Arles amphitheater as a set for some of the deadliest scenes.

There are also mock gladiator fights that take place in the arena at various times throughout the year. Interestingly, the last time I was in Arles, I ran into a gaggle of Italian high school students who were visiting Arles and the arena presumably to learn about their Roman heritage. Like most teens, they were trolling the shops and giggling as they licked their ice cream cones and gossiped.

I happened to be in one of the shops along with them; I was browsing for souvenirs. The very nice French proprietress kept shooing the students out of the store so she could ring up my purchases. Finally, the group wandered into the arena, leaving us alone. She leaned in and said conspiratorially to me in fractured English, "These Italian teenagers make my ears break!"

Later, I wandered into the arena after lunch. There, I saw this same group of Italian students lined up with their teachers in the mid-dle of the arena (shown). They were doing gladiator drills with plastic weapons! The man in the middle was teaching one side to stab and the other side to shield themselves with plastic armor. Then, they'd switch sides. I can only imagine what kind of stories the students took home.

Italian Twitter must have been on fire!

Hotel lobbies situated near the arena feature glass floors to view the ruins below; many of their façades feature a Romanesque motif. In April and September, Arles and Nîmes compete with each other for the best *férias*. Other Arles ruins are the Theatre Antique, Constantine's Baths (the largest

remaining in Provence), and the necropolis of Les Alyscamps.

Arles has inspired a number of creatives besides Vincent van Gogh, including Frédéric Mistral and novelist Alphonse Daudet. Modern Arlésiens making their mark in the world include fashion designer Christian Lacroix and the mega-popular salsa band the Gipsy Kings who were born in Arles (and Montpellier). They perform in Spanish with an Andalusian accent. (Their music makes great listening on a treadmill: hard charging and upbeat.)

But Arles's most famous visitor is probably painter Vincent van Gogh. He was truly inspired by the Provençal light, country people, and pastoral scenes in Arles. You can see his life and work represented at Espace van Gogh and the Fondation Vincent van Gogh Arles. The Foundation is a bit modern for my taste. It displays not only van Gogh inspired pieces, but works by Francis Back, photographer Robert Doisneau, and Arles native Christian Lacroix.

Other sights around Arles that are worth a visit are the Museon Arlaten, founded by the legendary poet Frédéric Mistral. This noted museum details Arles life in the 19th century; it's hosted by attendants dressed in traditional Arles costumes. The bright blue triangular building on the edge of the Rhône is the Musée Départmental Arles Antiques which also has a stellar collection of ancient art.

If you find yourself in Arles on a Saturday, you may enjoy visiting the lush market on Boulevard des Lices with its wide array of fruits, vegetable, oils, leather goods, knives, and colorful crockery.

Restaurateurs, foodies, and even cowboys of the nearby Camargue stop in for coffee and a chat about the next bullfight.

When you dine in Arles, you'll get a sense for the meat-based cuisine which includes roasting animals whole. Some restaurants have bull's meat on the menu, and there are more tapas bars than *brasseries*. Arles is sometimes called France's most "Spanish" town. You'll find huge *paella* pans filled with clams, saffron rice, and vegetables like those you find in Barcelona. Party lovers will also be able to enjoy flamenco and Cuban-style bars along the back streets that are filled with rumba, pop, and salsa sounds.

On a culinary note, Arles is known as the sausage capital of Provence. Sausage making is serious business in Arles. A special *Saucisson d'Arles* recipe was concocted in 1655 and has been handed down from generation to generation. It's still the gold standard by which sausage is made. It contains pork, beef, pepper, cloves, nutmeg, ginger, and red wine. One of the claims to fame for this Provençal sausage is that it's 100% meat—there are no bread fillers. My stay in Arles at the Hôtel de l'Amphitheater was practically next door to the amphitheater—and it provided some of these delicious sausages in their bright and sunny breakfast room.

There are many spots to grab a meal in Arles ranging from fast-food places to culinary sophisticates. Querida is a noted wine bar near the Arena. L'Atelier de Jean-Luc Rabanel is probably the best restaurant in town; it specializes in organically-based meals created with gourmet flavors. Many visitors like to lunch at the Café Terrace on the Place du Forum where van Gogh painted *Café Terrace at Night*.

Overall, Arles is a fairly central location from which to see the Camargue wetlands as well as Nîmes and other areas in the Languedoc. From Arles, you're also close to Les-Baux and Saint-Rémy-de-Provence for day trips.

The Camargue

The wild and wonderful Camargue, south of Arles, is Western Europe's largest river delta. The Camargue is a triangular area on the coast between the Languedoc-Roussillon region and Provence. It's basically a 360-square-mile river delta where the Rhône spills out onto a vast alluvial plain before it trickles into the Mediterranean.

The Camargue has large brine lagoons, cut off from the sea proper by sandbars, which are surrounded by reed-covered marshes. These lagoons teem with Camargue life. Included are 400 species of birds (plus pink flamingos), ferocious mosquitoes, wild white Camargue horses descended from prehistoric animals, and lithe little bulls—many of them no taller than 4.5 feet. There are also sheep and cattle and various kinds of fish. It has been officially deemed a botanical and zoological nature reserve.

If you travel to the Camargue, you can ride the white horses of the Rhône Delta or watch the Camargue cowboys (*gardians*) round up the famous bulls. You can enjoy a pleasant afternoon by taking a boat ride down the Rhône to see the unique Camargue ecosystem. This is a great way to glimpse the intricate network of marshes, streams, flora, fauna, and wildlife.

The Camargue produces a very interesting product that's shipped round the world: salt. *Sel de Camargue* is a superior type of salt that comes from the delta where it spills out into the Camargue. Today, more than 400,000 tons of salt is harvested there. And this is no plain crystalized salt tossed into paper bags.

This fine salt is sifted and packaged according to grain size and flavoring from *sel fin* (a fine-grained salt) all the way up to *fleur de sel* (course salt). The highest grade, *fleur de sel,* is gathered manually by a *saunier*. Often you can buy *fleur de sel* in cork-topped pots, and the seal will show the signed name of the *saunier* who harvested it. (Talk about the personal touch!)

The Camargue bull, a smallish creature known more for doggedness than prowess, lies at the heart of the bullfighting or bull running culture in Southern France. *Courses camarguaises* is the sport of men called *raseteurs* chasing a bull around an arena in an attempt to remove a rosette from between the beast's horns. The bull is not killed in this sport, unlike in Spain. Often, some of the same bulls take part in the games year after year. Some of these scrappy little creatures even get statues erected for them in their hometowns! The major bull-chasing event takes place in Arles on the first Monday in July. There are also *abrivados* where bulls are let loose on the streets, similar to Pamplona.

You can sojourn in the Camargue at hotels like Le Mas de Peint, a hotel and gastronomy center. My friends Cris and Lynn had a wonderful stay here on this ranch-cum-hotel with gourmet meals, swimming pool, and pleasing rooms. This hotel is perfect for various Camargue celebrations and learning how the Camargue cowboys tame the land and the beasts.

Aix-en-Provence

Aix-en-Provence is one the world's great art capitals. But it has a pleasing ambience due to its distinctive old town, university vibe, tree-lined streets, honey-colored buildings, and vibrant history. It's famed for its colorful characters, age-old culture, and above all for artistic master Paul Cézanne who was born here.

The Romans built much of the town around a thermal springs which still exists today. Aix has had several golden ages, particularly the 17th and 18th centuries when wealthy lawyers and business people built magnificent mansions and wide streets anchored by sparkling fountains and squares. Around old Aix, a new, bustling town has arisen that is a spa, an artistic center, and an industrial complex. Today, there's also a youthful enthusiasm to the area, much like the Left Bank in Paris. Here in university-driven Aix, the young are fueling the new Southern France.

The Cours Mirabeau is Aix's very appealing grand boulevard. Wide and welcoming, it's lined with shops, businesses, bookstores, and pavement *cafés*. It teems with Provençal life. As you meander along, you may see young artists displaying their crafts on the sidewalk or a violinist playing on a street corner. Aix is a walker's paradise. Winding byways off the broad boulevards lead to tempting shops, art installations, and statuary.

When visiting, you'll want to view the Cathedral of St. Sauveur, the Cézanne Museum, and La Rotunde, the spectacular fountain on the Cours Mirabeau. Along the boulevard, there are some wonderful façades of old hotels with finely crafted doors and intricate wrought iron balconies. Among them are the Hôtel Maurel de Pontevès (now the annex of the court of appeals), the Hôtel de Forbin, and Hôtel d'Isoard de Vauvenargues where the president of parliament murdered his wife, Angélique, because he wanted to be with his mistress.

While wandering along the Cours Mirabeau, I slipped into Les Deux Garcons at number 53 one late morning. Les Deux Garcons, known colloquially as the 2Gs, is a brasserie with an ornate First Empire interior and piano bar. It looks a little like the famous Les Deux Magots in Paris. Jean François de Gantès, a local dignitary, built the building in 1660. It became a chess club for gentlemen which turned into a focal point for Royalists during the French Revolution. Named after the two waiters who purchased it in 1840 and gave it its name, it became the watering hole for the *beau monde* (high society) of Aix.

Today, 2Gs serves up scrumptious Southern France fare: great wines (local and further afield); starters like homemade duck *foie gras*, smoked salmon, and *tarte Provençal*; main courses of shellfish platters, grilled sirloin, or *steak tartare*; and yummy desserts and memorable coffees.

But you don't go there for the food. You go to soak up the creative ambience that fueled the regulars. Regulars like Paul Cézanne and his school friend, Emile Zola. The pair would drop in to enjoy a three-hour *apéritif* between 4 and 7 pm. Years later, Pablo Picasso often wandered in. Jean Paul Sartre, Edith Piaf, Alain Delon, and Jean-Paul Belmondo stopped in for a drink, as did Jean Cocteau. Even more recently Jean Reno, Hugh Grant, and George Clooney have enjoyed a beverage or two here. If you visit and get too tipsy, there are rooms upstairs in the boutique Hôtel de Gantés.

June/July is a fabulous time to visit Aix when the music and opera festivals take place. The Festival d'Aix-en-Provence features performances of operatic masterpieces and classical music concerts;

prizes are given for various individual performances and direction, and new pieces are previewed at the festival The 2014 festival featured performances of Mozart's *The Magic Flute*, Handel's *Ariodante*, Schubert's *Winterreise*, and a staging of Bach's cantatas, for example. More than 20 composers presented their work, and 250+ young artists from many continents took part in workshops and productions designed to educate and offer them performance opportunities. Many of these took place in the Grand Théâtre de Provence, a magnificent curving theater.

You'll also find numerous street markets in Aix. They're split between four beautiful squares in two locations. First is the Place des Prèchurs food market brimming with local produce. In the Place de Verdun opposite, shoppers can acquire panama hats and Moroccan slippers, among other exotic goods.

Down in the town center, you'll find Place Richelme where a frenetic daily market offers local foods, wine, and wares. A stroll towards the cathedral to the beautiful Place de la Mairie set against honey-colored buildings will lead you to a beautiful flower market.

Aix is particularly known for its *calissons*. The *calisson* is a marzipan-like cookie confection in the shape of an almond made from sweet almonds and fruit preserves with "royal icing" on top. Aix's industrial area has numerous almond processing and *calissons* manufacturers; the delectable treat is a gourmet specialty that sells year round. *Calissons* are the symbol of the city. You can see the deliciously arrayed treats on serving dishes or in eye-catching boxes in bakeries and shops.

Aix is a great base from which to discover some of the sites Cézanne painted, as well as nearby locales like Montagne Sainte-Victoire, les Alpilles (little Alps), Arles, and Les-Baux. Before you leave the Aix area, you may want to stop into Château de Vauvenargues where Pablo Picasso and his wife Jacqueline are buried in a mound on the grounds of the estate they bought in 1958; it's topped with Picasso's 1933 sculpture, *Femme au vase*. The *château* sits on the slopes of Montagne Sainte-Victoire which Paul Cézanne painted dozens of times. "I have just bought myself Cézanne's mountains," Picasso told his real estate agent.

Provence in Sum

"There is something about Provence that I can't quite understand. It has a way of enveloping you...it makes you feel as if you are living life in slow motion...Provence has a magic, a special power, an unknown quantity that seeps into every part of my being and seduces in the best possible way."

–Vicki Archer, *French Essence*

Seductive is an apt term for Provence. Provence beguiles with its painted sunsets, lavender valleys, unconventional people, garlicky flavors, and bountiful zest for living.

The days are long and languid here. For this golden land—and lively people—has survived the charge of warring factions, the unyielding *mistral*, and the sweep of time. Like the *mistral*-bent trees of Provence, the versatile Provençaux have a way of letting the destructions of time simply slip around them. Here, the resilient traditions, homegrown cuisine, and time-honored ways resist the machinations of the mighty.

But the lively Provençaux open their doors to those who want to enjoy their lifestyle, but not dominate it. To partake, but with appreciation. And above all, to respect their Provençal harmony where beauty is in the air, atop your table, and in your psyche when you embrace the sounds, surroundings, and succulence of Provence.

Part Three: Languedoc

"So desirable is this hot rocky corner of southwest France, bordered by long beaches and the Spanish Pyrénées, that it's been called the new Provence."

—l.escape.com

Commanding Carcassonne, with its great walls and stately turrets rising like the Vatican amidst a sea of vines, greets you as you travel the route between the Mediterranean and Toulouse. Carcassonne, shown above, is the symbol of the mighty Languedoc. In stone and steel, it echoes the fortunes of this formidable region. This is a land—and a fortress—with parallel stories of turbulent conflict and majestic renewal.

When I first saw Carcassonne, I immediately thought of the Vatican in Rome. Each bastion dominates its terrain and those who live there. Eerily, these two seats of religious power clashed with each other in the Languedoc in an epic battle for the souls—and lands—of the Languedoc people in the 12th and 13th centuries.

Then and now, a pugnacious zeal characterizes the Languedoc. *"La Provence chante, le Languedoc combat,"* ("Provence sings, Languedoc fights") Frédéric Mistral famously said. But what a fight it's been! This land has been coveted, fought over for centuries. But even today, it remains untamed, boldly beautiful.

The Languedoc is a land of contradictions, known as much for its cave-living prehistoric inhabitants as its jetting sophisticates. Nowhere in Southern France is there as much diversity. Majestic coastlines. Wild-life preserves. Roman ruins. Dreamy villages. Space-age cities. Cave dwellings. Verdant vineyards. And the world's tallest modern bridge at Millau.

Its sister area of the Midi-Toulousain mirrors this unpredictable charm. It too is a land of contrasts where high-tech Toulouse dominates the European Airline industry, but medieval Cordes-sur-Ciel sits atop a hill nearby, suspended in clouds like some Medieval kingdom in the sky. For purposes of this section, therefore, we're exploring these paired territories of the Languedoc (10,000 square miles) and the Midi-Toulousain (17,000 square miles) under the general section heading "Languedoc."

The Languedoc/Midi-Toulousain is the largest region explored in this book. It's a fascinating terrain that stretches from the Mediterranean Sea and Provence to the east (west of Marseille) across to the Midi-Pyrénées in the west, then south from the border of Spain and Andorra to the edge of the Dordogne to the north. It's nearly impossible to see all of this region in a few days or weeks, since it's a land of great distances and diversity.

At the balmy Mediterranean coast, you'll find Riviera-like beach resorts without the high price tag and crowds. Above them near Avignon, you can walk the magnificent Roman Pont Du Gard and wander the massive Roman amphitheater in Nîmes. In the southwest you'll find Cathar country, where majestic Carcassonne dominates, a last stronghold of a stubborn people who challenged the power of the Pope. Across the land stretch huge tracts of vineyards that produce more wine than anywhere else in France.

Further south are the towering Pyrénées shared with Andorra and Spain. North of Carcassonne is cosmopolitan Toulouse of aeronautics fame and Albi where Toulouse-Lautrec is remembered. Still further northeast are winsome hill towns like Najac where chemtrails reach down to touch the town spires. And northwest are the magnificent Tarn gorges and Millau Viaduct, a masterpiece of bridge ingenuity.

The Languedoc is a fascinating area to explore. It benefits from a Mediterranean climate and a plethora of offerings. Mountains lapped by cool lakes. Beaches bordering warm seas. History-rich fortresses and bull fighting arenas. Dolmens and megaliths plus dinosaur bones and eggs. Relaxing thermal springs and hikers heaven national parks. It has appetizing cuisine, delicious wine, and engaging people. This simply is a grand place to visit, set down roots, or retire.

The Languedoc is a popular, yet in some ways, undiscovered area. It's a territory loved for second homes and delightful holiday-making sans the crowds of Provence or the Dordogne. As I meander around, I've some-times driven through the coun-tryside along a river and not seen another car for 20 minutes. It's simply an enchanting place to nestle into the soothing environment and enjoy a long swallow of Languedoc wine.

Since the area borders Spain, there's a startling blend of French and Spanish cultures. You'll see *paella* served alongside *foie gras*. Toreador t-shirts are sold beside *berets* and *baguettes* in the shops. And you might very well see a bullfight in the afternoon in Nîmes, then enjoy a French fête that night.

This Languedoc is wild, proud, futuristic, ephemeral, and ancient all at once. In some ways it makes my head spin to spend time here; at other times it feels raw and titillating, alluring yet aloof. Above all, it's an infinitely fascinating locale. And until the word gets out, it remains one of the hidden gems of France.

History & Landscape

The Languedoc area, indeed all of Southwest France, has been home to man since prehistoric times. Cave dwellings, bone fragments, crude implements, and rock paintings point to Homo erectus, Neanderthal man, and Homo Sapiens all being present here. The Neolithic age (9,500-3,500 years ago) is seen in polished stone tools and earthenware found here. In the Aveyron *département*, where the Millau Bridge spans the valley of the Tarn River, dolmens (slab tombs), probably built sometime between 2500-1500 B.C. dot the land.

Since the area sat in strategic position on the Via Domitia Roman trade route between Spain and Italy, the Languedoc was conquered and settled by Rome around 121 B.C. This was long before the rest of Gaul was established between 51-58 B.C. Narbonne, on the Mediterranean, was the first Roman colony built outside Italy in 118 B.C. Roman remains are prevalent in Nîmes at the amphitheater (still used today and pictured above). And of course the Pont du Gard aqueduct is a huge testament to Roman might.

Gaul fell to invading barbarians in the 4th century until Charlemagne ("the father of Europe") came to power and united most of Europe for the first time since the Roman Empire. Upon his death, the Treaty of Verdun divided Charlemagne's lands; Charles the Bold took over the area between the Rhône (Provence) and the Atlantic (Bordeaux). Upon his death in 877, the princely houses (Toulouse, Auvergne, Barcelona) that would come to rule Southwest France for several centuries split the spoils. Historically, this region was mostly referred to as the "county of Toulouse" since Toulouse acted as the seat of power. For a long time, this Languedoc territory remained independent from the Kings of France who ruled in the north.

Eleanor of Aquitaine controlled vast portions of this area during the 12th century. Upon her marriage to Henry II, who later became King of England, English interlopers stirred up trouble in the region. During 1140-1200, the Cathar religion spread in response to the excesses of the Catholic Church. The conflict between Catholicism and the Cathars produced a dark period in Languedoc history. And it became profoundly linked with the evolution of France as a country, since the warring sects became linked with the political machinations of land grabbing factions.

Catharism grew out of a deep dissatisfaction with Catholicism. The Cathars believed Catholic practices had become decadently corrupt. Catharism had roots in the Paulican movement in Armenia and Bulgaria. But it soon spread through Northern Italy and Southern France, particularly the Languedoc. The Cathars sought to free man from the material world (and the use of Catholic indulgences), while restoring him to divine purity. Four key bishops from Albi, Toulouse, Carcassonne, and Agen helmed this breakaway "Albigensian" church in Southern France.

Affronted, Pope Innocent III attempted to stamp out Catharism from his seat in Rome by first sending missionaries to the Cathar areas. His emissaries were tasked with convincing local authorities to act against this "evil" sect. The Pope sent special envoy Pierre de Castelnau to the Rhône Valley and Provence. Here, Castelnau became involved in the local conflicts between the counts of Baux (Les-Baux-de-Provence) and Raymond IV, the count of Toulouse. When Castelnau was returning to Rome after excommunicating Raymond—who refused to capitulate—Castelnau was assassinated. It was presumed that Raymond's henchmen did the deed.

Castelnau's murder was the start of the infamous Albigensian Crusade. In this bloody conflict, knights from the north fought knights of the south for land and holy dominance. This "crusade zeal" was partially inspired by a papal decree permitting confiscation of

Cathar-friendly lands by all comers.

Noblemen swooped in from Paris, Normandy, Flanders, Champagne, and Burgundy, then teamed with others from the Rhineland, Bavaria, and Austria under the command of Abbot Arnaud-Amaury of Cîteaux. Later, zealot Simon de Montfort helmed the crusade to systematically wipe out the religion—and confiscate the land. This Holy War lasted more than 20 bloody years. It led to the massacre of thousands of people in particularly vicious ways—plus the fall of Cathar Carcassonne and many other strongholds around Toulouse.

But Catharism was not extinguished. Soon a second Albigensian Crusade was launched, this time led by King of France Louis VIII. Thus the "Holy War" evolved into a classic power struggle. Catharism eventually went underground (and still exists in some forms today). But the power of the local lords of Toulouse and others withered. Within a century, the Languedoc became part of the French royal estate in 1229; this partially lead in due time to the unification of France as the country we know today.

This is a good moment to mention the Languedoc language in detail. The fusion of Vulgar Latin with the old Gallic tongue led to new "Romance Languages" during medieval times. In Northern France, this became *Langue d'oïl*. In Southern France it became *Langue d'oc*. Among other aspects, the two dialects were distinguished by the way the word "*oui*" was pronounced.

This "Language of Oc" was the language of Southern France troubadours and poets who used it to devise songs and poems for entertaining the nobility. Eleanor of Aquitaine was among its many admirers. The term *Occitan* eventually replaced the term; today *Occitan* refers to the dialects spoken not only in Languedoc, but Gascony, Limousin, Auvergne, and Provence.

During the Albigensian crusades, use of the dialect was discouraged. In 1539 when Parisian French became the national language, the dialect fell into disuse except for locals who clung to their mother tongue in secret. With the rise of reforms introduced by Frédéric Mistral and the Félibrige movement to restore the traditions of the *Occitan* people in 1854, the language and cultural associations of *Occitan* became popular once again. By the 1950s, *Occitan* was again being taught in schools.

Today, the Félibrige is enthusiastically celebrated in local villages around Southern France, particularly in March (Mistral's birth month). *Occitan* is also spoken in parts of Italy, Monaco, and Spain where *Catalan* is a cousin of *Occitan*. Note this dual *French/Occitan* sign.

By the 1300s, the Hundred Years' War was underway, with the area split between ever-changing French and English alliances. Fortified towns or *bastides* were built. Fortresses rose. In the middle of the century, the Black Death (plague) killed about one third of the population. Between the 1400s to the mid-1700s, various conflicts rent the region. But religious pilgrims still made their way through the Languedoc on the Way of St. James.

In 1746, Théophile de Bordeau's thesis on the efficacy of mineral springs helped promote the creation of mineral spa resorts throughout the Languedoc where mineral springs bubbled throughout the mountainous land. People rushed in "to take the water cure." This is one of the reasons spas and thalassotherapies are still popular in France to this day.

The French Revolution brought some newfound freedoms to the Languedoc; sadly, many of the old structures and fortresses were left to decay however. In 1858, the Virgin Mary miraculously appeared 18 times to a young girl named Bernadette Soubirous. Visiting a small grotto in the tiny town of Lourdes, Bernadette was astounded when the Virgin Mary came to her and waters began to flow where none had been before.

Soon, the grotto waters were deemed sacred. Hordes of pilgrims came to bathe in the holy waters. To this day, people travel to Lourdes to bathe in the healing waters; the tiny town has had to grow up to meet the demand. Large and small hotels now accommodate thousands of visitors a year. (Personal note: I have not visited Lourdes. But my good friend and mentor discovered she had lung cancer about 15 years ago. She was expected to expire within a year or two. A year after her diagnosis, a good Samaritan paid for her to go to Lourdes. My friend bathed in the healing waters for several days. I can't say definitively if this was the cause of her cure, but my friend made a full recovery. She's still remarkably active today well into her 70s.)

Languedoc wines became popular from the 1800s onward. During the Spanish Civil War, many refuges from Spain poured into the territory (perhaps accounting for its mixed French-Spanish heritage). During the world wars, many citizens served from the Languedoc, and the mountainous areas became vital for the French Resistance. (If you're interested in an authentic account of life in occupied France, see the French television series, *Un Village Français*. This show about a fictional French village under German occupation is so realistically mesmerizing, I've watched it repeatedly. It's usually broadcast with English subtitles, but even just watching it in French with limited understanding, is spellbinding.)

The aeronautic Concorde English/French initiative was launched in Toulouse. In 1969, the maiden flight of the Concorde took place over the skies of Toulouse. Toulouse soon became the center for the European aerospace industry; it's now where Airbus is based. (I prefer to fly Airbus whenever I can on Air France.)

Within subsequent decades, three massive regional parks were designated, and new motorways and an underground railway metro in Toulouse were built. The spectacular Millau Bridge was constructed over the Tarn River. And the Canal du Midi, which couples with the Canal de Garonne (Bordeaux) to link the Atlantic Ocean and the Mediterranean, became a UNESCO World Heritage site in 1996.

In recent years, the famous architectural treasures of Carcassonne, Albi, Nîmes, Toulouse, Narbonne, and Cordes-sur-Ciel have been refurbished. Among the most remarkable renovations are the fortress at Cité de Carcassonne, which now has beautifully restored towers; Albi, with its pristine downtown and sublime Saint-Cécile Cathedral (one of the most beautiful I've ever seen); the stunning Pont Du Gard, which is now a startling travel destination; and the Nîmes amphitheater which has morphed into a sporting complex and *ferias* (bull fighting) ring.

People & Lifestyle

This vast Languedoc is home to more than five million people. And it's also the fastest growing area in France. As the road network has improved over the decades, workers are increasingly living in the countryside and making commutes into the large cities. Second-home buyers are pouring in to snap up properties for holiday stays.

Similar to Bordeaux in the west, the Languedoc area has become a hotbed for high tech and service industries. Local farming and wine growing is done on a grand scale, but the individual estates are kept relatively small. Tourism is also a huge draw. It's the fourth most visited area of France after Paris, Provence, and the Alps. Many expats come to run hotels or tourism attractions.

The locals have a variety of professions. Aeronautics and the space industry are key, with some 80,000 residents employed in the aviation industry. Electronics firms like Motorola, as well as biotech, chemical, and computing (IBM) industries have presences in Toulouse and Montpellier. Castre has a large pharmaceutical group, Pierre Fabre.

Agriculture and food processing are important businesses. The vineyards of the region are now competition for Bordeaux; and of course Armagnac production is legion. Shepherds still shift their livestock in seasonal movements around the region, however. Small farms proliferate, as they're considered an asset since they guarantee high-quality products for consumers.

Other Languedoc natives are experts in local products like the fun "Candy Lady" who posed prettily for me (shown) in her delightful Albi candy shop. Naturally, I walked out of there with about two pounds of French goodies that I munched while driving through the picturesque Languedoc. Sometimes you'll run into friendly Cathars more than willing to cuddle up for a photo.

Craftsmen abound from the Laguiole *couteliers* who forge the famous knives with the bee symbol to the artisans of Martres-Tolosane who decorate earthenware as beautifully as their ancestors 200 years ago. And in every fortified town are wonderful products made only by locals: glazed pottery, rope-soled shoes, Pyrénées woolen blankets and pullovers, hand-made scarves and hats, lace products, hand-loomed tapestries, and fantastic art and sculpture. The village of Revel, situated between Toulouse and Carcassonne, is famed for fine furniture and cabinetry. Wool making and related crafts are based in Mazamet, and Durfort specializes in beaten copper and brass pots, cauldrons, and artwork.

Tourism has exploded as well. Of particular note are the huge seaside resorts at Cap d'Agde (where nudity is popular), Palavas-Les-Flots, and Le Grau-du-Roi on the French Mediterranean. Ernest Hemingway set the first part of *The Garden of Eden* in Le Grau-du-Roi where he spent the first day of his honeymoon with second wife Pauline Pfeiffer.

You'll never be bored in the Languedoc. Year-round activities abound, especially since this roughly 27,000 square miles offers so much varied terrain. In late winter and early spring, snow abounds for cross-country skiing or snowshoe hikes on the Aubrac Plateau. There's also Alpine skiing and snowboarding in the Pyrénées. In spring, biking and riding tours, as well as fishing and hawking are favorites. In the hot, relatively dry summer, there's golf and rock climbing, and in autumn a drive through the countryside or ride on a kayak down the Tarn is sublime.

Fearless flyers may like the hang-gliding and paragliding since the Pyrénées offer high-incline venues. The Tour de France sometimes runs through this region of spectacular, but challenging roads. And mountain biking and cycling is popular everywhere, especially in town.

In the Languedoc, you're in hiker's heaven. The national parks offer fantastic venues for walking or hiking. Windsurfing is also popular on the beautiful lakes, while canyoning and body surfing down the narrow gorges is trendy. Hydro speed is another novel sport where swimmers shoot rapids with a kickboard and flippers. (Wear a helmet!)

Other great family excursions include horseback riding or cave exploration in Padirac and the Ariège. The Cité de l'Espace is the wildly popular space exploration experience in Toulouse. Local festivals range from bull running to the Fécos (Carnival) in Limoux, and from sea jousting in the north to La Jour de St-Jean (Summer Solstice in June) in the south where you can try your hand (or feet) at lighting bonfires and fire jumping.

At the coast in summer, Sète hosts crazy water jousting tournaments in its Grand Canal. Two opposing teams perch on gondola-style boats with extended ladders. Then they try to push each other into the water using jousting rods. Noisy. Fun. AND wet.

For serene sailing, a cruise along the Canal du Midi is a delightful drift through the countryside. Noted jazz festivals are held throughout the warm months, particularly in Nîmes and Montpellier.

Rugby is VERY big here, unlike other areas of France were football (soccer) is more popular. Nearly every town and village has a rugby team; passions run high during game season. The Toulouse rugby club (Stade Toulousain) is one of most successful in Europe; it regularly competes for the French championship and has won four European titles in the 10 years of the European championship's existence.

Enjoying art and culture is a necessary part of a French person's life. Children are taught early on to value the beauty around them. I love seeing how much parents and teachers spend time escorting their children to cultural exhibitions. In Carcassonne, I toured the Torture Museum with a group of enthusiastic schoolboys for example. They were deep in a huddle next to a "torture rack" as I passed by. (I wondered if they were pondering ways to torture their teachers.)

Ultimately, this is a rural yet sophisticated part of France, with busy, interesting people who make the most of their vast territory with its historical past and space-age future.

Food, Wine, & Shopping

Food

"As in the Dordogne, this area has a rich gastronomic tradition that includes not only foie gras and confit, but honey from the Cévennes, nougat from Limoux, cured hams and charcuterie from the mountains...But it is not until you get to Castelnaudary—of the *cassoulets*—that cooking with goose-fat begins, and foie gras and truffles and the real haute cuisine of the Toulousain district and the real, high wines of the Bordelais. There too I remember eating..."

—Ford Madox Ford

Ford is talking about the Languedoc's signature dish, *cassoulet*. The town of Castelnaudary became famous for concocting the *cassoulet*, a thick, slow-cooked stew of meat, sausages, (often) duck *confit*, and white beans. The dish is named after its traditional cooking vessel, the *cassole*, a deep, round, earthenware pot with slanting sides. (All French cookware companies offer a *cassoulet* dish. I have one each from Le Creuset and Staub. Staub is easier to clean.)

The birth of *cassoulet* as a regional specialty dates back to the 14th century siege of Castelnaudary during the Hundred Years' War. With the city surrounded, starving citizen soldiers gathered their remaining provisions to create a communal dish hearty enough to power their counterattack. The battle was in fact lost, but *cassoulet* went on to become a key element of the area's *Occitan* identity.

Pictured is a *cassoulet* made for me at La Tartine, a bistro across from Albi's Lautrec Museum. You can see it's often served with *pomme frites*. (When in France, ignore the calories.) At home, I make this dish often; in fact, there was one sitting in my refrigerator as I wrote this passage.

I love shopping for other local foods at the local Languedoc street markets, then scooping up everything and taking it to a park, meadow, stone bridge, or balcony to have an impromptu feast. A rich

variety of foods abound in this area. The Mediterranean coastline along the Languedoc is particularly known for its fresh fish, shrimp, and lobsters, while the Étangs de Thau is famous for oysters and mussels. Collioure produces wonderful anchovies. Livestock (cattle, goats) are bred all across the Causses Mountains and plateau in the north. Local cuisine is based on dishes made from the animals or their byproducts. These include lamb, tripe, local cheeses like *Bleu des Causses* (blue cheese made from cow's milk) and *Pélardon* (traditional cheese made from goat's milk), and *Trénels de Millau* (sheep's tripe stuffed with ham, garlic, parsley, and egg).

Chestnuts are traditionally used to flavor soups and stews. And for those with dessert cravings, try some marvelous *soleils* (round yellow cookies flavored with almonds and orange blossom), *fouaces* (angelica-flavored brioche), *croquants* (hard almond cookies), or *nènes* (small aniseed biscuits).

At the Mediterranean coastline, the cuisine liberally uses spices, garlic, and olive oil, as well as fresh *aubergines*, tomatoes, *courgettes,* and peppers. *Aigo boulido* is a local garlic soup made with garlic, olive oil, and thyme. Some dishes add snails, wild mushrooms, and truffles. Seafood dishes are plentiful: *Bourride Sétoise* (fish stew), *Gigot de mer de Palavas* (fish baked with garlic and vegetables), and seafood pasties (small seafood pies). Other specialties include *Aubergines aux Cèpes* (eggplant cooked with mushrooms) and *Courgette Farci* (stuffed zucchini). Everywhere *foie gras* is served year round.

In Montpellier, most fish dishes are accompanied by *beurre de Montpellier*, a sauce of mixed herbs, watercress, spinach, anchovies, yolks of hardboiled eggs, butter, and spices. The cooking in Roussillon, the Catalan corner of the area near Spain, has a Catalan version of fish soup called *Bouillinade*, as well as spiny lobster stewed in wine, *escalade* (fragrant soup made with thyme, garlic oil, and egg), black pudding, pig's liver sausage, *Cargolade* (snails cooked over burning vine cuttings), *Fougasse au Pignons* (flat bread with pine nuts), and *Calamars Farcis* (stuffed calamari).

You'll see *paella*, often served with *foie gras* as an appetizer! Sweets are Catalan versions of *crème brûlée (crèma catalane)*, orange-flavored doughnuts (*bunyettes*), and small almond biscuits (*rousquilles*).

Wine

The wine-growing areas of the Languedoc produce more wine than anywhere else in the world. That's about two billion bottles a year. The Languedoc is responsible for more than a third of France's total wine production. It's a significant contributor to the "wine lake" (some call it a "glut") in Europe. Interesting fact: as of 2001, the Languedoc was producing more wine than the entire U.S.

Its soils are varied with pebble terraces, red clay, and layers of schist (metamorphic rock). The Greeks first planted vines near Narbonne in the 5th century. Phylloxera, the insect pests of commercial grapevines worldwide, sadly wiped out the high-end Languedoc vines in the 19th century. Replacement rootstock from America and elsewhere didn't take, so lesser quality Aramon, Alicante, Bouschet, and the Carignan grapes were planted—and thrived.

Today, the Languedoc-Roussillon area is home to numerous grape varieties, including Merlot, Cabernet Sauvignon, Sauvignon Blanc, Chardonnay, Mourvèdre, Grenache, Syrah, and Viognier. Chardonnay is a major white grape used in the famous sparkling wine, Crémant de Limoux.

The Languedoc is the main producer of French table wine (*vins de table and vins de pays*). Today, however, wine producers are upping their game, so to speak, to produce blended wines in a league with Bordeaux.

As a result, a number of AoC designations have been awarded such as the Coteaux du Languedoc, the Languedoc AoC appellation in the Hérault, Gard, and Aveyron *départements*. Particular vintages have also been awarded AoC designations such as Corbières, Faugères, and Saint-Chinian.

The world's oldest bubbly wine, Blanquette de Limoux, was invented in the 16th century in the city of Limoux. Wine historians believe the world's first sparkling wine was produced in this region in 1531 by monks at the abbey in Saint-Hilaire. This was a century before the Champagne region in Northern France became famous for a sparkling wine called Champagne. Local lore says that Dom Pérignon learned how to produce sparkling wine while serving in this Abbey. Later,
he reportedly moved to the Champagne region where he made and widely distributed a similar product that paved the way for Champagne. Today, Champagne clearly eclipses the sale of lowly Blanquette de Limoux. But it's still deliciously intoxicating.

Blanquette actually means "white" in the *Occitan* language—hence its name. Blanquette de Limoux can contain three grape varieties: Mauzac (90%) with Chardonnay and Chenin Blanc (10%). The new designation, Crémant de Limoux, created in 1994, is still sold under the AoC designation, but with the same basic methods, although the exact percentages of Chardonnay and Chenin Blanc vary.

Shopping

Few major shopping malls can be found in this region, except in the larger cities of Montpellier and Toulouse. But appealing shops are everywhere in the little villages and hill towns. And on market days, locals come into town to display their wares, and you can shop straight off the wagon, so to speak.

The narrow streets of Narbonne, Perpignan, and Carcassonne

are bursting with everyday shops that, in some cases, almost market too much to the tourist trade. Search out some of the wonderful wares to buy, but beware of the wide array of touristy loot like plastic broadswords, cheap armor, and "I was here" t-shirts. Shoppers CAN find some beautiful pieces though if you're discriminating. In Cordes-sur-Ciel, some delightful storefronts are selling French baskets, cheeses, wine, and bread so you can put together a picnic for example.

Finally, if your camera, phone, or video recorder breaks as my camera did in Nîmes, hurry over to Darty—the French version of Best Buy. They'll fix you up with anything electronic you could ever need. And they speak English!

Culture & Art

Culture and art abound in this vast region, although it's perhaps more rurally focused than in other areas of France. The original artists were perhaps the cave dwellers who left dozens of cave paintings in the underground grottos of the Languedoc.

One of the area's most noted artists is Henri de Toulouse-Lautrec. Lautrec was born in Albi in 1864. He was the first child of Comte Alphonse and Comtesse Adèle de Toulouse-Lautrec. The Count and Countess were first cousins, and Henri suffered from congenital health conditions attributed sadly to family inbreeding. Ultimately, he grew to only five feet tall, having developed an adult-sized torso but retaining child-sized legs. (He predeceased his father and thus never inherited the family title, derived from that of the ancient Counts of Toulouse. He offset his health issues by developing considerable art skills.)

In 1882, he and his mother traveled to Paris where he entered a professional teaching studio. In 1884, he settled in Paris's Montmartre district, immersing himself in the decadent cabaret life of the time. Montmartre was the hillside artist enclave just below Basilica Sacré-Cœur. Lautrec painted or sketched intimate depictions of dance hall girls, patrons, performers, prostitutes, and other artists like Vincent van Gogh. Like Lautrec, van Gogh was there with a circle of artisans creating works that would live through the ages. Edgar Degas provided encouragement that particularly inspired Lautrec. Japanese art also influenced his use of oblique angles and large swaths of color.

Lautrec sadly became an alcoholic and syphilitic over time. He died in 1901 at age 36. He's buried in Verdelais, a few kilometers from his birthplace. After his death, his mother and his art dealer, Maurice Joyant, jointly promoted his art. His mother later contributed funds for a museum to be established in Albi. Today, Lautrec is admired worldwide.

Other art and cultural icons have created here as well including Paul Gauguin, Vincent van Gogh, Henri Matisse, Pablo Picasso, Marc Chagall, and Salvador Dalí along with many modern day artists who depict the Languedoc lifestyle. One of the most splendid modern art venues is in Toulouse at Les Abattoirs. The popular Toulouse Art Festival runs from late May to late June.

The Languedoc offers many opportunities to enjoy the art, sculpture, architecture, photography, music, and pageantry that celebrate life. But modern sculpture and art abound also. Everywhere you look, there's much to enjoy in the Languedoc where culture and art are as highly prized as elsewhere in France.

Navigating the Area

Since it's such a vast region, visiting the Languedoc requires your typically taking a train or plane into the region. Then, you can rent a car or take a bus trip or excursion of some kind. The main airlines fly into Carcassonne, Nîmes, or Montpellier, or farther away in Toulouse or Barcelona.

Trains are a fun way to come into the region. Major railways go to Nîmes, Montpellier, Sète, Agde, Béziers, Narbonne, Perpignan, and of course Toulouse. One journey you might consider is aboard the Petit Train Jaune, the little yellow train that climbs to the highest reaches of the eastern Pyrénées. The views are incomparable.

To get off the beaten track, it helps to have a European-size car. You can rent vehicles at most of the main train stations or airports. (Pre-booking often earns you a discount.) Travel note: since this is very near Spain, you may be tempted to hire a car in France but drop it off in Spain. This can be very expensive. I've found it's easiest to hire a car and drop it off in the same country. But check your local car agencies to get the best deal. As always Trip Advisor, Michelin, and Rick Steves are all great resources for planning your time in the Languedoc.

Favorites

Nîmes, the Pont du Gard, Toulouse, Albi, Cordes-sur-Ciel, and Carcassonne. These extraordinary locales depict the many aspects of the impressive Languedoc. Nîmes, with its Roman heart, *paella-foie gras* cuisine, and bull-fighting arena, plus the mighty Pont du Gard near-by—are living testaments to Roman ingenuity. Stylish Toulouse, with its space-age zeal and contemporary panache contrasts with gentle Albi "La Rouge" that birthed genius Toulouse-Lautrec. And finally, majestic Carcassonne, a fortified castle, transports us back to the past as we traverse her mighty turrets—and perhaps a ghost or two joins us as we wander. Come along as we explore the mercurial Languedoc—an historical time capsule with its eyes on the stars.

Nîmes

Nîmes sits on the border between Provence and the Languedoc. It's the capital of the Gard *département* in the Languedoc-Roussillon region. Located on the strategic Via Domitia, it was built by retiring Roman soldiers who desired comfort and fine living.

Veterans of Julius

Caesar's Nile campaigns were given plots of land to cultivate on the Nîmes plain after their service ended. These veterans swiftly created everything they'd need for comfortable living: an amphitheater capable of seating 24,000 people, a circus, a gymnasium, baths fed by an aqueduct bringing water from the hills, and the stunning Maison Carrée temple. During Roman times, 50,000-60,000 people called Nîmes home. For this reason, Nîmes is often referred to as the "French Rome."

When Rome fell and the Visigoths invaded, it began several centuries of destruction that took its toll on Nîmes' infrastructure. In the last few hundred years, Nîmes stabilized and refurbishment of its surviving treasures began.

Today, Nîmes is a busy metropolis with a bit of Rome at its center. Nearly 175,000 residents live here, and it has every modern retail convenience. Interestingly, Nîmes has been one of the textile centers of Europe since the Middle Ages. One of its most famous fabrics was something called *serge de Nîmes*. Coarse, dense, and very sturdy, this fabric was used for ship sails, tarps, and other uses that required a fabric that could hold up to severe weather and long-term wear.

In 1873, Levi Strauss acquired a swath of *serge de Nîmes*. He planned to use it for tents for the California gold prospectors. Surveying the shabby attire of the gold miners whose digging, blasting, and hauling had ruined most of their clothing, he spied another niche for his sturdy French fabric. He, and a man named Jacob Davis, created durable trousers from the tarp-like cloth; they reinforced the key stress points with rivets so they would last longer. And they were an instant hit—not only with miners but also with the farm workers and cowboys who needed durable clothing to "win the West."

The name, however, was *très difficile*. Somewhere along the way *serge de Nîmes* got shortened to *de Nîmes*, then merely to "denim"—and the rest is jeans history. Various reports suggest there are roughly 4.2 billion pairs of jeans in the world. Ergo, many good things come from France, including the product I usually travel in when researching my books! (Press time note: I have mixed feelings about this "breaking" news. The sale of leggings are severely cutting into the global jeans market. This could be why "jeggings" are so popular—the best of both worlds. But don't tell the French. Many French women still prefer to wear dresses anyway!)

But back to Nîmes. When I first pulled into the center of town—which you can't miss since the gigantic amphitheatre is plopped right in the middle of downtown—I had two delightful surprises. One, there's easy-access underground parking nearby. Two, my delightful Nîmes accommodation, Hotel de l'Amphitheatre, was nestled in the center of a delightful square, down a marbleized walkway, within a block of the arena. Hauling my luggage from the car to the hotel was like going through an airport. Easy and fast. When I checked into the hotel, I was given a fantastic balcony room overlooking the square.

Other highly rated accommodations in Nîmes include the Hôtel Vatel and Acanthe du Temple Hôtel. Check Trip Advisor or other accommodation resources for others.

I've discovered a number of sites to visit in Nîmes. A stroll around the medieval quarter will take you past the amphitheatre (open daily except during events), the Esplanade Charles-de-Gaulle (bordered by *cafes* and the Palais de Justice), the Maison Carrée (open most days), and the Musée du Vieux Nîmes.

The Maison Carrée, set within an attractive square, is the best-preserved Roman temple in France. One of the reasons for this Vitruvian structure's stellar condition is that it has been used continuously since Roman times. It's been a consular house, stables, apartments, and a church. Thomas Jefferson fell in love with the Maison Carrée when he visited Nîmes as American minister to France in 1785; he had a stucco model made of it and carefully carted it back to Virginia, where it was the model for the state capitol building.

In the 1800s, the Maison Carrée became the home for the Roman Festival, celebrating the glories of Rome in opera and plays. Famed American actress Sarah Bernhardt played *Phaedra* there in 1903. It now serves as a theatre showing films on the history of Nîmes.

Nearby is the Musée du Vieux Nîmes that houses an impressive collection of artifacts in the former Bishop's Palace. Across the way is the modern Carré d'Art, built by Norman Foster who also built the Millau Bridge. These and other sites are accessible by individual tickets or by using the three-day *Pass Nîmes Romaine*, available at tourist offices or online.

But of course, the big draw in Nîmes is the arena, which was stunningly designed by Roman engineers 80 years before the amphitheater at Arles was built. It remains the best-preserved Roman amphitheater in Europe. The arena is perfectly symmetrical, designed to seat 24,000 spectators over 34 rows of terraces. The stones were cut from quarries nearby. Since 1853, the arena has been used for bullfights during the *férias* and occasional concerts and films. Rock band Dire Straits and heavy metal band Metallica have performed here, while François Truffaut filmed part of *Les Mistons* here.

Visitors to Nîmes are often puzzled by the appearance of an amazing creature, emblazoned in art and sculpture around town: the crocodile. You may particularly notice a chained crocodile emerging from a fountain pool at the Place du Marché. Photographer and journalist Paul Shawcross, whose *Provençal Roaming* is a terrific travel app for smart phones and tablets, explains: "It is believed that Julius Caesar, or perhaps Augustus as no one is quite sure, awarded plots of land in Nîmes...to the veterans from the Roman army who helped him to subdue the Egyptians during the Battle of the Nile (47 B.C.). The chained reptile so familiar to today's visitor is therefore a metaphor for a conquered nation!"

When you grow weary of hunting for crocodiles, you may decide a bit of lunch or dinner is in order. There's a multitude of bars, *cafés, bistros,* and restaurants in Nîmes to choose from. You may particularly enjoy Au Chapon Fin, l'Ancien Théâtre, or Le Cerf à Moustache ("the Deer with the Moustache"). Check with youraccommodations proprietor or the tourist office for the range of prices and food offerings. I quite enjoyed my lunch at Le Cheval Blanc with its bullfighter-themed *décor* and dishes. Great French onion soup.

Pont du Gard

Situated between Nîmes and Avignon, one of the most spectacular Roman structures ever created spans the Gardon River: the Pont du Gard. The Romans built this massive aqueduct/bridge in the 1st century to bring water from a spring at Uzès to the Roman colony at Nîmes.

It's a massive structure. When I first saw it, my mouth dropped open. It was three times the size I'd expected at 163 feet high. In the photo above, you can see tiny people walking across the lower level; that will give you some idea of the size. The actual water flowed not through the lower tier where people are walking, but through the third, top most tier!

More than an amphitheater or temple, this aqueduct is a stunning representation of Roman ingenuity, because it was so massively complex and efficient. The colossal, cream-colored blocks weigh more than eight tons each for starters. And they've each had to be lifted more than 131 feet—then set in place without the help of mortar. It's believed the aqueduct took about 15 years to build because it's exceptionally long (31 miles). The waterway that passes through it takes a meandering route through hilly terrain from the hillside spring across the gorge of the Gardon and on into Nîmes. Author Lawrence Durrell calls it "the crown of the Roman experience in this honeyed land."

The Pont du Gard has had a colorful history despite its staying power. It became clogged with mineral deposits and debris once the Roman Empire faded. By the 6th century, water had ceased to flow. It remained in use, however, as a toll bridge. Local lords and bishops exacted payment from all who passed here. By the 17th century, the crumbling structure was looted; pieces of stone were carried off to build nearby fences or cottages. The forward-thinking 18th century authorities, however, began to see its potential as a tourist destination. They initiated renovations that continue today. Interestingly, wealthy travelers on the "Grand Tour" of Europe (London, Paris, Rome, etc.) visited as part of their program. French masons-in-training studied the structure as part of their education.

Automobile traffic was still creeping over the Pont du Gard as late as the 1990s. Kitsch shops and cheap food consortiums lined the riverbanks. The French Government finally intervened and, with the

General Council of the Gard Department, cleared the tacky shops and pedestrianized the bridge. Soon, a new visitor center arose, complete with a full-scale bridge replica and exhibits showing how the structure was made. Nearby, inviting *cafés* were built to offer visitors a stylish place from which to gaze at the monumental bridge over an *apéritif.*

Statistically, the Pont du Gard is the tallest of all Roman aqueducts remaining on the planet. Along with the Aqueduct of Segovia, it's also one of the best preserved in all of Europe. It was added to UNESCO's World Heritage Sites in 1985. The old Uzès spring still exists; today a modern pumping station pumps the water though the water is now heavy with calcium carbonate from the surrounding limestone. If you're interested in a new perspective on the bridge, however, you can canoe or kayak down the Gardon River and sail right under the mighty arches.

Many writers have been inspired to write about the colossal grandness of this structure sitting for perpetuity in the stillness of the Gardon Valley. But I think novelist Henry James said it best in 1884: "...the unexpectedness, the monumental rectitude of the whole thing leave you nothing to say—at the time—and make you stand gazing. You simply feel that it is noble and perfect, that it has the quality of greatness...When the vague twilight began to gather, the lonely valley seemed to fill itself with the shadow of the Roman name..."

Toulouse

Toulouse, France's *"La Ville Rose"* (pink city), lies in the heart of the Midi-Pyrénées. Known colloquially as the "Gateway to Southwestern France," Toulouse is the fourth largest municipality in France. If you fly into Southern France, chances are you'll land here. If you take a train from Paris or elsewhere, chances are you'll pass through here. And chances are, if you seek cutting-edge fashion, space-age technology, or modern education, you'll go here. Toulouse is simply the New York of Southern France, with all the accessibility— and hubbub—implied.

But this IS Southern France. And of course, even big city Toulouse offers some serene settings. The Garonne River runs through the middle of this exuberant metropolis. The lazy Garonne is a port in a cyclone, providing refreshing picnic spots, unhurried strolling venues, and picture-worthy viewpoints. Like Albi nearby, Toulouse Renaissance merchants took advantage of the rich clay found at the riverside. From it they fashioned grand mansions and businesses of rich red brick and timber that still stand today as a testament to the city's prosperous resolve.

Toulouse has been at the epicenter of much of the *Occitan* history of the Languedoc since Roman times. Religious wars were fought from her environs in the 12th century. In 1229, the city finally submitted to the crown of France. The Hundred Years' War, famine, floods, and the plague took their toll. But by the 15th century Toulouse began to enjoy a golden age. She was a key player in plying the Bordeaux wine trade with England, as well as providing grains and textiles around the world.

Later centuries brought waves of immigrants and new industries. The French airmail system was first set up here. Today, Toulouse is the aerospace heartbeat of Europe. It's the exciting home for not just Airbus (and the Concorde) but cutting-edge Aerospace Valley and the Galileo positioning system. (Airbus is Boeing's main competitor, and by all accounts it's gaining some ground over its U.S.A. rival.) It's also ground zero for the European Space Agency. The European Space Agency, by the way, just landed a space probe from their Rosetta lander on a speeding comet! Mars could be next.

With its red brick façades, downtown Toulouse presents a very handsome face despite its commercial profile. Contemporary life and medieval antiquity adroitly intertwine. With a large university population (90,000), the buzz of *nouveau* France churns comfortably alongside Roman ruins and medieval churches.

There's much to keep a visitor busy. (See the tourist office for a *Toulouse en liberté* card that will give you access to multiple attractions.) Toulouse boasts 21 museums and more than 25 sights, monuments, and lovely parks and gardens—not to mention the wine bars, eateries, and nightlife. Most of the sights are on the right bank, where the lyrical Canal du Midi flows around the city's northeast segment.

Place du Capitole is Toulouse's handsome main square crowned by the majestic town hall. Day or night there's bustle since it's ringed by *cafés* and an "anything goes vibe." You can even get burgers delivered to you via motorbike!

A short distance away, the Basilique de St-Sernin is the symbol of Toulouse. It's the biggest Romanesque church anywhere in Western Europe; the interior is beautifully serene and ornate. Another locale worth visiting is Place de la Daurade where you can grab a drink or dessert or hop on a boat down the Garonne. I had the most fun exploring Les Jacobins, the rabbit warren of narrow lanes at the heart of Toulouse's old town. On the street signs, you'll see words in French as well as ancient *Occitan*.

Toulouse is filled with action-packed fun: rugby games and football (soccer) at the enormous local stadiums, cinemas, theaters, casinos and casino theatre, wine bars, pubs, discos, *cafés*, and *bistros* for entertainment and food. The French are champions of quirky urban renewal. Case in point: Les Abattoirs, located on the west bank of the Garonne. It's Toulouse's museum of contemporary art—one of the most respected in France. But there's more: it morphed from an old butchery in 1989. If you didn't know Les Abattoirs meant "slaughterhouse," you wouldn't have a clue.

And then there's interplanetary Toulouse. Star Trek and Battlestar Galactica have nothing on Toulouse. Home to the Concorde and now Airbus, Toulouse has its eye on the skies. As such, *Cité de l'Espace* (The City of Space) is a must see. Part theme park, part science exploratorium, it has a planetarium, IMAX theater, flight simulators, and all kinds of fun space-oriented activities for the whole family. (It's kind of a cross between Disneyland's Tomorrowland and Washington D.C.'s Air and Space Museum.) Great French fun!

When you tire of space, your stomach may call you

back to earth. And, in Toulouse, there's much to enjoy. You'll find all of the Languedoc specialties like *cassoulet*, but Toulouse throws in a special ingredient: violets. This dainty flower holds a singular place in Toulouse gastronomy. French soldiers who'd served with Napoleon brought home violets from Parma, Italy. This tiny purple flower enraptured the Toulousains, and the locals began planting them everywhere.

Today, the flower remains wildly popular in Toulouse. Violets show up in vinegar, condiments, laced in biscuits and cookies, melted into crystallized sweets like sugared violets, and added for a dash of pretty in salads. Naturally, the scent has been distilled in fine perfumes and colognes. And of course, you can sip violet *liqueur*. Nowadays, the greenhouses of Lalande, just outside Toulouse, produce great truckloads of these lavender darlings. And the city celebrates their violet emblem through the *fête de la violette* held in late February or early March every year.

Fashionistas will also have a grand time in town—especially if you've been out in the rural areas and feel ready for something trendy, expensive, or both. Toulouse is very fashion-forward; it's the birthplace of several famous brands including Kooples, Marchand Drapier, 7Robes, and my all time favorite, Comptoir des Cotonniers. (My daughter regularly wangles things out of me that I've purchased at Comptoir since their goods appeal to both moms and their daughters. And their prices are very reasonable.)

Young designers often get their start in this fashion hotbed; then they head to Paris! It seems like they practically spring full born from Fashion 101 classes into the international fashion spotlight. All the major chains like Printemps and Galeries Lafayette are in Toulouse off Rue d'Alsace-Lorraine and Saint-Rome. For urban chic, you'll find much to love on Rue Cujas, des Filatiers, and des Tourneurs. If you're a sophisticate, you'll love browsing Rue des Arts, Boulbonne, and Croix-Baragnon, as well as Place Victor-Hugo for *haute couture* and *les lingerie*.

Toulouse is also famed for vintage—and shoppers from all over France come here to troll the secondhand shops on Place de la Bourse, Rue Cujas, and elsewhere. (Follow the smart university girls who know exactly where to snoop out the best deals.) Antique lovers will adore the streets around the Saint-Étienne Cathedral quarter or at the secondhand market on Allées François-Verdier.

Accommodations abound in Toulouse. High-end venues (though really reasonably priced compared to the French Riviera or Bordeaux) include Hôtel des Beaux Arts, Hôtel Mermoz, and the Hôtel du Grand Balcon. Moderately priced places include the Hôtel Castellane (well suited for families), Hôtel de l'Ours (two locations), and Hôtel St-Claire.

Dining options are plentiful—from five-euro lunches to extravagant meals like at Brasserie Flo Beaux Arts (similar to its sister restaurant in Nice that I described previously). I quite enjoyed Le Colombier and Le Genty Magre. And for a light meal, I especially love the little wine bars like Le Mojito and Melting Pot that are flush with delicious wines, delectable bar food, and fun company. But beware—you'll be watching rugby on screen with a bunch of French fans! Denver Bronco lovers have nothing on these rabble-rousers. And if you get fired up after a night of sports fanaticism, you can pop in for a disco dance at one of the all-night clubs.

Don't be surprised at the Spanish influence in Toulouse. Toulouse is more Barcelona than Paris. But it's delightfully its own brand of French spice coupled with Latin passion. (As such, watch out for the regular barrel rolling competitions that break out on the streets when you least expect them.)

Albi

Alluring Albi (pictured) sits at the edge of the Tarn River less than an hour from Toulouse. As the sun rises over the tranquil Tarn, the early morning rays sweep down the red Renaissance buildings to the quiet streets below. The night dew glistens as the sun

rises further in the sky. And the Albigensians of *"La Rouge"* awaken to begin a new day in one of Southwestern France's most storied towns.

Albi—sight of a bustling mercantile city forged from the red clay of the Tarn—has a turbulent past but a business-savvy present. During the 12th and 13th centuries, Albi was the site and namesake of the Albigensian Crusade, where the Pope in Rome struggled to rid the world of Cathars. Once the conflict was over, Bishop Bernard de Combret began work on the Palais de la Berbie (Bishop's Palace) in the late 13th century. Built even before the Palais des Papes in Avignon, this palace—a fortress for all intents and purposes—fronts the town at the Tarn. Nearby, majestic Cathedral Saint-Cécile rises behind it, one of the most stunning Gothic-style churches in France.

The town enjoyed unrivaled prosperity during the Renaissance due to the cultivation of the plant *Isatis Tinctoria*, commonly known as woad. The plant's leaves produced a blue dye used for centuries in dying cloth. Merchants who dealt in the woad trade especially prospered in the Albi and Toulouse areas; the fantastic Renaissance mansions sitting grandly along the Albi streets are evidence of their prosperous legacy. Later, I'll talk about staying in one of the old mercantile complexes where woad was the "Apple" business of the day. (Clinical note: woad has been used in Chinese medicine for centuries. It was also used for dying Egyptian cloth wrappings used for mummies. Though no longer used for dying, it's now being studied for use in the treatment of cancer.)

Albi grew up around the original cathedral and the palace; the historic area of delightful winding streets lined with Renaissance brick and tile structures covers about 156 acres. In morning, noon, or evening light, there's a luminous glow to the entire Albi downtown.

Red clay was much loved by Albi builders since it could be shaped by hand; on some of the buildings, you can still see finger marks left by these ancient brick-laying artisans. Anchored by glowing street-lights, the gently curving roseate-hued streets offer an intoxicating stroll through perfectly preserved Renaissance France. If I blink, I can practically imagine I'm in England's Stratford-Upon-Avon, the birth-place of William Shakespeare which looks a lot like Albi.

Modern-day Albi has parlayed its colorful history into a tourist haven where art, architecture, and ambience meld into a memorable milieu. In 1864, Albi's favorite son, Henri de Toulouse-Lautrec, was born. Much of his remarkable life's work now rests in the Pope's Palace which became the Toulouse-Lautrec Museum in 1922. The palace environment lends a spiritual gravitas to the oeuvre of this Albi genius.

This meandering museum houses a stunning 1,000-piece Lautrec collection. Many of the pieces were created in *Belle-Époque* Paris. Climb the grand 17th century staircase of the Lautrec Museum, and for a small entrance fee you can enter this colorful archive of Lautrec's creations from his childhood to his death. These include *Au Salon de La Rue des Moulins, La Goulue Entering the Moulin Rouge, Divan Japonais, Jane Avril Dancing, Aristide Bruant*, and numerous lithographs of the Moulin Rouge. Some hail Lautrec as the father of modern advertising.

As you leave the museum and wander further up the colorful incline from the Tarn's edge to the old city center, you'll stroll along perfectly preserved Renaissance byways now prettified with street *cafés*, vibrant flower baskets, and quaint boutiques. As in Toulouse, the street signs are bilingual in modern French and ancient *Occitan*.

And, in the center of the old town area, you'll find yourself at Place St-Julien. It's lined with pretty shops and situated across from the grand Cathédrale Saint-Cécile, the pinnacle of the town. The building of Cathédrale Saint-Cécile was begun in the 13th century after the Albigensian crusade. It was painstakingly constructed over 200 years—a symbol of Catholic power. Saint-Cécile is considered the largest brick structure in the world today. At 370 feet high, it's a mass of gothic vaults and towering walls that culminate in a soaring bell tower.

The cathedral has a Gothic structure, but not the intricate outer stonework of Northern France churches. Perhaps reflecting the religious turmoil of the time, the impenetrable looking cathedral is more citadel than cozy place of worship from the outside. Inside, however, it's a splendid sanctuary of ornate beauty. Late flamboyant Gothic decoration is everywhere in the interlaced motifs, pinnacles and arches, rich multi-colored frescoes, iridescent stained glass, and bold Gothic statuary.

Old town Albi has a unique feature: it's spotless. And at night, it's tranquil and nearly empty of tourist frenzy. A wander around old

Albi, lit by luminescent street lamps that cast an angelic glow to every rose façade, is a rapturous experience. Outside the formidable citadel at night, Saint-Cécile casts an otherworldly glow over the entire town. And this isn't just visual. You'll hear choirs singing through the magic of stereo speakers from the eves of the lofty spires. It's as if heavenly Christmas choirs were heralding young and old—but here in Albi, you can enjoy the lovely strains all year long. Pure magic.

From the city center, day or night, you can meander happily for hours along the Albi byways viewing various mansions, museums, and attractions open to the public. You can also cross the Pont-View, Albi's arched stone bridge that connects right and left bank settlements, and wander through the other side of town. If you'd prefer a seated excursion, you can take a boat ride down the river, hire a horse and buggy, or board the local petit train that will take you all around Albi. Check the tourist office for further details.

I've found several Albi dining venues worth a taste. Among them are l'Épicurien, La Fourchette Adroite, and l'Esprit du Vin helmed by two-Michelin-starred chef Daniel Enjalran. If you can, stop in at the covered market near Saint-Cécile that's brimming with local goodies.

Accommodations are plentiful in Albi, from B&Bs to hotels. I suggest Hostellerie Saint-Antoine, La Réserve, Hôtel Lapérouse, among others. My personal favorite, however, is delightful Mercure Albi Bastides. This beautiful Mercure property is perched on the banks of the Tarn overlooking downtown Albi. It's housed in an 18th century water mill built from red Albi brick. The rooms have modern amenities and stellar views if you can snag a waterfront room (rooms 11 and 12 are particularly nice). The modern restaurant features local cuisine and wonderful service.

Less than an hour by car from Albi are two locales you may want to visit for their special charm. First, is the medieval hamlet of Lautrec, resplendent with its overhanging half-timbered houses built around a rock outcrop. Here, the famous purple garlic is grown. More than 4,000 tons are shipped out to a garlic-loving world which prizes this colored, aromatic vegetable for its flavor and shelf life. Favorite dishes for this plucky purple produce include garlic-crush sauces, garlic-rubbed breads and croutons, and garlic soups and stews. (Note: In ancient France, and perhaps still today, a handful of raw garlic and a hunk of bread was the favored lunch of local laborers.)

The second locale is Saint-Antonin-Noble-Val, the village where the *Hundred Foot Journey* movie was filmed. You can relive the scenes from the much-loved film by wandering the cobblestoned streets, going to La Halle (covered marketplace) where the main characters buy (or should I say co-op) their restaurant produce, and by stopping for a *café crème* at Café de la Halle where star Helen Mirren ponders her culinary fate.

Cordes-sur-Ciel

When I first headed toward Cordes-sur-Ciel, a hilltop village out of the way of the normal routes from Toulouse or Albi, I had some misgivings about what I would encounter. Would it be worth the drive?

What I found was a perfectly preserved medieval village crowning the Puech de Mordagne outcrop, similar to Mont St. Michel in the north. Both have a mystical skyline. And both are often misted with clouds as if they're in some Brigadoon-like suspension, only appearing once a day for tourists! In 2014, Cordes-sur-Ciel was voted "France's Best Loved Village." Now that I've stayed here, I'm in love too.

Cordes-sur-Ciel ("ropes on sky") was built by Count Raymond VII of Toulouse during the Albigensian Crusade in 1222 to be exactly that: a roped-off city, high in the sky. Due to its isolation and an avid artistic community that has rescued it century after century, this enchanting medieval village remains frozen in time.

Cordes-sur-Ciel has the distinction of being the first *bastide* in Southwest France. It was built as a shelter for people who had been displaced by the Albigensian Crusade when their village of Saint-Marcel was savagely burned down by Simon de Montfort in 1215. Though it's not fortified, Cordes was built on the crest of the crag to ensure its easy defense. Later, Cordes became part of France in 1271. Over the centuries, three ringed walls were built around the town, but only one survives today. Despite incursions during the Hundred Years' War and the religious wars, there remain some fine examples of 13th and 14th century Gothic architecture. Since Cordes is laid out in a perfect little diamond shape, it's also very easy to wander around in and not get lost.

The leather and cloth trades flourished in Cordes where flax (for linen), hemp, and saffron grew abundantly. The end of the 19th century found a boom due to the invention of mechanical embroidery looms. Fine embroidered linens were shipped all over the world.

But the commercial bounce didn't last. Cordes was destined for demolition in the 20th century until wealthy artists and others got some of the buildings classified as historical monuments in 1923. Soon after, craftsmen and artists moved in to the old shops, and today visitors will appreciate the booming craft and tourist trade. Additionally, the town holds music festivals several times a year in the covered marketplace. Shops like Les Délices du Terroir do a brisk trade in local foodstuffs and handmade products.

The town is now home to an ironmonger, an enameller, several sculptors and engravers, numerous watercolor and oil painters, figurine makers, weavers, shopkeepers, jewelers, and restaurateurs. You'll have a wonderful opportunity to watch artisans at work in Cordes. I watched an engraver for nearly an hour; he was hard at work in full medieval togs! (I couldn't resist buying one of his superb etchings.)

Cordes' Jardin des Paradis is an inviting wander through a "living garden" of medieval and oriental plantings maintained with organic methods. Afterward, you might pop in to the elegant Musée Les Arts du Sucre du Chocolat (Museum of Sugar and Chocolate) opened by *chocolatier* Yves Thuriès who lives here.

Yves Thuriès, twice an esteemed winner of the *Meilleur Ouvrier de France* (craftsmen of France), first created a sugar exhibition in 1988 after he moved to Cordes-sur-Ciel. Subsequently, he opened the Sugar and Chocolate Museum (with a boutique of Thuriès goodies). No surprise, it's the most popular attraction in town.

Thuriès is a whirlwind of chocolateering. He opened his 55th Yves Thuriès chocolate store in Paris in 2012 (you can find his *chocolatiers* all over France, as well as east coast U.S.). In 2007, he teamed with legendary chef Alain Ducasse to take over the National Pastry School. Last year he launched the "chocolate train," a unique exhibition in a high-speed train dedicated to the art of chocolate that tours France.

This mouth-watering sugar and chocolate museum in Cordes is housed in the rose-hued Prunet mansion. It contains art entirely made of sugar on a variety of subjects like mythology, nature, and the Middle Ages. You'll also find one of Thuriès signature creations, the Cordes-sur-Ciel *croquant*. The unique *croquant* is a cookie devised in the 17th century by the Count of Cordes when he found that he had an excess of almonds from his bounteous almond trees. Chefs discovered that if they crushed the almonds and mixed them with honey and egg whites, they could be rolled out, cooled, and then broken into candy pieces or kept intact for cookies. Variations are made by adding ingredients like chocolate and sugar, then forming the mixture around cups or cylinders to create "cups" to hold other ingredients—or simply eaten. Today, *croquants* are made all over Europe; they're often used as a pastry shell for sorbets or puddings or eaten as airy cookies.

Thuriès is famous for saying; "I create my chocolates for my customers, my neighbors, my friends…Chocolates as I love with a soft heart, breakable crust and a pronounced flavor. [I] blend less ingredients but remain close to the raw products and to the original flavor." Some of his other creations are a dark chocolate fondue and chocolates shaped like *macaron* cookies in multiple flavors. www.yvesthuries.com

Visitors to Cordes can park in the lower town down below, and either walk up the incline or take the petit train that chugs you up to the old town on the hill. I also found the "new" town at the bottom of the hill to be a cute place to shop and dine.

Accommodations are unique in Cordes; hoteliers maximize the sublime vistas and couple them with medieval ambience. Hostellier du Vieux Cordes and Le Secret du Chat are two stellar properties located in the middle of Cordes. But, one of my favorite overnight experiences has been at inviting Aurifat, a *chambres d'hôtes* slightly down the hill from

Cordes. (The city center is about a block up the hill).

My now favorite Languedoc hoteliers, Matt and Kay Noble, run Aurifat. Aurifat is a multi-room B&B housed in a 13th century Cordes-sur-Ciel watchtower. The Nobles and their effervescent five-year-old daughter, bought the property when they decided to move to France from their native Yorkshire England.

When I arrived, Kay was hard at work mowing the lawn out front, while Matt was inside replastering a wall. Within minutes, this pair had me installed in their most splendid room at the top of the bell tower, with adjoining balcony overlooking the Cérou Valley. Down below, I saw the lush garden where breakfast would be served overlooking an inviting swimming pool. I couldn't have been happier.

Kay and Matt told me their daughter had just spent a few days in an elementary school nearby and she was already speaking some French. The French teachers suggest this is a perfect time for a child to become bilingual with ease.

As dusk began to fall at Aurifat, my husband and I wandered up the hill to downtown Cordes. We purchased a basket of goodies— *baguette*, cheese, wine, *croquants*—and then made our way leisurely back down the hill to spread our picnic out on the deck table on the balcony.

Candles lit, we watched the farmer below haying his field as we finished the last of our food and wine. Later on, we walked leisurely up the hill a second time as the sun set to see locals out tending their gardens or simply enjoying a sip of wine. It was a magical twilight experience that still lives in memory.

Carcassonne

"Each time I round the final bend of the long…auto route leading to Carcassonne, I hear myself unexpectedly catch my breath yet again. There, on a distant hilltop, stands the perfect medieval fortress—as magical as the very first time I saw it…the citadel seems to rise out of the vineyards like an apparition from a fairy tale. Indeed, it is said that the fortress city's massive double ring of stone ramparts, towers and barbicans so mesmerized Walt Disney that he used it as the model for Sleeping Beauty's castle."

—Suzanna Chambers

At the heart of the Toulouse-Montpellier-Barcelona triangle, stands legendary Carcassonne. Carcassonne is both a fortified medieval city (*La Cité*) and a walled castle. Situated at this critical crossroads between Spain and France, the town's strategic importance made it the site of many fierce battles over the centuries.

The settlement around Carcassonne dates back to 3500 B.C., but the hilltop structures of this imposing walled city began taking shape as early as 100 B.C. when the Romans built fortifications. They dubbed their city Carcasum.

When Rome fell, the Romans ceded the location to Visigoth King Theodoric II in the 5th century who built additional fortifications. Attacks came from Frankish King Clovis and Saracens from Barcelona, but the castle remained in the control of local medieval lords.

Legend has it that Pepin the Short, King of the Franks, attacked the castle in 760 A.D. He believed the inhabitants would eventually starve to death if he waited long enough. Dame Carcas, wife of Carcassonne's ruler, however, had other ideas. She fattened up the last pig of the stalwart citizens and had it thrown over the ramparts. The enemy figured if the castle controllers could waste such valuable meat, they must be well provisioned; they eventually gave up and slunk away. Dame Carcas rang all the bells in the city in celebration as they departed. And *"carcass soone"* (Carcas rings the bells) became the new name of the city.

The breakup of Charlemagne's empire was the beginning of the feudal era. In 1067, Carcassonne became the property of Raymond-Bernard Trencavel, viscount of Albi and Nîmes. Allied over the following centuries with either the counts of Barcelona or Toulouse, the Trencavels built additional structures, including the Château Comtal (castle), which you can tour today and the lovely Basilica of St. Nazaire. Pope Urban II blessed the new cathedral. A *ville basse* (lower town) grew prosperous at the feet of the citadel.

But the Cathar religion became popular in Carcassonne. And

in 1209, the Pope's crusading army, bent on quashing all Cathars, imprisoned upstart Roger-Raymond de Trencavel (son of Raymond-Bernard). Trencavel later died mysteriously in his own dungeon. Violent Simon de Montfort took possession of Carcassonne and built additional fortifications.

In 1247, Carcassonne finally submitted to the rule of France. Both King Louis IX and his successor Philip III built outer ramparts to fortify Carcassonne as a border fortress. Edward the Black Prince attacked but failed to conquer Carcassonne. However, the Inquisition was active here; many Cathars were tried and executed within the castle walls.

By 1659, Carcassonne's military significance waned. The city above and below the great walls became focused as an economic center on the woolen textile industry. Under Napoleon and the Restoration, Carcassonne the citadel fell into disrepair. The French government was about to demolish it in 1849 when there was a huge uproar by local authorities. Ultimately, support rallied and the government agreed to restore Carcassonne to its former for glory as a historical monument.

Eugène Emmanuel Viollet-le-Duc (1814-1879), French architect and restorer, was hired to oversee the renovation. Chief among his repairs were the tower roofs and ramparts. He was criticized in the day since he used a modern design for the towers. He produced numerous spectacular architectural drawings, including many of Carcassonne which are actively studied even now.

The results are stunning. Carcassonne now has a double row of fortified walls that run almost two miles long and are accentuated by 56 majestic watchtowers. The castle environs include a moat and drawbridge. The *lices,* the flat, empty space between the inner and outer walls, have returned to their verdant past when they were the site of tournaments where knights dazzled their ladies-in-waiting. And the ramparts, inner chambers, and turrets are fantastic for exploring their raw power and legendary past.

Nighttime Carcassonne is particularly ethereal. I had the opportunity to stay inside *La Cité* on a recent visit. I can tell you that there's nowhere on earth like Carcassonne when the moon is up. Obviously, much of the history of the Languedoc is mirrored here. Many have lived and died within the walls of *La Cité*. And I can report that moonlit nights are thick with the feeling that others walk these paths.

If you've read about orbs, you may know that they're either considered retro-reflection off dust particles during low-light photography OR supernatural phenomena pinpointing paranormal energy fields of other beings. I'm not offering an opinion one way or another. But notice this photo of me around midnight in Carcassonne on one of the ramparts. I felt completely unafraid, by the way. You may be able to see at least nine orbs in the photograph swirling around me. You be the judge.

In 1997, Carcassonne was classified as a UNESCO World Heritage site. Today, it welcomes more than three million visitors annually. Several Robin Hood films have used the vivid ramparts as background. And many historical fiction and non-fiction books have been  written about this enchanting place.

The city outside the castle proper (but inside the fortified walls) meanders along several medieval streets lined with souvenir shops, eateries, and accommodations, as well as parks, the entertaining Torture Museum, and the majestic Basilique St. Nazaire. If you can get to Carcassonne during July close to Bastille Day (July 14), you'll find the city at its most glamorous, with a spectacular light show, pageants, costumed performers, and heart-pumping music.

A variety of accommodations exist inside the old city walls. Among them are Hôtel Donjon and Hôtel de la Cité. Yet my favorite is the Hôtel de la Cité. They have fabulous rooms, a fine wine bar, and sumptuous dining at the La Barbacane where I still recall the seven separate desserts I tried to choke down after a gourmet meal. (Even in France you don't have to eat everything they serve you. But I gave it the old college try.)

Other dining opportunities include Chez Saskia, Auberge de Dame Carcas, and Brasserie Le Donjon. For a quick bite, wander into Place Marcou where you'll find half a dozen choices, among them Le Trouvère.

Carcassonne has its own airport which offers free shuttles to and from the city May though November. The airports at Carcassonne and nearby Toulouse and Nîmes are all serviced by inexpensive carriers from Paris and a number of British airports. But Carcassonne's easily reachable by car. Just outside the outer wall at the Porte Narbonnaise gate is plenty of parking. From there, you can walk up into the walled city or take a carriage ride or *petit train* up the winding streets.

Outside the old city in the attractive town below, you'll find a busy wine trade in full swing since the entire area is a sea of vineyards. Along with wine consortiums are stylish boutiques, lively markets, and a thriving arts scene. The picturesque Canal du Midi traverses the countryside which now produces excellent wines including Minervois and Corbières. And, of course, it's only 75 km (47 mi) from the Mediterranean coast. In addition, plenty of venues offer medieval dining; at some of these restaurants, you can slip on medieval costumes for the full effect.

Ultimately, legendary Carcassonne may be the crowning glory of the Languedoc. Should you visit? Many others have heeded the simple advice of 19th century French songwriter Gustave Nadaud who wrote, "You should not die without seeing Carcassonne."

If you haven't the resources to actually visit Carcassonne yet, you might enjoy Kate Mosse's transporting novels set in the area such as *Sepulchre* and *Labyrinth*.

Languedoc in Sum

"The Languedoc Roussillon Region of France is an undiscovered Gem filled with a breathtaking coastline, some of France's best cuisine, rich medieval history and amazing architecture like *châteaux* (castles) and cathedrals…

—gofrance.about.com

The Languedoc. Land of high art, medieval majesty, soaring drama, wines aplenty, space-age savvy, verdant vistas, commercial zeal, and stalwart people who know how to live life to the fullest.

Not quite Provence. Not quite Dordogne. Not quite Spain.

It's Southern France at its best: hard to pin down, but so delightful to discover.

Part Four:
Dordogne

"I believe that this great peaceful region of France will always be a sacred spot for man and that when the cities have killed off the poets this will be the refuge and the cradle of the poets to come…France may one day exist no more, but the Dordogne will live on just as dreams live on and nourish the souls of men."

—Henry Miller

The Dordogne, and its adjacent community of Quercy, is a verdant agricultural and historical area located in the eastern segment of the Aquitaine province. It's named after the great Dordogne River snaking through it (pictured). This is a wildly diverse land filled with farmlands of sunflowers, vines, orchards, walnut groves, and tobacco crops. It's thick with gently wooded hills edged by craggy outcrops where hanging villages, colorful bastides (fortified towns), and rough fortresses anchor the land. Ancient castles are built on stony peaks. And deep below the earth, lay prehistoric limestone caves adorned with primitive cave drawings—evidence of man's habitation dating back 30,000 years. In the "the valley of 1,000 castles" life is alive and thriving.

The Dordogne is especially famed for its market towns like Sarlat-la-Canéda where agricultural abundance overflows in open-air markets. It's loved for its dramatic hanging villages like La Roque-Gageac and Rocamadour where art and religion, fine cuisine and wine, mingle in a marvelous *mélange* of sensory experience. But it's best known for its magnificent castles like Beynac and Castelnaud where medieval life lives on in ancient stones, magnificent weaponry, and captivating history.

Beloved by gourmands, the Dordogne is a feast for the palette as well as the eyes. Exquisite *foie gras* and duck products lead the way in favored foodstuffs, while the region brims with black diamonds (truffles), succulent strawberries, tasty walnuts, and rich wines from Cahors and Bergerac. In and around Limoges, skilled artisans craft fine porcelain. And for spelunkers, world-famous cave dwellings and rock drawings lay deep in the earth for exploration.

If you see the movie *Timeline* from the Michael Crichton science fiction novel, you'll experience a little of what visiting the Dordogne is like. The film tells the story of history students whisked back to 14th century Dordogne on a quest to rescue their time-traveling professor played by Billy Connolly. They start the story in a time-travel lab in modern day New Mexico one moment. Then seconds later, they're fending off medieval French knights wielding broadswords as the students struggle sans modern technology to complete their quest and return to the future.

When you land in the Dordogne for your own adventures, you'll undoubtedly use your electronic devices to GPS your way around this rustic region. But the living history will nevertheless time-travel you to the past as you climb the ancient battlements, squeeze through rustic turrets, breathe the smells of thousand-year-old tapestries, and stand alongside ancient *trebuchet* that rained fiery terror down on enemies long ago.

The Dordogne doesn't just preserve history. It weaves medieval life into modern living to form a kind of French multiverse. It may be the closest you'll ever come to actual time travel when you walk here. But you'll have the advantage of knowing your modern jet or smart car will transport you handily in and out of this magnificent time capsule with ease.

In the Dordogne, you'll come across quaint villages at practically every bend in the road. In the whole country there are 152 *Les Plus Beaux Villages de France*, 10 of which are found in the Dordogne—more than any other *département* in France. These pretty villages are delightful for strolling. They're fun to photograph. And they're intriguing for their historical significance. In springtime, the fruit trees in blossom perfume the air with the most gorgeous scents. Orchids and wild flowers spread like a beautiful blanket over the land. And the many Dordogne lakes, ponds, and rivers invite visitors to take a dip or a canoe ride.

However, in fall and winter, the medieval architecture and grand churches are fascinating. Sometimes, they're dusted with snow as the winter sun sparkles through the ancient stained glass. And of course the fresh truffles, *cèpes* (mushrooms), and *foie gras* appear in the winter shops, tempting one and all for the holidays or early spring *fêtes*.

Good living is very accessible here I've found. On any given day in the incomparable Dordogne, you can take a hot-air balloon, sailing high over magnificent Rocamadour. Then, you can hop over to La Roque-Gageac for a kayak run down the river to Beynac. There, once you alight, you can climb the steps to the ancient Beynac castle for a wander through 14th century France. Later, you can descend for lunch in the lovely town below which overlooks the sparkling river. Afterward, you can climb back onto a boat for the return trip to La Roque— and cycle back to Rocamadour if you like for dinner.

Or you can meander at a more leisurely pace—my preferred style of exploring the multifaceted Dordogne. You can stroll the striking gardens at Clos des Sources or Château de Marqueyssac for a few hours. Next, you can browse the Saturday market stalls in Sarlat-la-Canéda and enjoy delectable *Duck à l'Orange* paired with dark Cahors wine in fetching Saint-Cirq-Lapopie that evening.

Stunning, serene, sumptuous, exciting, raw. You'll never go wrong spending a few days or weeks in the Dordogne. But I guarantee this mesmerizing place will draw you time-traveling back again and again.

History & Landscape

The castle-strewn area known as the Dordogne follows roughly the parameters of the old province of Périgord. It sits east of Bordeaux and roughly northwest of the Languedoc region. The terms "Dordogne" and "Périgord" are basically used interchangeably in modern day. The Dordogne territory is split into four distinct regions: Périgord Noir (Black Perigord) which is dense with forests and legendary castles; Périgord Blanc (White Perigord) which has bright outcroppings of chalky limestone and "black gold" (truffles); Périgord Vert (Green Perigord) known for its lush countryside favored by landscape painters; and Périgord Pourpre (Purple Perigord) with its beautiful vineyards and wine growers. For purposes of this section, I'm including Quercy, home to Rocamadour and more, along with the Dordogne destinations herein.

The Dordogne has been a favorite locale of man since prehistoric times. This accounts for the abundance of prehistoric remains and caves along the Vézère Valley and elsewhere. Many of the caves have colorful rock drawings and etchings that tell the story of primitive man who lived in the Dordogne thousands of years ago.

The Romans, then Vandals, Visigoths, Franks, Moors, Vikings, and English all occupied portions of this territory over the ages. When Henry II ascended to the English throne in 1152, English troops too occupied the land, fueling a French-English conflict that lasted hundreds of years.

During the Hundred Years' War (1337-1453) which actually lasted 116 years, the area was fraught with conflict. English Edward, the Black Prince, held sway over the area in the 1300s; he ultimately captured French King Jean II at the Battle of Poitiers in 1356. For years afterward, various English and French factions defended their positions through bastides and castles built at strategic positions along the valley. Many of these well-maintained structures remain today. They make for dramatic visits—if you have the stamina and desire to climb the ancient steps to some of these embattled fortifications. Within, you'll find medieval weaponry, rustic furnishings, fading tapestries, and all the trappings of medieval life. These dramatic backdrops often show up in modern films like *Chocolat* and *Jeanne d'Arc (Joan of Arc)* since they remain fixed in the past—except for all the tourists with smart phones and digital cameras taking selfies at the ramparts.

Still later, the area weathered the Wars of Religion and Henri IV's reign. Henri converted to Catholicism in 1593 and was soon crowned King of France. The County of Périgord became part of the royal domain during his reign. He's considered by many in France to be *Le Bon Roi Henri*—the good king. He's remembered for bravery on the battlefield, for his "love of love," and for his care for the common people via *"la poule au pot"* (a chicken in every pot). He was the first king from the Bourbon branch to take the throne of France. His father was Antoine de Bourbon-Vendome of the Capetian dynasty; as a stylish prince, Antoine introduced the idea of wearing earrings and bracelets for men (perhaps a precursor to the notable Frenchmen's fashion sense).

Henri inherited the throne after the last three kings of the Valois branch expired: Francois II (first husband of Mary Queen of Scots), Charles IX, and Henry III—all died without male legitimate heirs. His son Louis XIII and the Louis heirs reigned until the French Revolution. Post-revolution, the Dordogne was pro-Napoleon, and many of Napoleon's best generals and marshals came from this region. Two World Wars sadly brought destruction and occupation to the area. But the French Resistance was very strong.

In 1940, some boys searching for a lost dog discovered Lascaux Cave with its magnificent cave drawings—the first of hundreds discovered in this "cradle of man." In the late 1900s, 15 prehistoric sites in the Vézère Valley were registered as World Heritage sites. And in 2010, the remarkable International Prehistory Centre in Les Eyzies opened to great fanfare.

There's much to experience here—and since the Dordogne is so varied, it may take a lifetime to savor. For those of you who want to make good use of your smart phones and your time while visiting, I'd highly recommend downloading Paul Shawcross's handy app, *Dordogne Explorations*. I found myself onboard a tiny boat cruising the Dordogne River between La Roque-Gageac and Castelnaud, for example, as I reviewed Paul's recommendations. Without lugging around an armload of travel books, I accessed the app to hone in on tips to help me pick my photography spots, choose dining and accommodations, and grasp the history behind the sights I was visiting.

People & Lifestyle

Yet it's not all history interests in the Dordogne. The Dordogne is a wonderland of activities for young and old. Life is busy with cycling, river activities (canoeing, kayaking, boating, fishing), balloon rides, hiking, horseback riding, camping, outdoor markets, garden visits, and wine tasting. You'll also enjoy the wealth of festivals featuring ancient traditions. River activities thrive since much of the river remains wild, with kingfishers, otters, and herons hunting along the banks, while freshwater eels congregate in great numbers, and packs of migrating wild salmon ripe for harvesting swim upstream.

The friendly locals add to the ambience. They work in the infrastructure of the communities in the agricultural or wine-growing industries, practice creative endeavors, or make their living in tourism. They speak more and more English these days, and perhaps because they have so many eager visitors, they're most welcoming. They're high-tech savvy too. I spot many locals with smart phones and laptops, even as they're dusting off 500-year-old castle furniture.

I've had several experiences in the Dordogne with friendly locals very willing to accommodate my needs. Later on I'll tell you a truly remarkable story about a wonderful French craftsman who kept his word to get a set of hand-crafted Laguiole forks across thousands of miles to my husband. Many of these artisans run shops or market consortiums—and they make a brisk euro or two maximizing the hungry tourist trade for their fine goods.

The locals jump through time too. Many of the residents dress up in traditional garb if the *fête* or pageant warrants it. Colorful medieval events get played out in mock battles and Renaissance-type fairs that dot the Dordogne. Food fairs are popular here. In January and February for example, food and wine lovers from around the world arrive for the *Cahors*
Malbec & Truffle Festival. In Sarlat-la-Canéda (Sarlat), January marks the *Fête de la Truffe* (truffle festival), and February celebrates the *Sarlat-la-Canéda Fest'Oie* (goose festival). In July, visitors enjoy the *Cahors Blues Festival* while they sip red wine and groove on the sounds of artists like the Original Blues Brothers Band and Johnny Gallagher. And of course, around Bastille Day in July, the region explodes in a variety of dramatic celebrations that last for weeks.

The trendiest enterprise in the Dordogne—indeed all of France— is using the majestic castles and fortresses for backdrops in sensational light shows. These are often accompanied by rock music or symphonic strains to fit the period or the presentation. Nighttime illuminations are a specialty of the French. Even when there's not a light show taking place, wandering around the Dordogne towns at night is one of my favorite things to do. The enchantment is everywhere.

Food, Wine, & Shopping

Food

Like many other regions of France, the Dordogne has an abundance of local flavors. Dordogne cooks value age-old ingredients that are both thrifty and delicious. Every part of an animal is used from pig entrails to duck gizzards. Duck and goose fat are used extensively, especially to make heavenly Sarlat potatoes (potatoes fried in duck fat and seasoned with parsley and garlic) or as a basis for roasting chicken or frying cabbage.

With its wines, mushrooms, truffles, and preserved duck and goose products, the Dordogne supplies nearly half of France's finest foods. Ducks and geese (pictured) have an honored place in the Dordogne. Duck livers make their way into tins and jars sold everywhere—even at roadside stands. *Foie gras* is found in most shops and open-air markets. Duck and goose *confit* is another specialty; to create the *confit* the bird's legs and thighs are salted and flavored with herbs, then simmered in rendered poultry fat that preserves the meat as the *confit* cools. Later, the *confit* is crisped and typically served with green salad and mouthwatering Sarlat potatoes.

Sarlat is also renowned for poultry products like *pâté* and *magret de canard* (duck breast) served with a variety of sauces. Many countries have banned *foie gras* due to the *Gavage* (force feeding) of the birds required by geese farmers, however. I was puzzled about why France persists in making this controversial product until I learned this: Apparently during the WWII occupation of France, the Nazis found the practice of *Gavage* unseemly; they resolutely banned the products. (Psychologically this is about as incongruous as it gets; I can't fathom the value system that favored geese over people, but that's off topic.) The impact on the French however was this: *foie gras* became a proud symbol of the French Resistance. Thus, there's a great deal of emotional attachment to the notion of *foie gras* as a national symbol.

Walnut and chestnut trees flourish in this bounteous land. Evidence exists that groves of walnut trees have grown here for at least 17,000 years. Walnuts have been much prized over the ages: 10th century peasants paid their debts with bushels of these nuts. Thirteenth century merchants sold walnut oil as a precious commodity. Today, many French families sell nuts as a second income. And despite modern machinery facilitating cracking and processing of truckloads of Dordogne walnuts, the *denoisillage* is still practiced. Elderly women called *les dames denoisillenses* take the precious walnuts and crack them by hand as they gather around the fire in the evenings. They use boxwood mallets that help keep the nutmeat intact. Interestingly, many of these industrious ladies' hands are permanently stained brown—which helps you spot them in the market places.

Now a major crop in the Dordogne, walnuts figure into a number of famous dishes, liquors, and even furniture. In 2002, an official AoC was launched guaranteeing the high quality of the nuts from specific producers. Like AoC wines, the nuts are grown within specific parameters and must meet rigorous cultivation and taste tests.

Among the bounteous Dordogne walnut products are chocolate-dusted walnuts, walnut cakes and breads, mustards, jams and spreads (often combined with honey), and fine walnut oil. Chefs sprinkle them on salads or mix them with Roquefort cheese or butter for a delectable spread on artisanal bread. And they're used in tasty stuffings for poultry. The nuts are also macerated in alcohol to make the famous *vin de noix*, walnut wine. Handsome furniture is made from the hard walnut wood. And even the tons and tons of shells don't go to waste: they're ground into kitty litter! I've recently noticed walnut-based kitty litter adverts in American television commercials as an alternative to clay litter. French influence even extends to your *chat* (cat)!

As a nut lover, I happily munch my way through the Dordogne enjoying these flavorful snacks particularly in the local walnut cake which I find irresistible. I'd add that walnuts are very healthy for us. Périgord locals have the second-lowest heart disease rate in the world; many ascribe at least part of this phenomenon to the lowly walnut which lowers cholesterol and is bursting with potassium, zinc, copper, and magnesium the last of which particularly fights stress and imparts energy.

The fields and forests of the Dordogne abound with other local delicacies as well: strawberries in early summer, mushrooms in mid-summer and fall, and prime black truffles found at the feet of oak trees by enterprising truffle hunters in winter. Some of the other well known Dordogne dishes include *bréjaude* (pork rind and cabbage soup garnished with rye bread), lentil and *foie gras* salad, *cèpes* (porcino mushrooms) tart with herbs, breast of duck with fresh figs, *soufflé* with truffles or morel mushrooms, *crème brûlée* with chestnuts, *salade landaise* (smoked duck breast, duck gizzards, pine nuts, and cherry tomatoes on a green salad); *axoa* (a ground veal dish served with potatoes), and *cabécou*, a goat cheese specialty of Rocamadour that I find perfectly compliments a black Cahors wine.

Wine

"This impenetrable area skillfully hides many secrets, starting with the profound and ebony color of its wine...this Lot Valley, which accumulates legends and mysteries as if they were stacked archives, tied up with spider webs."

—Jean-Charles Chapuzet, *Cahors,*
The Black Wine Novel

The popularity of the wine from this region dates back to the Middle Ages—even before the noble grapes of Bordeaux were popular. First planted by Romans 2,000 years ago, the Cahors Malbec grape vines produce a dark, rich wine that's been loved by "popes, kings, and tsars." Huge barges originally took this *vin noir* up the Dordogne to Bordeaux; from there it was shipped to the great capitals of the ancient world. It became so popular, that by the 13th century Cahors wine represented almost 50% of the wine exports out of Bordeaux. Having survived both a phylloxera devastation and competition from Bordeaux and Saint-Émilion, today's Cahors calls itself "the historic and spiritual home of Malbec."

Cahors is a highly prized AoC "black" wine with flavors of black currant, cherry, and licorice, and an aroma accented by notes of truffle and eucalyptus. It's made with 70% Malbec grapes, supplemented by up to 30% Merlot and Tannat. The region's place as the Malbec capital of fine wines has been challenged in recent years, however. Argentina (planted with Cahors Malbec vines in the 1800s), Chile, and New Zealand, as well as California and other U.S. states are denting the Malbec market. In the U.S., the Malbec grape is a favorite for blending into a "Meritage" (Bordeaux-like blend).

The flavor of Cahors wine is earthy, sometimes very strong on the tongue until it's aged for a dozen or so years in the bottle. The Malbec grape, called *auxerrois* or *côt noir* in Cahors, has an inky dark color and robust tannins. Its plum-like flavor goes best with game, roast meats, and strong cheeses. If you plan a visit here, you can acquire a list of vineyard addresses at Union Interprofessionnelle du Vin de Cahors (www.vindecahors.fr).

Bergerac, which is northeast of Cahors, is also a leading wine-producer of the region; it has 12 different AoC-designated wines. Bergerac plants largely Sauvignon grapes which are used in making red and white wines; Cabernet Franc, Merlot, Cot, and Sémillon grapes can also be found there.

Monbazillac, the sweet white AoC wine created with the effects of *Botrytis cinerea* (noble rot), is one of the area's most famous products. Its honeyed tastes go well with *foie gras*, dessert, or as an *apéritif*. Other flavorful wines include the dry, fruity whites Montravel and Bergerac, that are excellent with seafood and fish; the sweeter whites like Côtes-de-Bergerac, Rosette, and Saussignac that are excellent as *apéritifs* or with white meats; and long-in-the-bottle Red Bergerac and Pécharmant that are best paired with hearty meals. There's a delightful wine-route through the vineyards for your tasting pleasure. You can find info at the Maison des Vins de Bergerac (www.vins-bergerac.fr) or the Cave Coopérative de Monbazillac (www.chateau-monbazillac.com). The best news is that you can take home some of these wonderful wines for a mere $10 and up.

Fans of the eloquent, long-nosed Cyrano de Bergerac, who pined for the beautiful Roxane in Edmond Rostand's play, can find two statues of Cyrano in the town of Bergerac. Be aware, however, that the real Cyrano never lived here. Interestingly, Rostand first used the word *panache* in his play written in rhyming couplets. "My panache" is Cyrano's last utterance as he dies. Numerous translations and reworkings of the story have appeared on stage and screen, including the Hollywood flick *Roxanne* starring Steve Martin in a rather magnificent schnoz. I fantasize that Rostand was sipping a fine glass of Monbazillac as he penned his play. Perhaps he "intoxicated" that it takes a rather large proboscis to appreciate the fine aromas of Bergerac wine—and the idea of Cyrano was born!

Shopping

You'll encounter numerous shopping opportunities in the Dordogne. Most of the towns like Sarlat, Rocamadour, Saint-Cirq-Lapopie, and La Roque-Gageac have an abundance of shops selling everything from food to crafts and home goods to antiques. Many have weekly markets jam-packed with *foie gras*, fruit preserves, wine and liquors, soap and bath products, *bric-à-brac*, and souvenirs. You can also buy farm-grown products straight off the farmer's table such as mushrooms and strawberries collected that morning or, if you're lucky, some truffles with the soil still hanging off them.

Since each area has something special to offer, you'll find a lot of variety. For example, Rocamadour is famed for its religious heritage and pilgrimage center. Here, you'll find many religious themed gifts that are beautiful even if you're not a devotee of any one religion. What's more, I was amused to see kitchen witches in some of the Rocamadour souvenir shops. Spiritually, I guess, this is an egalitarian effort to cover all bases.

In Sarlat *foie gras* is king. And there are ample opportunities to buy duck and geese products galore. Not only do the Wednesday and Saturday main square markets offer table after table of duck and geese goods, but whole shops are dedicated to the Sarlat mascot.

In Bergerac and Cahors, you'll find fabulous wine consortiums. Not only will they offer you plenty of wares, but most will even let you do wine tastings—even in the grocery stores. I can't tell you how happy this made my husband. He could taste while I shopped!

Despite its teeny size, Saint-Cirq-Lapopie is teeming with places to spend your euros. I particularly like the Musée du Vin, which is a high-volume kitsch store, wine museum, home goods consortium, and wine merchant all rolled into one. I would be tempted to call it a "French mini market," but it clearly aimed higher.

Some of my treasures from the Dordogne include a wonderful collection of hand-illustrated French recipes bundled together in a colorful French portfolio. I also picked up some intriguing medieval French baskets and a clutch of French keys for some enormous castle lock somewhere. (Sometimes I wonder: Are they keys to an ancient dungeon where English interlopers were fed the dregs of medieval soup? Or were they manufactured in some factory in Toulouse or China? I prefer the first fantasy.)

If your interest is authentic porcelain, there's much to love in the Dordogne. Porcelain, particularly the magnificent products created in Limoges, is available in a variety of types and styles. Among these are True Porcelain (hard paste, resonates when tapped), Artificial Porcelain (soft paste), Bone China, Faience Fine (white earthenware, very durable), Stoneware (gray, glassy in appearance), and Terracotta redware. Limoges itself has factory outlets, workshops, and many showrooms. It's also the place to find beautiful enamelware. All of these products are available throughout the region's outlets if you can't get to Limoges specifically.

Suffice it to say, you'll find ample opportunity to run up your credit card—and most shops and stalls take them. The problem will be in getting your collectibles home! Most large towns have extra suitcases to sell—and I once went twice to a La Poste in Sarlat to ship my goods home. The staff was all too happy to prepare yet another big orange box for me to send home—and they cheerfully took my euros each time!

Culture & Art

Art and architecture are closely aligned with the turbulent history in this region. The architecture itself becomes part of the manifestation of creative endeavors employing various Italian and French influences through the ages. There are only a few Roman ruins here. But the medieval and Romanesque periods are represented not only in the design and structure of dwellings, churches, fortresses, and town infrastructures, but in the beautiful stained glass, tapestries, and sculptures beautifying the squares.

The vaulted ceilings, ribbed arches, bell towers, church naves, square ornamentation, patterned sandstone, and enamelwork make many views seem like paintings. During the Renaissance and the reign of François I, the Italian style was much favored. This style shows up in the inner courtyards, busts in high relief, statuary, and intricate staircases.

Later, the 17th century designers began copying the beauties of Paris and Versailles. One of the most beautiful places to view art, sculpture, and landscape creativity together is in Rocamadour. This ecclesiastical city, known for its chapels and churches, has a magnificent Way of the Cross walkway that gently leads up the steep climb from the town to the castle at the top of the ridge.

Lined with the Stations of the Cross, it's a serene, spiritual walk along gentle switchbacks canopied by beautiful trees and magnificent art. I found it peaceful and calming, especially as the sun set. In the late afternoon, just a few pilgrims were making the journey up the hill. My companion and I had it virtually to ourselves.

Modern art, particularly sculpture, pops up throughout the Dordogne, reminding us that French sensibilities lean toward visual art. I particularly like the tender couple sculpture in cosmopolitan Périgeux (shown above).

Navigating the Area

The Dordogne and Quercy are easily accessible. Bergerac has its own airport, and trains come in daily to various stations throughout the area. Ultimately, you'll most likely rent or hire a car, van, or motorcycle to get around. The roads are well marked, and around almost every bend are stunning vistas.

Once you arrive however, I'd highly recommend you sample the abundance of travel modes. Though I usually arrive by car, I've enjoyed a refreshing boat ride down the Dordogne, sampled the hot-air balloon rides, and glided down the river in a kayak.

Hardy cyclers are everywhere. Of course, I joined the groups hiking up and down the hillsides and wandering through the bastides on foot. Small and large bus tours are offered however if you prefer a guided group. You can also hire a private guide who'll ferry you around in a local vehicle and offer personal insight.

Most of the castles and fortresses are accessible without advanced reservations. But I'd suggest getting there early or arriving after 3 pm to avoid any large tour groups. If you visit the various caves like Pech-Merle and Lascaux, you may arrive early but will most likely be required to view the cave with a group. My group experience at Pech-Merle caves was very easy; we arrived, bought tickets, then joined an almost entirely French-speaking group. However, we were offered an English booklet so we could follow along without any problems. (And we could practice our French with the others.) I particularly enjoy visiting these attractions with French families; it always affirms my belief that kids are kids no matter their language, and that the parents who take them on these excursions love sharing real-time history no matter where they are on the planet. I'm always fascinated by watching little ones look at cave drawings and engravings. Some of the French children in our group thought the etchings looked like *dessins d'enfants* (drawings done by children like themselves). To the cave people, however, I'm sure they thought their etchings were masterpieces!

Visitors can follow many "historic routes" or themed itineraries to see specific Dordogne sites. Local tourist offices have maps of these specific routes. For example, the sign-posted *Route Historique Jacques-*

Cœur guides you to an abbey, 10 private *château,* and six towns exploring the life of the famous 15th century merchant. Other routes include the *Route des Vins* (wine), *Route des Métiers d'Art en Périgord* (stone cutters, potters, glass blowers, leather workers, and other craftsmen), and others as well. There's also an abundance of cooking classes, equestrian tours, donkey-treks, and horse-drawn carriage rides. You may opt to join a river cruise or take a tourist train.

I confess my favorite mode of transportation here is the hot-air balloon. You might recall that the hot-air balloon was actually invented in France. Brothers Joseph-Michel and Jacques-Étienne Montgolfier first developed a hot-air balloon in Annonay, Ardeche, France. They made an unmanned flight on September 19, 1783 lasting 10 minutes. Soon, humans climbed into the basket, and the rest is flight history. (I'll talk more about aeronautics in the Bordeaux section. The Wright Brothers, followed by a long line of aeronautical enthusiasts, finished out their years in Southwest France after they made their first airplane flights in North Carolina in America.)

Despite my initial fears of getting off the ground in one of these colorful but intimidating balloons, I felt wildly exhilarated once I got up in the air. I could see everything at once—castles, rivers, forests, people. I couldn't stop taking pictures; my companions even seemed a little concerned about my hanging out of the basket. I had no fear whatsoever. And my pictures are fantastic.

One of my favorite memories in Rocamadour was around 6 am one Sunday morning (when I was on the ground in my hotel

room). I heard familiar bursts of whooshing sounds, but couldn't place them at first. Suddenly, I remembered: This was a hot-air balloon filling for take off! As I ran out to my balcony, I beheld the beautiful sight of these hot-air balloons rising up to meet the morning sun. It was marvelous.

Lest you think I'm some sort of fearless adventurer, let

me assure you I'll do a balloon ride in France, but you'll never get me up again in a helicopter on Maui! I nearly lost my lunch on one of those mechanical mosquitoes. Yet a flight in one of the beautiful French balloons is like nothing else on the planet. And when the handsome crew serves you champagne upon landing, what could be a better way to see France?

Favorites

Sarlat-la-Canéda, Castelnaud, Beynac, La Roque-Gageac, Rocamadour, Saint-Circ-Lapopie, Lascaux/Pech Merle/Les Eyzies, and Périgueux. The Dordogne beguiles with its cliff-top castles, undulating river, delectable *foie gras*, mystical black wines, and cradle of ancient man. Come with me as we meander the attractive marketplaces of Sarlat and dine with music by tableside troubadours. Climb along as we scale the ancient fortifications of Castelnaud and Beynac with armor-suited knights and lovely ladies-in-waiting. Ride with me as we glide down the Dordogne at La Roque-Gageac and sail the skies in a hot-air balloon over Rocamadour. Rise with me above the Saint-Circ-Lapopie valley then climb deep into the earth as we gaze upon the etchings of prehistoric man. And finally, join me in Périgueux, the seat of Dordogne power where unforgettable cuisine and bustling commerce awaits.

Sarlat-la-Canéda

"Sarlat-la-Canéda—a film set with probably the best market in France."
—Paul Shawcross, *Dordogne Explorations* app

In the center of popular Périgord Noir sits the most amazing town: Sarlat-la-Canéda. Commonly called Sarlat, this atmospheric little township (pictured) with its grand Place de la Liberté, circa 1500 Renaissance edifices, and delightful avenues with abutting passageways is enchanting. Some travel pros claim Saint Cirq-Lapopie is the cutest restored town in France. For my money, Sarlat beats it hands down.

I've spent many an hour wandering through Sarlat, exploring the labyrinth of passageways and courtyards. I'll shop a little, take some pictures, linger in a quiet garden or church, or stop for a drink or a meal. Then I'll mingle with the locals, who I find fascinatingly modern in this medieval hamlet that nevertheless offers fast WiFi . The town is a model of French ingenuity. But a French ingenuity that's put vast resources behind honing the town's ancient infrastructure—while subtly installing modern conveniences. A black knight in silver chainmail galloping along main street Rue de République would not be out of place here for passersby—who might offer a bow to the intrepid knight, then nonchalantly step into l'Atelier du PC for a computer repair.

Sarlat's had a long colorful life that's now been burnished to a medieval sheen. But it's not some Disneyfied fiefdom. It retains a raw medieval luster. And, if you wander through Place de la Liberté at dusk or after dinner, I swear you can glimpse a 15th century halo softly glowing around the 21st century streetlamps.

The town grew up around a Benedictine abbey founded in the 8th century. It was designed to store the relics of St. Sacerdos, Bishop of Limoges. The abbots ruled this area until corruption led to their downfall in the 13th century. The abbey church became a cathedral when Pope John XXII proclaimed Sarlat the Episcopal see. The 13th and 14th centuries saw the town rise and grow as a busy marketplace. But the Hundred Years' War devastated the populace. To thank them for their loyalty against the English, Charles VII showered the little town with privileges and tax exemptions so the people could rebuild.

The mercantile town's building boom lasted between 1450 and 1500; it resulted in an architectural uniformity that forms the town's charming skyline today. During this period, sturdy townhouses sprouted for the bourgeois class using fine, golden sandstone. These were crowned with heavy limestone slab roofs necessitating a steep pitch to hold the heavy weight. Most of these fetching houses have interior courtyards, lantern turrets, picturesque gables, and slate-topped spires.

Often these structures have ashlar masonry that gives each façade a finely dressed appearance. Some of the stonework is intricate, depicting medieval characters, Templar symbols, mythical beasts, and particularly the salamander, the historical "symbol" of the town. The salamander symbolized resistance and resurrection during the Middle Ages. It's everywhere in Sarlat—except where displaced by images of the 21st century "mascot," the goose.

Sarlat's old town was eventually cut in the 19th century by the modern Rue de République thoroughfare. There's much to be seen on either side of this busy street; it serves as a general main street, making it hard to ever get lost in Sarlat. In 1962, Sarlat became the trial locale for the new loi Malraux law enacted to provide money for the restoration of specific French towns. Funds flowed into Sarlat to refurbish the fine buildings and edifices.

Now, the town has the highest density of historic and classified monuments in France. Of particular note is the project of Pritzker Architecture Prize winner Jean Nouvel. Nouvel, who was born in Sarlat, undertook the restoration of the Church of Sainte-Marie in the center of Sarlat. He added enormous steel doors to the front of the building and restored the arch and nave inside. The building now holds a tempting covered market plus a glass elevator which opens at the top of the bell tower for panoramic views across Sarlat.

Sarlat is a magnet for historians and tourists alike. As a municipality, it's at the center of the region of the Périgord Noir where Beynac, La Roque-Gageac, Castelnaud, Les Eyzies, Lascaux, and Souillac are only minutes away (unless you get waylaid behind a line of tourist buses). As Paul Shawcross observes in *Dordogne Explorations*, "this magnificently restored Gothic and Renaissance town has been the location for two Hollywood films, *The Duellists* and *Timeline*. But it is much more than a film set. It's a busy small town with an extensive Saturday market to die for which is arguably the best in France."

I first stumbled upon this busy Saturday Sarlat market one morning after I'd driven in from Saint-Émilion. After I parked, I wandered into the *vieille ville* (old town) to the Place de la Liberté (I just followed the crowds). A palatial Saturday market unfolded before me.

It not only overflowed the square, it spilled over into virtually every offshoot byway.

I discovered a vast array of seasonal produce plus all manner of area specialties—breads, cheeses, truffles, cherries, mushrooms, biscuits, fresh fruits and vegetables, and of course, *foie gras*, hams, and meats. The market also had fine wares like French clothing and Laguiole knives.

I've returned several times since that first visit and was fascinated to see another interesting aspect to this fabled Place de la Liberté marketplace. It undergoes a dramatic transition once the market disappears around 1 pm. I once sat at the edge of the square for about two hours (nursing a glass of Cahors) as I watched this extraordinary transition take place.

Huge trucks lumbered into the paved square. Strapping French men hopped out and loaded up all the market tables and wares in a matter of minutes. Poof, they were gone. Then, another set of more slender, but equally robust, Frenchmen appeared from the restaurants ringing the square. Each one dragged a huge stack of tables or chairs behind them. Like some kind of table ballet, they swung out clusters of stacked furniture. Then, they'd artfully array them in front of the eatery. Again and again they repeated the ballet until the square was ringed with tables.

Within minutes, these same energetic fellows had set the tables with white tablecloths, china, glassware, and menus. Then, they popped back inside once more. Soon, they emerged in aprons and jackets— *voilà*—as the wait staff. (I had a strong urge to film the whole thing. This wasn't the first time I've witnessed boundless French energy when it comes to restauranteering. I'd love to use it as a training film for American servers who think they have it hard!)

In December, the Sarlat market is especially pretty. It becomes a wonderful Christmas fair with 40 or more wooden chalets selling arts and crafts. Skaters even enjoy an outdoor ice rink. If you miss the big Saturday market however, visitors can sample the smaller version on Wednesday. The main street, Rue de la République, is a wonderfully wide shopping street nearby, however, that's open daily and brimming with clothing and shoe stores, *bric-à-brac* sellers, jewelry stores, kitchen shops, and my husband's favorite, Maison Mérilhou. I have two amazing stories that involve this remarkable little Sarlat shop.

Maison Mérilhou is a *coutellerie* (cutlery) that carries all major brands of knives, blades, sommelier's tools, and shaving equipment. It also restores and repairs knives. Brands include Laguiole, Opinel, Cabatier, and Douk-Douk. Once inside, my husband was mesmerized. He quickly snapped up a beautiful set of handmade Laguiole steak knives with deliciously aromatic pepperwood handles (pictured).

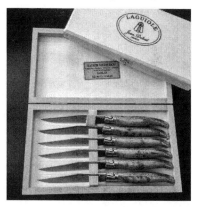

Laguiole knives are highly prized in France. This beautifully crafted knife comes in a variety of pocket or table knife formats; it originates in the Languedoc town of Laguiole, France. Probably taken from similar knife designs used by shepherds and cattle herders in Spain, the distinctive French version appeared around 1829. Pierre-Jean Calmels created the sinuous Laguiole version featuring a forged bee symbol on the top of a curved knife handle. Soon, the design was used on corkscrews, spoons, steak-knife sets, and sommelier paraphernalia.

My husband had admired these fine knives for years. Now, he had a magnificent set in his possession. However, he wanted to use them as we continued on our trip. So instead of shipping this precious box of cutlery home—which in retrospect I would highly recommend to anyone reading this book—we decided to carry them with us. At the airport, we planned to put them in our checked bags.

All went well until we headed for Spain. (I'm relating this cautionary tale even though we appear completely idiotic. I want to help you avoid this same embarrassment.) We prepared to board a train in Valencia and innocently loaded our luggage onto the metal detector conveyor belt. Blam! All hell broke loose. Red lights flashed. Sirens blared. And the police came running.

Soon, I found myself frantically explaining in bad high school

Spanish why we were NOT terrorists trying to smuggle knives into the country for nefarious purposes. I plead with the Spanish officials to let us into our reserved cabin along with the knives. "*Usted está de suerte, señora*," they answered. (You're out of luck.) We were finally able to board the "milk" train (that stopped in every little village between Valencia and Alicante) with our steak knives. But the crew definitely kept an eye on us. (I have no idea why we were kicked off the high-speed train but allowed to go on the everyday train, though I think I spied a cowboy or two in our train car who were probably carrying sheep-sheering tools as well.) Our steak knives ultimately got home safely. And we use them with pleasurable memories of Sarlat each time we smell pepperwood.

Fast-forward a couple of years. We returned to delightful Sarlat, and I found my husband standing yet again in front of Maison Mérilhou. He had a winsome look on his face. Now what, I thought.

"I want to buy matching forks. To match the pepperwood knives," he told me.

"Oh no," I groaned. Not again.

"Let's just go inside and see if they have them. If they do, we can ship them home—natch!"

Once inside, we wandered around looking; there were none to be had. Luckily, I had a picture of our beloved Laguiole knives which I whipped out to show the delightful proprietor—the same little Frenchman who'd sold us our original set. We asked if he could locate matching forks.

"*Oui*," he said. "*Naturellement*." But it would take time he explained.

"And we want them shipped home…" I quickly added.

After handing over about $300 via credit card (yes I know—pretty expensive), we left our home address and continued on our trip. Once home, I murmured to my husband one evening, "I wonder if we'll ever see those forks? Maybe we've been had." (Even I can sometimes be suspicious of the French.)

"No," he answered. "I have complete faith they'll come." Then we forgot about them.

A few months later, our local post office called. The postmaster told my husband he thought he had a package for him. Now I want to state up front that we live in a rather large metropolis of many thousands of people. The postmaster didn't know us personally.

"I have this package here," he began. "It's from Europe somewhere. We weren't sure what to do with it."

"Is it from France?" my husband shouted.

"Not sure. But it has your last name on it, our town, and the words 'USA.' No street address. No first name."

"No address?!" my husband exclaimed.

"Nope. We found you in the phone book."

"Oh gosh," my husband sighed. "I think they're forks from France. Can you smell pepperwood?"

"Sure do smell something," he said casually.

Within days, the package arrived. My husband tore off the wrapping. In it were the Laguiole forks the wonderful Monsieur Mérilhou had forwarded. How they got to us from France without an address seems like a miracle. But somehow I'm not surprised. Miracles do happen—especially in Sarlat.

As for Sarlat dining, my favorites include Le Quatre Saisons, Restaurant le Grand Bleu, Le Regent, and Restaurant le Tourny. Le Tourny is particularly fun since a modern-day troubadour keyboardist serenades you with lovely French ballads interspersed with Broadway show tunes.

Hotels and B&Bs abound in and around Sarlat, including La Villa des Consuls, Hôtel Bon Encontre, and Clos La Boëtie. Whether you stay in Sarlat or nearby, many travelers find Sarlat an excellent central base from which to see the rest of the Dordogne. If you select a B&B or *chambres d'hôtes*, you may get some opportunities to interact with the locals more than you would in a hotel. Many of these smaller accommodations usually expect visitors for breakfast—but many also offer dinner as well. I find if you have at least one dinner with your hosts, you may save money during your trip. Off-season in the Dordogne is typically October to May; you can enjoy as much as 20% off on prices and you'll avoid crowds. However, always bring an umbrella.

Above all, I've learned to take my time meandering through the central areas of Sarlat itself. Look for the excellent tourist office near the cathedral that provides a helpful walking map. There are churches to see, gardens to discover, the *La Lanterne des morts* bullet-shaped tower (Lantern of the dead) to explore, and little nooks and crannies where French life unfolds. Early morning light or dusk brings a marvelous, luminous quality to this precious town. So enjoy it day or night—and everything in between.

Castelnaud

Château de Castelnaud is a formidable castle built in the 12th century. It's located a mere eight miles or so from Sarlat at the confluence of the Dordogne and Céou rivers. The *château* is situated above the small village of Castelnaud-la-Chapelle, one of *Les Plus Beaux Villages de France*. Its original owner supported the Cathars. Ultimately, barons from Northern and Southern France came to blows—and many opposing knights confiscated the lands of Cathar-friendly noblemen. Hence, Château de Castelnaud fell into the hands of mighty Simon de Montfort during the Albigensian crusade.

Later, when the castle fell into English hands during the Hundred Years' War, the *château* served as a base from which to monitor (some say "harass") the neighborhood. In this photo with the *trebuchet*, you can see the enemy Beynac castle across the river. These two opposing castle occupiers fought back and forth through the ages—often changing allegiances—as each fought to maintain dominance. When the wars dissipated, the Caumont family repaired Castelnaud's crumbling turrets and added spacious new living quarters while keeping the battlements ready.

During the French Revolution, the castle was neglected and fell into ruin. The stones were used as building materials for neighboring structures until 1966 when the castle was listed as a Historic Building and renovations began as a major renewal.

Today's Castelnaud (pictured)

is still fairly rustic, but the huge castle rooms have been refurbished to allow for wonderful viewing of its ancient weaponry, artillery tower, donjon and kitchens, twisting staircases, and panoramic Dordogne Valley views. There's a Museum of War and Middle Ages on site which has full-sized models of medieval *trebuchets, perriers* (catapults mainly for rocks), *mangonels* (pitching cannons for tossing burning pitch), battering rams, cross bows, armor, and hand weapons. Most interesting to families may be the gift shop, which has a stunning collection of toys, miniature *trebuchets*, comic books, and other products on medieval history.

In July and August, you can visit the castle at night where a historical play is performed every year in the torch-lit rooms. Other times, medieval pageants are staged where you can witness medieval life in the flesh. In a corner of the courtyard, a blacksmith primes his bellows before fashioning a metal sword on an ancient anvil. Nearby, an armorer surrounded by vests and hoods crafts chainmail rings for an entire suit of chainmail. Across the way, a serf demonstrates the method for loading a *trebuchet* catapult while a lovely lady-in-waiting in traditional garb admires him. Soon, the catapult is sprung and the fiery projectile shoots over the ramparts. Such is a typical scene at the marvelous Château de Castelnaud.

Beynac

Across the river from imposing Castelnaud, its archenemy for hundreds of years, sits the equally commanding Château de Beynac. Built at the top of the tiny village of Beynac-et-Cazenac, another of the *Plus Beaux Villages de France*, Beynac sits glowering at Castelnaud.

"Beynac is arguably one of the most impressive castles in the whole of France," states

Beynac from Dordogne, Beynac
Copyright © 2014 Paul Shawcross

travel expert Paul Shawcross in *Dordogne Explorations*. "The original castle fell into the hands of the redoubtable Richard the Lionheart during the late 12C; but [it] was later destroyed by Simon de Montfort. Rebuilt by the Lords of Beynac, it was strategically very important during the Hundred Years' War." I found it amusing to see a plaque listing the castle's pedigree (or shall I say "occupations") at the castle entrance. You'll see English King Richard the Lionheart's name on the list, surrounded by Frenchmen!

All of this historical squabbling gets very confusing for visitors to Beynac. Suffice it to say, the Dordogne River marks the traditional medieval dividing line between the (usually) French stronghold of Beynac and the (often) English fortress of Castelnaud. Over the warring decades, each castle changed hands between the French and English several times. Hence, the waters get a little muddy when determining each castle's allegiance. Both currently reside in the solidly French Dordogne. But a bit of the old wrangling still remains.

Interestingly, 3,000 years before Christ, farmers began tilling the slopes of this rocky outcrop overlooking the nurturing Dordogne River. A mere 500 residents live in Beynac today, but they're reportedly inundated by more than 500,000 visitors a year! When you enter the village of Beynac prettily bordered by the river, it may feel vaguely familiar. The tiny town is a series of handsome but rustic shops, *bistros*, art galleries, and rough stone homes forged seemingly out of the very rock they rest upon. You can wander through the town, then begin the picturesque climb up to the castle from the center of town. Or, as I discovered later, you can drive up to a within 50 yards of the castle entrance from the other direction. (I discovered this after my steep climb up medieval stairs to the *château*; it had to be at least a 26% grade. No pain, no gain I guess.)

However steep the "stroll" up to the top was, I finally realized why I recognized my surroundings. Parts of the movie *Chocolat* starring Johnny Depp and Juliet Binoche were filmed here. The medieval nature of Beynac's stark architecture was perfect for the movie's depiction of the 40 days of Lent where all the residents were supposed to be fasting. Binoche's tantalizing chocolate shop, however, was tempting the townspeople to undertake all kinds of scandalous behavior. As I climbed, I felt that same bleakness—although there were some patches of brilliant color from attractive red flowers, red shutters, and bright tablecloths.

When I got to the top of the castle, I found a no-frills fortress of raw beauty. The feudal castle was abandoned at various times during history, but it was finally rescued by Lucien Grosso in 1962. He's spent a lifetime restoring it with the help of the French Ministry of Culture.

Inside, I found a massive keep ringed by ramparts and watchtowers. The medieval castle—cutting edge for the time—used the latest techniques for repelling invaders: defensive pinch-points, reinforced artillery turrets, and a network of hidden holes from which boiling oil, tar, and arrows could be dispatched.

I also found several magnificent structures, courtyards, living quarters, a guard room, a rustic kitchen, a delightful chapel (still in use by the town), and some ancient stables (where Luc Besson filmed part of his *Jeanne d'Arc* film in 1998).

A large section of Beynac was remodeled in the 17th century. This "upgrade" installed a baronial meeting room, an oratory, some ornate frescoes, a stunning Florentine Renaissance staircase, and some rather ancient tapestries. I was actually rather concerned about this massive, fading tapestry. It was clearly hundreds of years old, but it was completely unprotected. This, however, is part of the unique charm of Beynac castle. It's splendidly raw—which adds to the realism of the place and my vivid impression of it.

The owner and his family live in the 17th century portion of the privately-owned castle, and he has certain restrictions for visiting. We were shooed out of the castle precisely at 11:30 one Tuesday morning. I couldn't understand why. I learned later that the owner doesn't like tourists disturbing his lunch! (If 500,000 visitors are always interrupting his two-hour *dejunier* every day of the year, who can blame him!)

As we were leaving the front entrance of the castle, however, a young Frenchman letting us out the massive castle doors took special interest in my husband and me. He asked us in English, "Where are you from?"

I answered that I was from the U.S. He then looked at my husband who replied that he was originally from England. The young

Frenchman studied us both for a moment. Then he said to me, teasing, "Well then you can go. But you (looking at my husband), we will have to lock up!" I still rib my husband about his narrow escape from Beynac—and medieval France.

Just outside Beynac is a town called Vézac, where the spectacular Château de Marqueyssac sits on the hillside. An elegant 17th century *château,* Marqueyssac is also noted for its whimsical gardens that feature a marvelous collection of terraces, alleys, kitchen garden, and garden peacocks who greet you as you wander through the maze of plantings, hanging gardens, and cascading water. There are 150,000 boxwoods all pruned into delightful shapes: domes, hedges, balls, and quirky shapes like flocks of sheep. Since it opened to the public in 1997, it's become one of the most visited gardens in the area. From the *café* terrace, you can look down the Dordogne to Château de Castelnaud. Other lovely gardens to visit in the area are Les Jardins du Manoir d'Eyrignac, Les Jardins de l'Imaginaire, and Les Jardins Panoramiques de Limeuil. I find these Dordogne gardens serene places to enjoy the beautiful vegetation of the Dordogne, as well as to relish the magnificent views across the valley.

La Roque-Gageac

La Roque-Gageac (La Roque) is another one of *Les Plus Beaux Villages de France.* It nestles along the rock-face looking down on the beautiful Dordogne. Castelnaud and Beynac are within a short distance; all three are within minutes of Sarlat.

This is a tiny community with no grand castle looming above. But it does have handsome shops, open-air terrace restaurants, and stone cottages huddled together surrounded by delightful plantings that make it look practically like one big garden. Since the Dordogne is steps away, this tiny town has maximized its allure with craft-for-hire opportunities galore: canoes, kayaks, or one of the traditional *Gabarres* riverboats (pictured at the front of the Dordogne section) fashioned on the old river trading vessels.

I had a delicious ride in one of these "Norberts" (the company's name for their small fleet of passenger boats). I say delicious because I had been clomping through limestone caves and up and down castle steps for hours on a blisteringly hot May day one year. When I drove into La Roque, I saw this fabulous river vista open before me. Ahead was the languorous Dordogne River, filled with bobbing boats and sleek kayaks loaded with deliriously happy people bobbing along. Within minutes, I was aboard one too.

Riding in a riverboat is one of the most enjoyable things I've done in the Dordogne. It's refreshing, cool, serene, and exhilarating all in the same moment. Frogs croak, songbirds sing, swallows dart across the water, and swans paddle slowly under weeping willows dipping into the river. From the comfy seat of my quiet Norbert, I relaxed and shot vivid, river-reflected photographs of the great *châteaux* and troglodyte fort we passed. Takes about an hour and runs April to November. Superb.

Many of the kayakers near us were drifting further down the river to Beynac or beyond. You'll discover various little consortiums in this area of the valley that will teach you how to use a canoe or kayak. Then, they'll guide you down the river and bus you back to your car at your starting point. Once you disembark, you'll find plenty of irresistible eateries for lunch or dinner—or just an *apéritif* so you can sit and watch the river roll by. Later you can hop back onto your kayak until the next stop!

Rocamadour

As you come along the winding road toward Rocamadour (about an hour southeast of Sarlat), you may think you're lost in a wild forest. Suddenly, you'll come around the bend, however, and see one of the most stunning views on the planet: Rocamadour. Rocamadour is a glorious town, perched on the edge of a massive cliff, with chiseled buildings and a magnificent castle towering at the top of a limestone cliff. It absolutely takes your breath away.

Rocamadour is the second most visited site in France (after Mont St. Michel in Northern France). It's filled with revered chapels, ancient dwellings, quaint hotels, and fetching shops. Rocamadour seems to have literally been carved from the cliff face overlooking the unspoiled Alzou canyon below. Indeed, it's a beloved pilgrimage site that draws thousands who come for the spiritual succor or who simply want to soak up the beautiful ambience.

Here's how the legend of Rocamadour began. In 1166, a local man expressed interest in being buried beneath the threshold of the Chapel of the Virgin. But when the townsmen began to dig the grave, an older body was found. This body was placed at the altar to be honored with prayers, and from that time, miracles began to happen.

Conflicting stories suggest the body was that of disciple Zaccheus of Jericho who fled Palestine and set up home in nearby Limousin. In his later years, he retired to the Alzou Valley to preach. Ultimately, he was buried here. Other stories tell of a saintly hermit named Amadour who sought shelter in the magnificent outcroppings and finally died there. Soon, the *Occitan* expression *roc amatar* (he who likes rocks) came into the language. Others eventually came to live or pray here, and the name of this rocky sanctuary that grew into a village became Rocamadour.

Soon after the news of the miracles spread, Rocamadour became a famous Christian pilgrimage destination. Benedictine monks built a fortified abbey on the holy site plus a defense fortress on the top of the cliff. The Abbey of Rocamadour became a major stop on the pilgrimage road to Santiago de Compostela in Spain.

Thirty thousand people would show up on plenary indulgence days in the Middle Ages to be pardoned. Henry Plantagenet, King of England (and Eleanor of Aquitaine's spouse) was miraculously cured here when he knelt before the Virgin. Many, royal or not, have made the journey to Rocamadour over the centuries.

Like other important places in France, Rocamadour was invaded, plundered, and laid waste at various times, including the Wars of

Religion and the French Revolution. The only untouched elements were the miraculous Virgin statue and the church's bell which would spontaneously ring in acknowledgement of each miracle. In the 19th century, the Bishops of Cahors tried to revive the pilgrimage and ultimately rebuilt the abbey, the castle, the Saint-Amadour Sanctuary, and the Black Madonna shrine. The former episcopal palace now houses the Museum of Sacred Art.

Today, Rocamadour is basically a pedestrianized, ecclesiastical city. But there are delightful hotels (10 by last count) and fanciful shops if you're not partaking in the religious offerings. You can reach Rocamadour from the plateau above at Hospitalet Village or down below near Alzou Valley. There's a tiny train that can take you up and down from the  valley parking lots below. And there are various elevators and walking paths up and down the village. If you're bold, you can even drive up the steep hill into the village and park within it—if you can find a parking place! I happened to stay within the town at a hotel called Grand Hôtel Beau Site Notre Dame (Best Western) that thankfully offered onsite parking.

As you enter the town, you'll find yourself on a one-way main street lined with souvenir shops, restaurants, and boutique hotels. This leads you a few blocks further to the Grand Escalier or Via Sancta stairway that climbs up the episcopal city in 226 steps. At the top of the steps, you'll enter a beautiful *parvis* (open space) square that opens onto seven churches: Saint-Saviour's Basilica; Saint-Amadour's Church; the Chapel of Our Lady (home to the Black Madonna, so called because the silver plating has worn away and she's turned black from oxidation and candle smoke) rebuilt in 1479 as the Chapelle Notre-Dame; the three chapels of Saint-John the Baptist, Saint-Blaise, and Saint-Anne; and the saintly Saint-Michel Chapel.

I guarantee you'll have a marvelous experience if you decide to climb the Via Sancta up the hill to these churches. Pilgrims, to this day, often make this ascent, saying their rosary and kneeling at every step. (But it's not required!)

The Stations of the Cross walkway greets you after you continue the climb up the hill. Built with tree-lined switchbacks, this is truly a heaven-inspired pathway. As previously mentioned, I walked this path leisurely early one evening. Since there were very few people taking the path up to the top, I seemed to enter a serene bubble of contemplation as I strolled.

After passing the grotto of the Nativity and Holy Sepulchre, visitors walk the paved path to the next bend of the switchbacks. Each bend is marked with one of the magnificent Stations of the Cross. Finally at the top, the Cross of Jerusalem stands tall. The Penitential Pilgrims brought the cross all the way from the Holy land. Rocamadour is classed as a World Heritage Site by UNESCO as part of the Saint-James Way pilgrimage route. Even if you're not religious, this walk is a tranquil experience. I often think of it when I feel stressed—and it immediately calms me.

As for accommodations and dining opportunities in Rocamadour, there are lots of choices. You can choose from hotels and B&Bs up on the plateau above the town near or in Hospitalet. Within Rocamadour, are a variety of places to stay. One of my favorites is the Grand Hôtel Beau Site situated right in the middle of things.

The delightful Ariadna at the Grand Hôtel Beau Site saw to it that we enjoyed a most palatial room in the building overlooking the river. For a mere $45 dollars extra, our upgrade gave us a nearly 800-square-foot second floor suite with a magnificent jetted tub that opened onto a patio with French doors. Here, we could languish in the bubbles with the doors wide open and not be seen. Heaven. It was from this room that I watched the hot-air balloons rising just off my balcony. (It was a perfect respite for enjoying a glass of Bergerac wine as well.)

Rocamadour is the proverbial must-see locale in this vicinity. Just keep your wits about you when you visit. As you enter and leave Rocamadour, you'll encounter a number of turnouts that offer a stellar opportunity to pull over and snap some terrific photos. Be aware, however, that everyone else will be doing the same thing—so be careful not to get rear-ended as you stop to ponder spectacular Rocamadour. Above all, try a hot-air balloon ride from Rocamadour. You'll have a view of the Dordogne like nowhere else. And you'll fly unfettered in the quiet sky above this most celestial place.

Saint-Cirq-Lapopie

South of Rocamadour sits the most extraordinary village of Saint-Cirq-Lapopie (pronounced "San-Sear-La-Poopie"). It's located in the Lot region of the Dordogne. Saint-Cirq sits perched on the top of a rocky escarpment facing chalky cliffs. It's named for the young Saint-Cyr who was martyred along with his mother in Asia Minor during the reign of Diocletian. His effects were allegedly brought back by Saint Amadour. The La Popies, medieval lords, had a castle above the town that spread at its feet. The name was soon hyphenated to Saint-Cirq-Lapopie. As one of *Les Plus Beaux Villages de France*, many suggest Saint-Cirq is France's most pleasing locale.

During the Middle Ages, the town became a center for woodworking and related crafts. Until the late 19th century, craftsmen could still be seen at their lathes and tables in the tiny shop fronts set in small archways sprinkled throughout the town. Today, you can see some of these craftsmen's tiny alcoves abutting stone cottages; many of them have morphed into souvenir shops or enlarged to form inviting restaurants or ice cream shops. Cottages lining the streets often have corbelled façades, exposed beams, or bays with mullioned windows popular in the Renaissance.

Saint-Cirq was particularly loved by post impressionist painters like Henry Martin; many creatives came to live here, including famed writer and poet André Breton. Breton is most well known as the founder of Surrealism. The town is so petite you can see it in an hour or two unless the crowds are thick. More than 400,000 visitors come every year, so go early in the day. Of special note is the cliff next to the town where the ruins of the castle can be found. The view from the top gives you a marvelous view of the valley and all of Saint-Cirq.

On the adjacent hill as you wander through the tiny town, is a lovely fortified church clinging to the cliff face. Down below, boat rides are offered from Les Croisières de Saint-Cirq-Lapopie. Similar to the boats from La Roque-Gageac, these *gabarres* take riders along the river to see the "Seven Wonders of the Lot Valley" which includes Saint-Cirq up on the hill.

I particularly enjoyed Saint-Cirq's Musée Du Vin which is a wine shop, gourmet center, and wine museum all rolled into one. You can buy many treasures here, as well as wine in this alluring shop brimming with French treats. Some of the "booty" I carried home from this tantalizing shop appears in the section on shopping.

I also had a memorable lunch at Lou Bolat Restaurant where the wait staff moved as if on roller skates since it was so busy. This delightful *bistro* is perched prettily at the top of Saint-Cirq, offering you a panoramic view of the gardened village below. It was here I also met Kiki, France's most hyperactive pooch.

She arrived about 20 minutes after my companion and I sat down. Kiki's French "parents" were a very attractive French couple who'd arrived in a sleek Aston Martin. For a time Kiki, in her fetching red bandana, cavorted around the restaurant; all of us were entranced by her unfettered affection as she sniffed her way around our feet under the tables.

Finally, Kiki whizzed past my table for about the fourth time. Suddenly, she turned back and leapt into my arms. My photographer snapped this surprising picture. How cute is that? After lunch (during which Kiki was restrained at her owner's feet where I noticed she was fed bits of duck *confit*), we rose to leave. As we passed by her, Kiki's little body wiggled so hard with glee she starting pulling the table across the floor. Talk about French affection!

The town boasts a variety of accommodations. Of particular note are the Hotel le Saint-Cirq and the country inn Auberge Du Sombral.

Other dining venues include Le Gourmet Quercynois and L'Oustal. You can reach Saint-Cirq via various picturesque roads from Cahors, Sarlat, or the Languedoc. I especially advise taking your time arriving here. These country roads are so beautiful you'll want to stop frequently to enjoy the views!

Cave Systems (Lascaux/Pech Merle/Les Eyzies)

A young French lad named Marcel Ravidat was hiking through the Montignac hills one morning in 1940 with his dog, Robot. Robot, a born canine spelunker, nosed around some interesting dirt. He suddenly discovered a hole leading to a long cave shaft. He promptly fell in.

Tracked by Marcel and his friends, Robot quickly had company when the boys decided to follow him into the hole. (Are you surprised?) Inching along the dark shaft inside, Marcel and the others lit some oil lamps. They soon discovered they stood in a vast cave plastered with crude wall drawings. Life-like etchings—herds of horses galloping across the walls, great bulls suspended in action, reindeer raising horned heads in rich shades of reds, black, and yellows—stared back at them.

The boys had discovered Lascaux, one of the "artistic wonders of the prehistoric world." Known as the "Sistine Chapel of Cave Art," the Lascaux cave contains 2,000 individual images more than 17,000 years old. There are also mysterious signs and geometric symbols, as well as a human figure with a bird's head known as the Wounded Hunter. Man was apparently creating art here long before the Pyramids or Stonehenge were even ideas.

Man has occupied the Dordogne since humans first appeared on earth it seems. While Medieval French knights and their damsels left evidence of torrid medieval life in the great castles on land, much earlier men and women of France etched colorful evidence of themselves in the deep caverns below. In these subterranean art galleries, primitive man satisfied an irrepressible urge to depict the world around him. And he used what crude tools he could find: bone, rock, berry juice, soot, water, spit, and blood.

One of the great intoxications of the Dordogne is the chance to ponder primitive man in his own setting. To learn how he evolved through trial and error. To see how he projected himself into his art, etchings, and tool inventions. Many of the Dordogne cave systems are open to the public, and the visits are vivid experiences. Descending into one of these Dordogne caves where prehistoric man actually lived and created makes ancient history real. But when you visit his artistic habitat, where his *own hand* appears before you as in Pech-Merle cave, you'll come face to face with the flesh and blood of your ancestors.

Talk about a time warp. If you too decide to take the journey through one of dozens of cave systems, you'll find the Dordogne area honeycombed with them. The Vézère River Valley—the Valley of the Caves—in Périgord Noir is permeated with spectacular rock dwellings, grottos, and caverns knit together in a huge underground network. Here are the caves of legend: Lascaux II (a "copy" since the original Lascaux I has begun to degrade), Grotte de Rouffignac (where a tiny electric train chugs through six miles of caverns), La Grotte de Bara-Bahau, Grotte du Grand Roc, Grotte de Font-de-Gaume, and several others. Inside are hundreds of Paleolithic cave paintings.

Nearby is Les Eyzies-de-Tayac, another UNESCO World Heritage site. It's affectionately known as the "World Capital of Prehistory." This is a tiny village tucked under a vast limestone cliff that carries a big reputation. Five skeletons of Cro-Magnon man were discovered in a rock shelter here in 1868; thus began the quest that uncovered hundreds of sites throughout the Dordogne. Today, the Musée National de Préhistorie is located in Les Eyzies where you can learn everything about prehistoric man and also see the fantastic stalactite displays. All of these caves are easily accessible by car; many visitors choose to bike along the valley and enjoy the *confit,* truffles, *foie gras* and Bergerac wine along the way, however. Lascaux Hotel in Montignac is particularly good for cave lovers.

Slightly north of Saint-Cirq about seven miles (and about 30 miles south of Rocamadour) lies one of the many extraordinary cave systems in the greater Dordogne area. It's called Le Grotte du Pech Merle. www.pechmerle.com/english/. There's an excellent video on the website under the Caves & Prehistory tab that will give you a look inside Pech Merle and the specific artwork and natural limestone "sculptures." Despite the commentary being in French, ignore the over voice and simply enjoy the spectacular visuals.

My group tour of Pech Merle was remarkable since the museum staff has gone to great lengths to create a very personal story arc around the cave and the museum pieces. Once down inside the remarkable dripping caves penetrated by only our guide's lights, we learned how family groups clustered in certain areas of the cave chambers, maybe using the stalactite pillars as room dividers. The cave drawings here not only depict mammoths, bison, horses, fish, and more, they depict prehistoric life 20,000 years ago: love, romance, birth, tribal rituals, family life, reverence for nature. You'll also see a variety of hieroglyphics of unknown meaning.

We witnessed ingenious examples of personal creativity here: animal drawings using the crevices and crannies to create three-dimensional art; vivid colors ground from plants or rock dust, then splashed on walls in deep black, blue, red, ochre, and yellow; pooling limestone "pearls" piled together to create limestone "sculpture;" etched human figures in full form; and footprints and handprints pressed into hardening floor mud or pressed into crude pigments, then slapped onto the walls, floors, and ceilings like signatures.

These ancient "selfies" are the remains of man's drive to record his presence. To say, I WAS HERE. I found Pech Merle captivating, chilling, and above all, profound. The experience took me back to a visit I made as a teenager to Carlsbad Caverns in New Mexico. I was only mildly interested in those stalactites and stalagmites

shaped by dripping limestone. Psychologically, I was pretty detached.

But when I saw Pech Merle, where prehistoric man intimately depicted his life and the world around him, it became personal for me. I reacted subjectively, intuiting what it must have been like to dwell here. And this was relatively easy. I stood in the same chambers, on the same cold, dank stones, where primitive man etched his life despite the inhospitable conditions. I sensed the creeping dampness penetrating my coat. And I felt the airless claustrophobia that primitive man must have experienced even as he scratched out his crude drawings by firelight. The urge to create clearly overwhelmed him.

Soon, we came into the most important Pech Merle chamber. The guide shined his flashlight on the wall, and we beheld an extraordinary sight: a pair of prehistoric handprints. It was as if they'd been placed there an hour before. We've all seen cave drawings of bison, cattle, and horses. But to see a flesh and blood handprint of a real person on the wall caused a chill to snake up my spine to my head. I could almost feel prehistoric man's breath on my neck.

Interestingly, there's a startling development regarding these cave drawings and handprints (shown) which have always been believed to have been painted by men. Archaeologist Dean Snow of Pennsylvania State University analyzed hand stencils found in eight cave sites in France and Spain, including Pech Merle. By comparing the relative lengths of certain fingers, Snow determined that three-quarters of the handprints were female. He suggests that cave*men* probably did most of the hunting, but it was most likely the cave*women* who were hauling the meat into the cave, and while they were cutting, cooking, and serving the spoils, they were taking a little time to etch their lives on the walls. Early French *décor*? Or sacred art? Most likely both.

Unfortunately, photography is not allowed inside the actual caves for obvious reasons. But the Museum of Prehistory at the cave entrance provides copies of many of the underground images. There are two permanent exhibitions of more than 1,000 artifacts (tools, weapons, jewelry), plus a film, as well as temporary exhibitions and events that change seasonally. Don't miss the opportunity to visit one of these spectacular caves. The experience is incomparable.

Périgueux

The very busy municipality called Périgueux is the largest city in the Dordogne and also its capital. Located in the River Isle Valley, Périgueux has two distinct sections. First, is the Saint-Front with its Byzantine-style Cathédrale Saint-Front and busy downtown area brimming with old houses, shops, and restaurants. Second, is the Cité with the Church of Saint-Etienne at its center; here Roman remains can be found at the Vésunna Museum. The two sections merged, creating today's thriving metropolis of 30,000 residents. Périgueux reminds me of Lyon due its high volume of traffic and citification. But it has a more intimate feel—and far less traffic.

On the other hand, like many of the small towns in the Dordogne, Périgueux has a delightful bustling downtown in St. Front that's pedestrian-friendly and filled with fun shops and bistros. This enclave is located in the tiny streets between the remarkable Cathedral Saint-Front and the Musée d'Art et d'Archéoligie du Périgord.

To get there, you'll pass through the old artisans and merchants St. Front district that's being given a major facelift. A conservation program is under way to restore the Renaissance façades, medieval houses, courtyards, staircases, and ancient shops. (This is similar to what occurred in busy Sarlat, but Périgueux is just now getting the "star treatment.") As I mounted the steps through this organized chaos, carefully dodging the cement mixers and jackhammers, an 80-year-old French lady passed me, then stopped. She apologized for her downtown being such a mess. I was struck by how kind she was as an "unofficial ambassador" of Périgueux—and of how much she wanted her beloved city to be presentable to strangers like me. I almost thought she was going to invite me home for tea!

I was following one of two historical walks that a pair of friendly gals in the tourism office recommended. (Always go by the tourism office in each town or village if you can. These people always have the list of places to see, maps, and favorite restaurants. Tip: I often ask them where they go for lunch or dine for special occasions. Then I go there. No tourist haunts for me!)

Today, I was on the Medieval/Renaissance walk that wends its way through the downtown (about one to two hours walking). On this delightful walk, you'll pass a variety of popular sights, including the Mataguerre Tower, St. Louis Square (where from November until March the "fattened poultry" and truffle market is held), the market squares of Place de L'Hôtel de Ville and Place du Coderc, the Fayolle Residence, The Consuls House, Cloiseter Square, and the sublime Cathedral Saint-Front.

I enjoyed a serene morning in stunning Cathedral Saint-Front. The Cathedral is one of the largest in Southwestern France. Several previous churches had risen, then fallen on this site. A third basilica was completed in 1173 in an uncommon (in France) Byzantine style with a dome and ground plan in the form of a Greek cross. This cathedral, therefore, somewhat resembles Saint-Mark's church in Venice. During the Wars of Religion, the church was pillaged. When restoration began around 1852, it was reconstructed in Second Empire style by Abadie. Abadie would later use this same style for the design of the Sacré-Cœur Basilica in Paris. So it has a remarkable appearance combining radically different architectural styles.

Inside, I had the lovely opportunity of watching a very patient priest tutoring a group of elementary school children about the spiritual path. The French teachers had seated this little group of about 15 at the feet of a large dais; the white-robed priest was trying in vain to hold their attention. (Trying to focus a group of kids this age looks a lot like herding cats no matter what country you're in.) Unfortunately, I was unable to take any photos of this classic—and hilarious—scene.

My second memorable Périgueux experience was with delightful chef and restaurant owner Patrick Fuega. His restaurant, Le Clos Saint Front, was highly recommended by our hotel (the Mercure Périgueux Centre.) And I had a double recommendation from the gals at the tourism office who nodded approvingly when I said I was headed there for lunch.

Despite the fact we were the first guests to arrive, Chef Patrick was so delighted to see us that he seated us himself at his best table. Then, he chatted with us throughout our entire two-hour lunch. Chef Patrick explained what and how he was cooking each dish AND then served it to us himself with a special flair. Course after delicious course came and went. But I confess my favorite was dessert—chocolate mousse cake with pomegranate sorbet. Chef Patrick did not disappoint.

Le Clos Saint Front also features the fine artwork of sculptor Jean-Alexandre Delattre. This is another example of multiple artisans combining efforts to create a beautiful ambience for French cuisine. Above all, Chef Patrick was a delight from start to finish. I'd highly recommend this pretty restaurant where you can get fine French cuisine at an affordable price.

The other popular walking tour in Périgueux is the Gallo-Roman ruins to the west. Here you'll see the remains of the Roman Amphitheatre, the Norman Gate, the Barrier Castle, and the Vésunna Temple. The excellent Vésunna Musée Gallo-Roman containing first century treasures is also situated here. When you stay in Périgueux, it's perhaps best to seek out accommodations between both the Roman ruins side and the urban downtown.

While you're there, you can enjoy high- and low-end shopping at all the regular French shops. And of course the town hosts a variety of open-air markets to choose from on any given day for your Gariguette strawberries, fresh vegetables, pungent cheeses, cured meats and sausages, and freshly baked breads.

The Dordogne in Sum

"The southwest of France is a treasure trove of bijoux villages, spirit lifting landscapes and superb food and wine experience...You can sleep in fairy tale *Châteaux*, meander through the region's spectacular rivers, visit picturesque hamlets and taste some of the best traditional cuisine in France. Best of all, this is an exceptionally friendly area where you will receive a truly warm welcome."

—Cellar Tours

"*La Dordogne*"—some call it the cradle of civilization in France. It's certainly a spell-binding locale where much of the best that France has to offer is within a few miles end to end: rich food, dramatic history, *châteaux* galore, enchanting villages, breathtaking caves, rock paintings, lovely gardens, delightful wines, and convivial people.

Most of all, the Dordogne has atmosphere. Many who travel here come back again and again—or even return to retire here. Or buy holiday homes. Or stay for three months at a time—or more. It's a destination location with an infinite variety of experiences to offer.

I find it fascinating that travel pro Rick Steves says he thinks the Dordogne "seems to draw a more sophisticated traveler...low-key and thoughtful people who appreciate nature, culture, and cuisine." I don't know if he's right, but I do know I very much like the idea.

Many people, especially those of other European countries, even come to marry here, such is the allure. They plan a destination wedding—and take a house for all their guests. Then they book a *château* for their nuptials. They cater in the finest French cuisine. They're married with a castle as a backdrop. And they depart in near-royal splendor with a cache of Dordogne memories to cherish for the rest of their lives.

Still others come for the biking, hiking, kayaking, and canoeing. They rise to the challenge of the rustic Dordogne. Others come on spiritual pilgrimages, for there's much that's sacred about this land. Or they come to sample the fine wines. Or the fragrant cuisine built around the noble goose and duck.

Most of all, families come to enjoy the fine family living here. You can rent delightful *gîtes* (cottages or apartments or small homes) that can accommodate your whole brood. There's fun for all ages—and the offerings are endless for every age group.

Above all, this is a place to "just be." To sit on your balcony or in a sidewalk *café* and watch Dordogne life saunter by. One visitor wrote, "If you love to lose yourself in the life of the places you visit, this is the perfect place for you."

I couldn't have said it better myself.

Part Five:
Bordeaux

"Bordeaux...fascinating, magnetic, even hypnotic. Our region and its riches cast a spell that captivates every corner of the world."

—Bordeaux Tourism Board

The lush Bordeaux region sits regally on the edge of the Atlantic in Southwestern France. It's a magical nexus of wine-based delights found nowhere else on the planet.

Bordeaux is a verdant territory, nourished by gentle rivers and anchored by hectare after hectare of splendid vines. It's also bounded by vast stretches of resort-friendly beaches, hailed by many surfers as one of the best surf locales in Europe. While Bordeaux's beachfront dunes are home to succulent oyster beds, its inland acreage is festooned with ancient forests and rich agricultural enclaves. But primarily Bordeaux is one of the world's top wine-growing regions, fueled by a thriving viticulture that arguably leads the wine world today.

As a region, Bordeaux is the seat of an historical and religious power shaped by the adventures of many: the intrigues of great queen Eleanor of Aquitaine, the exploits of Gascogne musketeers, the travails of religious pilgrims, and the machinations of English and French patriots who spilt their blood on this regal land for centuries.

As a city, Bordeaux is also many things. It's a splendid modern capital with high-speed trains, urban trams, delightful walking paths, and modern shopping streets that feature the likes of Galeries Lafayette and Etam. But it's also "the jewel of Southwestern France" with an elegant 18th century architectural profile now burnished to a 21st century luster.

A legendary political focal point, Bordeaux city served as the seat of the powerful Aquitaine territory even before the 1100s when mega-landed Eleanor married her soon-to-be-king of England Henry. Soon, the two reined over a French/English empire famed as much for courtly love as cruelty and bloodshed. Later, in the 20th century, Bordeaux became the go-to capital of France when Paris was eclipsed in two world wars.

Though Bordeaux's political power has given way to the Paris powerhouse, she enjoys a formidable position in France tourism and wine culture. In the modern era, a youthful culture permeates urbane Bordeaux. The downtown bubbles with modern nighttime excitement as well as classical daytime elegance. What's more, it's the fifth largest tourist destination in France.

Visitors come for the fine wines. They arrive for the gastronomic abundance in its oysters, cheeses, delectable desserts, and local beef. They linger for the endless variety of activities that appeal: water lovers come for the boating, surfing, kayaking, water skiing, and windsurfing; land enthusiasts arrive for the hiking, canyoning, cycling, golf, and horseback riding through the spectacular countryside; and spa goers rejuvenate with the sea-based thalassotherapy, hydrotherapy, and vino therapy. Spiritually minded travelers can navigate pilgrimage routes like the ones taken by Saint James that traverse the land while bolstering the soul. And of course, wine worshippers have more than 10,000 wine producers bottling close to 70 million cases of wine per vintage to make the pilgrimage for vast quantities of liquid heaven.

When I first made my way to Bordeaux—part pilgrimage, part wine adventure—I drove in from Barcelona, Spain. I sped west toward the setting sun along the superhighway that stretches across Southern France. My little European Citroën soon entered the Bordeaux region via small roads cutting through the wine fields of Saint-Émilion.

Grapes!

Around my head swirled grape aromas and earthy smells of soil, freshly mowed grass, and fermenting juices. It felt like ripe molecules were seeping into my pores as I passed by the wine *châteaux*. When I finally sped over the sun-drenched Pont de Pierre Bridge that arches into Bordeaux city proper, it was like coming into a succulent world apart from the rest of France.

Glancing over the bridge's edge, I saw the languorous Garonne River rolling beneath. And, as I came off the bridge and sped along the city's long quay, I beheld the regal 18th century Bourse buildings and Cailhau Gate fronting a most magical of French "kingdoms." I soon discovered that Bordeaux is a kingdom whose power lies mostly now in the noble grape, but whose fairytale history makes it ripe for discovery.

History & Landscape

The complex Bordeaux region consists of several distinct areas. First is the bustling city of Bordeaux perched on the banks of the Garonne, coupled with the fabulous Bordeaux vineyard areas like Saint-Émilion.

Second is the legendary Médoc peninsula, home to world-renowned vineyards like Château Margaux and Lafite Rothschild, plus Arcachon, the sandy home of oyster and shellfish production. Third is the Landes des Gascogne Regional Park, a 5,000-square-mile wild-life preserve with a strip of forest that protects the precious vineyards from the winds off the Atlantic. Fourth is the Le Pays de l'Adour area (southern section of Les Landes) encompassing the spa towns of Dax and Aire-sur-l'Adour. Fifth is the Basque coastline including resort and surf towns Biarritz and Saint-Jean-de-Luz.

Sixth is the sparsely populated French Pyrénées just east of the coastline at the border with Spain. It stretches into the Béarn further east in the Pyrénées; this area is famous for dramatic backdrops and cultural history. And last is the Lot-et-Garonne further inland where the Lot and Garonne Rivers meet and where delectable local produce like Pruneaux d'Agen is grown. The general area (plus parts of the Languedoc and the Dordogne) is referred to as the "Aquitaine." The Aquitaine was historically both a kingdom and a duchy, with wildly fluctuating boundaries throughout the centuries.

Located in the southwest corner of France, the Bordeaux area sits at the 45th parallel. It's edged by the Atlantic Ocean which brings the salty air and warming Gulfstream to the peninsula. The peninsula is cut by the Gironde River (actually an estuary) whose mouth provides a port to the sea. Then, its meandering path divides the land as it spills southward into Left and Right Banks.

The flat, low-lying Gironde southland is called the Left Bank. It encompasses the wine-growing regions of Médoc and Graves. The sloping land on the north side forms the Right Bank, from which two tributaries, the Garonne and Dordogne Rivers, flow into the fertile areas of Pomerol, Saint-Émilion, and Entre-Deux-Mers.

The Garonne continues on past Bordeaux City proper, then flows south to the districts of Graves, Pessac-Léognan, and Sauternes. In general, gravel soil dominates the Left Bank; it holds the sun's heat and warms the Cabernet Sauvignon grapes that are crushed to become the heart of the much-worshipped red Bordeaux wines. The Right Bank soil leans toward limestone and clay. Like a thirsty sponge, the soil makes a succulent host for Merlot grapes, as well as Cabernet Franc, plus Sauvignon Blanc and Sémillion grapes that go into making dry white wines. All of these rich but varied wine growing areas work to produce today's most pedigreed vintages; but all have their origin in a tumultuous history of blood, sweat, and sacrifice.

The 3rd century B.C. saw raids in Bordeaux by Germanic tribes and Celts. The Celts particularly brought with them the beginnings of civilization through active trading and wine cultivation. They eventually established a thriving settlement called "Burdigala" on the banks of the Garonne River. Later, it grew into the international darling known as Bordeaux city.

Julius Caesar's forces conquered this coveted land in the 1st century B.C.—but only after a ferocious fight with local tribesmen. Aquitania, probably named after a local Roman settlement "Aquae Augustae" or from the Basque word "Aquis," became one of the four provinces of Roman Gaul. At the time, these provinces stretched from the Pyrénées to the Loire River (west of Paris). Roman roads soon cut through the Aquitaine terrain. Massive stone settlements grew block-by-block, while vast tracks of wine vines were sown into the fertile soil. Christianity spread. Retired Romans and their families settled on the rich land as the mighty Roman Empire declined and multiple invasions pummeled Bordeaux.

By the time Charlemagne was crowned Holy Roman Emperor in 800, he'd created a relatively united kingdom of Aquitaine. His successors regularly had to fight off gutsy Norman invaders, however. Though various counts ruled as powerful barons of the region, the undaunted raiders continued to destabilize the area. When the newest Duke of Aquitaine, the "troubadour Prince Guillaume IX," came to power in 1086, he fathered a great dynasty that would reach its zenith in the adventures of his granddaughter, Eleanor of Aquitaine.

Eleanor was an extraverted, worldly young woman reared in cosmopolitan Poitiers in northern Aquitaine. An effervescent girl, she was reared to hunt, ride, and hawk. Though her native tongue was *Poitevin* (one of the regional *Langue d'oïl*), she was also taught to read and speak Latin. She was well versed in music and literature. When her brother and mother tragically died in 1130, pretty Eleanor became the heir presumptive to the Duchy of Aquitaine—nearly one third of France. Deluged with suitors, Eleanor ultimately was married off by her grandfather in 1137 to Prince Louis, the 17-year-old Dauphin of France.

In that moment, the entire future of France shifted.

Duchess Eleanor came to the marriage with her huge dowry consisting of Aquitaine, Gascony, and Périgord. The marriage contract, however, stipulated that Eleanor's lands would remain in her hands, independent of France, until her oldest son became both King of the Franks *and* the Duke of Aquitaine. Within days of the marriage, her new husband's father, "Louis the Fat," expired.

When the newly married prince suddenly became King Louis VII of France, the couple came to great power. Eleanor made a dazzling new bride; Louis reportedly adored her. She could sing the songs of the troubadours and even wrote music and lyrics herself. The royal couple settled in Paris, but Eleanor maintained a court in Bordeaux which she visited often. But she drew criticism from the church elders for her flamboyant behaviors. Louis too began to question Eleanor's rebellious ways.

In 1145, the pious Louis declared he would go on crusade—and Eleanor insisted on going along. Stories abound that she and her ladies-in-waiting dressed as Amazons—perhaps an early French fashion trend. Records do confirm that she had loads of cumbersome baggage which may have contributed to the disastrous outcome of the crusade.

Besieged on all sides by attackers, the crusade failed. Poor military strategist Louis and headstrong Eleanor grew estranged. When rumors floated that Eleanor was having an affair with her flirtatious Uncle Raymond who ruled the court at Antioch, Louis had had enough. In 1152, the king annulled the marriage—remarkably after two children. Eleanor was still delightfully young, however—rich and powerful at a mere 30 years of age. Much to the consternation of the French royals, she also retained her massive land dowry.

Marriage-eligible Eleanor now became a prime target for kidnapping; in those days bride snatching was an acceptable way of securing a wife—and her lands. It was no surprise when two determined suitors accosted Eleanor as she made a dash for Poitiers. Theobald V, Count of Blois and Geoffrey, Count of Nantes, fought hard, but Eleanor outwitted them. Barely escaping, Eleanor quickly sent word to

Geoffrey's more dashing brother Henry Plantagenet, whom she'd met and flirted with at court. (Some reports indicate that Eleanor, in fact, had engineered the divorce from gloomy Louis so she could marry captivating Henry. This was despite his being several years younger than she was.) "Come and marry me—now," she ordered. Henry must have obeyed forthwith, for just eight weeks after her annulment, Eleanor and Henry were married in regal splendor in Bordeaux.

In a second shrewd political stroke, Eleanor had wed Henry Plantagenet, Duke of Normandy and Anjou—thus uniting the Aquitaine with the Angevin Empire which now ruled England. (Henry ignored the rumors that Eleanor had also had an affair with his father, Geoffrey V, Count of Anjou; but anyone who's seen the movie *The Lion in Winter* knows it perhaps became a bone of contention later on.)

Eleanor, whose greatness was not to be denied, became an even greater queen when young Henry became King of England in 1154. By that time, Eleanor's vast dowry extended from the Atlantic coast to the river Rhône—including the ancient lands of Périgord, Quercy, and parts of Gascony. Together with Henry's large holdings, the pair controlled a massive tract of land extending from the English Channel to the Pyrénées.

The union was conflicted, but fruitful. As Queen of England, Eleanor bore Henry five sons and three daughters. Throughout their fractious marriage, Henry philandered. Eleanor distracted herself with feeding her considerable political appetite and cementing her power over the Anjou power brokers. These power brokers mostly despised Henry. But they revered Eleanor as one of their own. Reports vary, but history suggests Eleanor and her grown daughter Marie also presided over the famous "Court of Love" at Poitiers where troubadours sang of courtly love and ardent knights perfected the art of chivalry.

Henry was constantly absent, fending off potential usurpers throughout England and France. Eleanor grew more powerful year after year. Soon her adolescent sons—young Henry, Richard, Geoffrey, and John—were chomping at the bit to steal some of aging Henry's power. Eleanor sided with the boys.

Inevitably, Henry, Eleanor, and their sons became entrenched in a power struggle within and without the family that reverberated through hundreds of years. In 1173, Henry ultimately imprisoned the meddling Eleanor in a drafty castle in England; she remained locked up for 16 years. Meanwhile, her sons young Henry, Richard the Lionheart (her favorite), Geoffrey, and John squabbled for power.

Old King Henry II finally expired in 1189. Richard, then later, John, became kings of England. (Richard made Bordeaux wine his everyday beverage by the way. Most of the subsequent kings of England followed suit.) Both Richard and John struggled with the machinations of their relative and frenemy, King Philip II of France who wanted the Aquitaine for himself—and for France. Various English and French factions in the Aquitaine continued to fight for dominance. History lovers will know that a kowtowed King John signed the Magna Carta near Windsor, England in June of 1215; this great document serves as the first inklings of constitutional law granting non-royals legal rights in England and elsewhere.

And Eleanor, who lived to the advanced age of 82, left her mark as one of the most formidable women of the ages. She lived flamboyantly, bucking the prevailing traditions of the day—particularly for women. In the end, she humbly plead the case for her legacy, especially to the clergy:

"Pitiful and pitied by no one, why have I come to the ignominy of this detestable old age, who was ruler of two kingdoms, mother of two kings? "

— Eleanor of Aquitaine, *Third letter to Pope Celestine* (1193)

But all remained bloody chaos in France in the centuries after her death. Parts of France saw themselves as English; others saw themselves as French. Warring *bastides* (fortified towns) and castles sprang up as various French or English factions claimed dominion over certain areas of Southwestern France during the tumultuous years to come. This is why perpetually-at-war Beynac and Castelnaud castles were built, for example, in the Dordogne.

By the late 1300s, Bordeaux had become a large city—so large that, after London, it was the second most populated British-controlled municipality in the world. Despite the political turmoil that continued throughout the Aquitaine over the years, the Bordeaux region itself essentially stayed under British oversight for more than 300 years; in fact, it was the Brits who worked to commercialize the Bordeaux wine industry. Enterprising British wine distributors began exporting vast quantities of the highly prized Saint-Émilion wines to England around 1302. This was primarily done to quench the bottomless thirst of King Edward I who loved the rich wines. (At this time, the Médoc hadn't really been developed.)

The Hundred Years' War and the Wars of Religion continued to destabilize the area until the 16th century—but the wine trade boomed. Soon, entrepreneurial Germans and Dutch merchants joined in the marketing and distribution process. The burgeoning wine trade was soon delivering product at record levels, especially to the interconnected royal families of Europe who loved the formidable wines.

The next two centuries saw the growth of maritime and colonial trade in Bordeaux, plus an ever-expanding viticulture and significant swell in popular spa resorts for the wealthy. Bordeaux became a port overwhelmed by busy merchant ships.

The Dutch were especially instrumental in getting Bordeaux on track to produce great quantities of wine for thirsty consumers who by this time also included anyone—royal or not—who could afford it. By the 1600s, the clever Dutch had come up with the idea to burn sulfur in barrels. This aided the wines' ability to last as it made its way in great ships across the Atlantic to England, Holland, and elsewhere. Interestingly, it was not until the 1800s that Louis Pasteur explained the benefits of sulfur as an anti-bacterial agent that could protect the wine. All the Dutch knew was that they'd transformed a perishable product that "had to be drunk quickly" into a *vin de garde*, a "wine to keep." They also stumbled upon the beneficial effects of wine aging that gives vintages such a remarkable bouquet after years in a cellar.

The Dutch additionally tackled the problem of getting the wine across the swampy, marshy land that plagued much of the Bordeaux area at the time. It was they who figured out how to drain the unusable Bordeaux lands through a series of dikes and pumping stations. This pumping network made it easier to transport goods and people.

In doing so, they also created much more land for vines and other plantings. (You can still see this system of dikes and pumping stations in operation today across Bordeaux.)

The Dutch, as well as Germans and entrepreneurial Brits, particularly enhanced the role of *négociants*, or wine developer/ distributors. A replica of one of the hardy *négociant* merchant ships is located in the *Bordeaux Musée Vin et du Négoce* (Négociant Museum). These wine merchants provided the marketing pipeline to produce and package the wines for the vineyards; the vineyards at the time only produced the grapes and placed the blended juice in barrels. (Most of the wine estate owners were members of the royal family during this century. They were not interested in the mundane aspects of bottling and distributing their harvests "for the people.")

The *négociants* would take the barreled wine and either bottle it or sell it on to auction houses who would in turn sell downstream to wine merchants. By the late 1600s, specific regions and brands like Haut-Brion, Margaux, Lafite, and Latour began to develop name recognition with this merchant stratum, as well as the general public.

The *négociant* idea expanded in the early 1700s with such founding firms as Nathaniel Johnston, Schröder & Schÿler, and Lawton that remain in business today. They established their business operations on the edge of Bordeaux city in an area called the Chartrons district. In narrow, multi-storied brick warehouses, they handled the packaging and distribution of the wine all over the world. You can still visit some of the original *négociant* enclaves in the Chartrons at the museum that's practically within walking distance of downtown Bordeaux. More than 300 successful *négociant* firms still operate in Bordeaux today, plus 93 wine brokers.

These early wine brokers had to deal mostly with wine in barrels at first. The invention of the glass bottle to store wine and the cork stopper to seal it didn't occur until the 18th century, and it was not widely used until the 19th century. (The wood barrel has been a hardy invention. The Gauls were the first to use them 2,000 years ago to replace the Roman amphoras or jugs that were impractical for transporting on ships sailing across vast bodies of water. A modern oak Bordeaux barrel contains about 60 gallons of wine or the equivalent volume of 25 cases of 12 bottles each.)

By 1725, specific wine appellation boundaries were drawn. The congregated areas were known as the *Vignoble de Bordeaux* (vineyards of Bordeaux). Consumers and merchants began to buy wines from their preferred appellations whose labeling began to show the region and area where the wine was produced. Wealthy Bordeaux land owners and members of the royal family quickly began building fabulous estate buildings and expanding their vineyards. The Bordeaux coastline was rapidly developed with new road construction, new businesses, and homes of all sizes. The marshlands were managed by planting pines in such places as the Landes region. The population tripled in size.

When the French Revolution broke out in the 18th century, the common people rose up to take power over their Aquitaine. They marginalized the aristocracy and created a commerce system built for the people, by the people. Bordeaux *châteaux* and vineyards were soon confiscated from the royals. Sometimes the *négociants* themselves took over the estates or arranged to buy them outright.

Influential Americans also found their way to Bordeaux. While Thomas Jefferson served as ambassador to France, he visited Bordeaux in 1787 for a week on horseback, tasting wine all over the region. Then, he journeyed home to Virginia and compiled his own guide to the Bordeaux vineyards. He particularly enjoyed Château Rauzan-Ségla's wines and ordered several cases to take back with him. Jefferson is known today as "America's first wine connoisseur."

Jefferson's visits to Bordeaux are recorded at several Bordeaux wineries—among them are many of those that made the 1855 *Grands Crus Classés* classification list. Jefferson was a particular lover of red wine—and he spared no expense when it came to drinking the best he could find. In his book *From Undaunted Courage: Meriwether Lewis, Thomas Jefferson, and the Opening of the American West*, Stephen E. Ambrose notes several facts regarding Jefferson and his wine interests. Jefferson—philosopher, politician, and farmer—took up residence in the president's house in 1801 after his inauguration as the 3rd President of the United States. And, as Ambrose notes: "Jefferson ran the place with only 11 servants (Abigail Adams had needed 30!) brought up from Monticello. There were no more powdered wigs, and much less ceremony. Washington and Adams, according to Republican critics, had kept up almost a royal court. Jefferson substituted Republican simplicity—to a point. He had a French chef and French wines he personally selected. His salary was $25,000 per year—a princely sum—but the expenses were also great. In 1801, Jefferson spent $6,500 for provisions and groceries, $2,700 for servants (some of whom were liveried), $500 for [Meriwether] Lewis's [explorer] salary, and $3,000 for wine."

The golden age of Bordeaux is considered to be the 18th century. Many downtown buildings (about 5,000), including those on the quays, are from this period. Victor Hugo reportedly found the town so captivating that he said, "take Versailles, add Antwerp, and you have Bordeaux." Baron Haussmann, a long-time prefect of Bordeaux, used Bordeaux's 18th century big-scale rebuilding as a model when he was asked by Emperor Napoleon III to transform the chaotic, slovenly medieval Paris into a "modern" capital that would make France proud.

During the industrious 19th century, the development of railways boosted tourism as well as trade in Bordeaux. The fertile wine-growing areas had expanded by this time to many hectares of profitable vineyards. The first classifications of wine, drafted in 1725, were expanded in 1855 with the *Grands Crus* of the Médoc. The vast wine estates were taking maximum advantage of the maritime climate and fertile soil to produce some of the best wines on the planet. The English were also busy reaping the wine profits of the area; they were shipping massive quantities of the much-prized red wines—dubbed "claret"—to

thirsty connoisseurs back in the British Isles.

When World War I broke out in the 20th century, many young men from the Bordeaux region lost their lives, and the population waned. Later, Bordeaux city became the stopgap capital when Paris went to war in 1914 and again in 1940 (until Petain moved his government to Vichy). During World War II, German troops marched into Bordeaux after the capitulation of France. But much of the countryside remained unoccupied until 1942. The rugged forests and vast countryside proved perfect hiding places for the French Resistance; guerrilla war ensued with the occupying Germans until peace was declared in 1945. Many modern museums in the area hail the Resistance heroes and heroines.

Bordeaux and its environs also have a legendary history as the site for many religious pilgrimages. When the tomb of Saint James the Great, the first apostle to be martyred, was rediscovered in Santiago de Compostela in Northwestern Spain, a church was built in commemoration. Soon, pilgrims were flocking to the site via Southwestern France, resting in hostels and visiting holy places along the way. These hardy souls, often dressed in heavy gray capes and broad-brimmed hats, carried long staves with a scallop shell as a badge. These scallop emblems are called *Coquille Saint-Jacques* to this day. And the symbol marks the trail of Saint James at various places along the way.

Many individuals still make the pilgrimage from Northern France through Southwestern France on their way to Spain. Today's pilgrims, however, are sometimes in mini-cars or on high-tech racing bicycles—but some still traverse the holy roads on foot. On the whole, I'd suggest a certain religious zeal characterizes the entire Bordeaux area whether it's for the heavenly insight, *vinoble* delights, or culinary ecstasies.

People & Lifestyle

As both a city and a region, Bordeaux has a multi-faceted character. The old city itself was long called *La Belle Endormie* (Sleeping Beauty) due to its winding, unnavigable streets and soot-coated 18th century build-ings. She found a 21st century prince to reawaken her beauty in the form of Alain Juppé, former French Prime Minister. Juppé became Bordeaux's

visionary mayor in 2006. He spearheaded a major revitalization of downtown Bordeaux (shown), modernized the transportation system, and helped create an environment for modern commercialization while maintaining the city's status as an historic marvel.

Today, Bordeaux is a glistening, urbane metropolis. She has burnished neo-classical buildings, pedestrian-friendly byways, and fabulous shopping streets like Rue Sainte-Catherine that remind me a lot of Paris. (Rue Sainte-Catherine is the longest pedestrian-zone shopping street in Europe today.) The city has delightful riverside jogging paths that invite a stroll or a run any time, day or night. Elegant parks open up every few blocks. And there's the high-tech public transport system that whisks 240,000 *Bordelais* citizens around town.

The city's extensive collection of ancient buildings number 362. These *monuments historiques* have earned Bordeaux the UNESCO World Heritage designation. (Only Paris has more.) Among these are the Esplanade des Quinconces (the largest public square in Europe), the Porte Cailhau Bridge, the Grand Théâtre (a large neoclassical theater built in the 18th century), the Place de la Bourse, and Saint-André Cathedral built in 1096. One modern addition to the Bordeaux beautification was the installation of the water mirror fountain (Miroir d'Eau de Bordeaux) opposite the Place de la Bourse. This fountain is a marvel, day or night, since it sometimes spews water delicately up in varying patterns. At other times, surreal fog wafts up creating a smokey effect perfect for photography.

But 21st century wine-centric Bordeaux is also a modern working capital with San Francisco-like hustle. More than 20,000 aeronautics workers along with 70,000+ university students lend a cutting edge vibe to the area. The city is home to high-tech manufacturing and automobile companies. It offers a variety of educational opportunities from the University of Bordeaux to various engineering, business, and management schools.

Aviation holds a revered position in Bordeaux due to its aircraft history and aviation-based businesses. After they'd successfully flown their own plane as the pioneers of flight, the Wright Brothers came to Bordeaux in 1909. They were attracted to the favorable climate for flying. The brothers created a flying school north of Pau (south of Bordeaux city). They paved the way for French aeronautics which today is a multi-million dollar enterprise for the region (along with neighboring Toulouse). The Wright Brothers are buried in the chapel of the Mémorial de l'Aviation in Lescar, just outside Pau.

Bordeaux city is sometimes called "Little Paris" due to its beautiful 18th century architecture, elegant life style, and superb cuisine and wine. To me, it feels more like a little New York rather than Paris, however. Yes, it's French, but it's also very continental, with a modern hum to its diverse environs.

The city population is a sophisticated mix of mostly French individuals, along with sizable groups of Italians, Spaniards, Portuguese, Turks, Germans, North Africans, Afro-Caribbeans, Asians, Brits, and Americans. One of my wine tour guides, Adam, hails from Paris where he worked at the highly-esteemed George V Hotel; like more and more French  businesspeople these days, he's struck out on his own with some partners in an entrepreneurial effort in wine tourism. In my *Intoxicating Paris* book, I mentioned that entrepreneurialism has typically been frowned on in France in the past. But with the explosion in worldwide commerce and social media, the French too are jumping into the fray, seeking more business autonomy like my friend Adam (pictured).

Bordeaux city is naturally the urban gateway to the world-renowned wine region. It reminds me somewhat of San Francisco, if San Francisco sat at the mouth of the famous Napa Valley, home to California wineries. In Bordeaux, the mega-powerful wine economy takes in about 14.5 billion euros a year—and most of the lifestyle of the residents is touched in some way by viticulture.

The city's port is newly renovated; nearly 9 million tons of goods and wine products run through the busy port every year. Tourism continues to grow, and cruise companies like Viking River Cruises ferry thirsty visitors up and down the rivers, off loading them to sample fine wine or dine on succulent *Bordelaise* cuisine.

When I visit Bordeaux, I'm always amazed at the growing number of wine tours, wine stores, wine-tasting venues, and general wine events that are available. But the Bordeaux lifestyle is not just about loving grapes. Bordeaux is a seat of fashion and culinary excellence too. And, like Paris, it hubs a splendid countryside which feeds it an abundance of fresh produce, fish and game, local cheeses, and delectable local sweets like *Broyé* cake (delicious butter cake) and *cannelés*, the small French pastries with soft custard centers.

Culture oozes from Bordeaux. Like Paris, Bordeaux is a cultivated hub for those who wish the elegance of a city with opera, theater, and arts activities with the rural vibe of the countryside nearby. The high-speed TGV train whisks passengers from Paris to Bordeaux in a matter of a few hours. Or, you can head south into Spain via train, plane, or car (or even bicycle) and be there before the sun sets. Some locals tell me that since the airline and train systems are so good, they can live in Bordeaux but work in Paris, Madrid, or as far away as London or Rome without too much trouble. (I once flew out of Bordeaux seated next to a talkative medical instrument sales rep named Hans. Hans told me he was born in Holland, trained in London, and now lives in Bordeaux, rearing his two daughters and enjoying life with his lovely British wife in a *maison* in the heart of the Médoc. But he worked mostly in Dubai— his final destination on that flight. Talk about transcontinental!)

With a mild, steady climate and occasional frost, plus more than 2,000 hours of sunshine a year, there's ample dry, warm weather for nurturing not only vines, but fun and frolic in action-packed Bordeaux. Outdoor loving tourists can partake of miles of pristine beaches, beautiful lakes, vast conifer woods, and splendid resorts for golf, recreation, or therapy. Boat lovers enjoy fun on the seas, rivers, and lakes for water skiing, canoeing, kayaking, and house boating. Cyclists head out daily on the many bike paths along the sandy beaches, through green forests, and over the flat plains and moors. Hiking, ballooning, fishing, diving, and *péche à pied* (digging for shellfish) are popular pastimes. I've also learned there's a large horseback riding community in the area.

The *Bordelais* people are above all cultured and wine savvy. Dining across from the National Opera House at Comptoir Cuisine one Friday at lunchtime (next to the Grand Hôtel de Bordeaux), I noticed the Friday lunch crowd descending.

Like this couple (pictured), they had Parisian-style sensibilities but the bustle of intrepid New Yorkers as they lunched. Yes, the *de rigueur* multi-course French meal with wine was being served; but most of this crowd was definitely going back to work after a *café crème*.

Other *Bordelais*, like my bartender friend at the Frog & Rosbif in downtown Bordeaux or my clever wine guide Anna at Château Pontet-Canet in Pauillac, are typical of the new breed of *Bordelais* citizens. Each was born to one English parent and one French parent. Hence, they were raised completely bilingual; both carried on a long, friendly conversation with me. And both moved nonchalantly between English and French. They liked wine of course—but like many young people under 30, they told me they often preferred beer. I discovered that each knew as much about Facebook and Twitter as their ancient family histories. And they were much more interested in what they were going to "tweet" next rather than what the stock market or wine futures were reporting.

(Note: I met my bartender friend at the Frog & Rosbif one noon in downtown Bordeaux. My companion and I had just visited the Musée de Aquitaine up the street. We'd meandered down to the river port for lunch. Suddenly, we spied his darling pub which is part of a British chain that offers mostly bar food and craft beers across France. We plunked ourselves down for a down home lunch of bacon burgers, beer, and fries. I confess it was refreshingly delicious! I can only take so many days of baguettes and French cheese before I long for something homey.)

Many expats retire or move to this bewitching region. Many work in local organizations or retail operations like my delightful new British friend Clare. Clare tends one of the tapestry and accessory shops part-time; she enjoys her retirement the rest of the week. Clare hails from Yorkshire in Britain, speaks basic French, and loves selling these beautiful tapestries and clothing products. (I bought a hand-made scarf from her knit by an artisan in Cordes-sur-Ciel where I had just visited the week before.) I also bought a wonderful cloche (1920's style knitted hat) from her to match the scarf. Yes, she was a terrific saleswoman!

Along with locals and tourists, students are everywhere. They bring a young French intoxication to the area similar to that you see around the Sorbonne in Paris. Some of the shops cater to their style and budget. You will also see them on the street corners as mimes and performance artists, lending a lively carnival atmosphere to Bordeaux.

Many Americans make a living in Bordeaux too. Patricia McBain, for example, is an American urban planner from the San Francisco area who moved with her architect husband and young son originally to the Dordogne area about 10 years ago. The couple became expert at revitalizing French homes. Ultimately, they moved to Bordeaux when their son was ready for middle school and high school. Now a savvy Bordeaux city guide, Patricia runs a remarkable company called Bordeaux Walking Tours.

Patricia is an example of someone with the zeal to experience a different lifestyle and rear her son in a culturally varied environment. All three of the family members speak French (although Patricia says she is more "fluid" than "fluent"). Her son entered first grade in France, speaking almost no French. Within weeks he was rapidly becoming completely bilingual. Ten years later, he easily switches back and forth between French and English. Patricia tells me he often coaches his parents on their French; they still have a little trouble with verb conjugation and complex pronunciation, she admits.

Patricia, and her colleague Hela Soula, offer five kinds of Bordeaux Walking Tours through their company: *Landmarks of Bordeaux*, *Wine in the City*, *Gourmet Tour*, *Farmer's Market*, and customized tours. Tours are offered in English, French, Spanish, and Arabic on request. In the wine section, I'll detail my day with the witty, knowledgeable Patricia as she explored the delights of the Bordeaux wine industry with me.

Food, Wine, and Shopping

Food

"Do I recall the night we met?
You wore a bandeau on your hair and with the coq au vin
Produced a magnum old and rare of Chambertin.
Château d'Yquem, a last surprise, was climax, crown and seal.
I might forget your lovely eyes, but not that meal."

— Eric Chillman, *Gourmet's Love Song*

The Bordeaux region, with its fertile soil and temperate climate, is noted for its area-based flavors that fuel the recipes of *haute cuisine*. The fabulous local wines are only an accompaniment to the sumptuous cheeses from the Basque country, for example. Or the succulent oysters from Arcachon Bay nearby. Or the *foie gras* from the Landes. I've tried lamprey, sturgeon, and salmon from the waterways, as well as Aquitaine caviar, Pauillac lamb, and Basas beef. Bordeaux is also home to famous dessert confections like the original *macarons* of France (sans filling) and *pralines* (almonds browned in sugar) first concocted in Blaye in 1649. I never miss a chance to munch some Bordeaux *macarons* that are only produced locally.

Downtown Bordeaux makes dining an accessible pleasure. I've found plenty to choose from whether I was in the mood for fast food or high-end dining. Michelin stars were once scarce in the region, but in the last 10 years a burst of stars have been awarded in Bordeaux to such exquisite dining venues as Le Gabriel and Le Chapon Fin.

Other famous foods of the Bordeaux region include dried sea asparagus, *nougatines*, *Broyé* cake, chocolate sardines from Royan, prunes from Agen, and Basque tart. There's also the delectable Gironde caviar, Bressuire beef, Callan poultry, Basque cured meats, melons and potatoes, as well as *chabichou* goat's cheese. One of France's most famous dishes, *Poule au Pot* (chicken in a pot), hails from the Aquitaine. It was a favorite dish of Henry IV and consists of a trussed chicken stuffed with goodies like chicken livers, Bayonne ham, beaten eggs, and decrusted bread; the stuffed chicken is then boiled in water, and later traditional *pot-au-feu* vegetables are added (carrots, turnips, leeks, celery) to make a tasty stew. I make this dish often at home since it's easy to prepare and satisfying.

Cannelés are the famous tiny cinnamon cakes from Bordeaux. They're so special that they have their own regulation system to ensure authentication. And I can't leave the region without trying some Bayonne chocolates. Other sumptuous desserts include *goxua* (a rum baba cake coated with custard and caramel) and *gâteau* Basque cake with a cherry or almond cream center.

Wine

"The Wines of Bordeaux give tone to the stomach, while leaving the mouth fresh and the head clear. More than one invalid abandoned by the doctors has been seen to drink the good old wine of Bordeaux and return to health."
— Comments by members of the jury judging Bordeaux wines

Bordeaux has an incomparable reputation around the world for fine wines and oenological excellence. The famous Bordeaux wine-growing region covers about 284,000 acres in multiple regions: Médoc (Southern Haut-Médoc and Northern Bas-Médoc), Graves (Pessac-Léognan and Sauternes), Libournais (Saint-Émilion and Pomerol), Bourg, Blaye, and Entre-Deux-Mers. All combined areas produce about 700 million bottles of wine a year of red wine (89%) and white wine (11%). Bordeaux is the largest wine-growing region in France followed by the

Rhône Valley which is about two-thirds the size.

The Médoc essentially covers the Left Bank area of the Gironde Estuary. Haut-Médoc includes Saint-Estèphe, Pauillac, Saint-Julien, and Margaux. Pauillac is home to three of the original 1855 First Growth properties: Château Latour, Château Lafite-Rothschild, and Château Mouton Rothschild. (The other two are Château Margaux, which is located in Margaux, and Château Haut-Brion found in Pessac.) This is the area most famous for the big red wines known throughout the world.

Graves includes the sub-regions of Pessac-Leognan and Sauternes (and its sub-region of Barsac). The Libournais has the sub-regions of Saint-Émilion and Pomerol where Pétrus and Lafleur are located. Incidentally, Pétrus was not one of the first growths originally designated in the famous 19th century classification. But it currently is among the most highly-priced wines in all of France! The Entre-Deux-Mers is the area between the two rivers, the Garonne and the Dordogne, which combine to form the grand Gironde River. Most of these regions (except the Libournais) have their own *Appellation d'origine Contrôlée* designations (AoC).

The majority of red vines planted in the region as a whole are Merlot (63%), followed by Cabernet Sauvignon (25%) and Cabernet Franc (11%). Malbec and Petit Verdot are also grown in small amounts, but they're used mostly as a seasoner; the red blends are primarily made up of Merlot, Cabernet Sauvignon, and Cabernet Franc.

The majority of white vines (about 11% of Bordeaux's total wine market) include Sémillion (53%), Sauvignon Blanc (38%), Muscadelle (6%), and Ugni Blanc, Merlot Blanc, and others in small quantities. Entre-Deux-Mers produces the lean dry white wines while Pessac-Leognan and Graves produce the rounder, more complex whites. Château d'Yquem, producer of some of the most expensive wine being made, bottles sweet wines of stunning quality that are highly prized.

Without getting into too much detail regarding Bordeaux wine, suffice it say that there are various classifications of wines from the top *Grand Cru* to table wine. The area boasts more than 7,800 wine growers locally and various wine farms. As I've mentioned, most of the Bordeaux wines are blends of more than one variety of grape. Unlike California wines, which focus on certain grape varieties, French wines are intricate blends which may vary from year to year. The French bottle labels therefore indicate classification, region where the grapes were grown, the estate, the vintage, and the AoC designation rather than the type of grape(s).

Wine buying note: I learned something deceptively simple about choosing a good bottle of Bordeaux wine on my last trip to Bordeaux. If the label has a *château* depicted, chances are it's a very good wine! In France, the lesser wines are not allowed to show any *château* picture on the label. Here's a note about the term *château*: Although *"château"* means castle, it may also be a mansion or a little house next to a vineyard that meets the requirements for winemaking, with storage facilities on its property.

The year 1855 was particularly significant for the wines of Bordeaux. This was the year of the official classification of the top wines from the Médoc—by then, the premiere wine producer in the region. The eligible areas on the Médoc peninsula were Margaux, Pauillac, Saint-Estèphe, Saint-Julien, Haut-Médoc, and Pessac—except for the already legendary Château Haut-Brion from Graves. (At this time, fine wines like Pétrus and other wines from Pomerol and Saint-Émilion either were not producing wines in great quantity or were considered "simple wines.")

The Wine Brokers Union of Bordeaux developed this 1855 classification called the *Grands Crus Classés du Médoc* or Classified Great Growths for Médoc wines; the classification was revealed with great fanfare at the Exposition Universelle de Paris (similar to a world's fair.) The purpose of this official classification of these *Grands Crus* was to inform consumers of the ranking of these very fine wines, as well as to inform them of a reasonable price to pay for the individual wines. The "classes" indicated by the designations (*premiere, secondaire,* etc.) didn't denote quality at the time; in fact, they referred to price. Thus the "first growth" wines were the most expensive with the second, third, etc.

classifications being less and less expensive.

The 1855 classification was the beginning of the *l'aristocratie du bouchon* ("cork aristocracy") that the estates struggle to maintain year to year in modern day. The hereditary privilege of this designation is passed down, not by a family line, but by the estate itself.

The 1855 classification divided the wines into five categories. The top was First Growth (*Premiers Crus*), of which only four originally made the cut: Lafite Rothschild, Margaux, Latour, and Haut-Brion (Mouton Rothschild was added later). The other four were the Second Growths (*Seconds Crus*), Third Growth (*Troisièmes Crus*), Fourth Growth (*Quatrièmes Crus*), and Fifth Growth (*Cinquièmes Crus*). I've had personal tours of some of these *Grands Crus* estates which I'll cover later in the section.

In addition to these robust reds, Bordeaux is home to some of the world's finest dry and sweet white wines. The sweet Sauternes and Barsac varieties, with Château d'Yquem in the forefront, also are much in demand worldwide. Thomas Jefferson particularly loved Château d'Yquem for its ambrosial flavors. He wrote, "Sauterne. This is the best white wine of France and the best of it is made by Monsieur de Lur-Saluces [at Château d'Yquem]." Jefferson ordered 250 bottles of the 1784 vintage for himself and additional bottles for George Washington.

The other regions of the Bordeaux area such as Graves and Entre-Deux-Mers also have their classification systems with full AoC criteria that must be maintained. While many of Bordeaux's finest wines sell anywhere from $150-$2,000+ per bottle (and much more), you can still purchase good vintages for under $100. If you can't afford the time or trouble to go out and visit the *châteaux* personally, there are still excellent ways to find wines in Bordeaux.

Here's one final wine factoid. Recently, the French government announced officially that the long-standing AoC (*Appellation d'origine Contrôlée*) system is being replaced by a new quality tier. This new tier system is supposed to be adopted by EU countries over the next years. For wines already labeled and bottled, there will be no repercussions. But for new vintages the new labeling will look like this:

Appellation d'origine Contrôlée (AoC - top step) = (new)
Appellation d'origine Protégée (AoP - top step)
Vin Délimité de Qualité Supérieure (VDQS) = (same)
Vin de Pays (VdP) = (new) *Indication Geographique Protegée* (IGP - replacing VdP)
Vin de Table (VdT) = (same) *Vin de Table* (VdT)

In the Bordeaux area, most towns have a Maison du Vin (house of wines) where the wines of the particular locale are explained and sold to individual consumers. I enjoyed visiting the very modern Maison du Vin de Bordeaux that sits right in the heart of Bordeaux; it's housed in a stunning 18th century building across the street from the Office of Tourism. The tasting room is filled with beautiful stained glass, handsome sculpture, and a grand mahogany bar.

This Maison du Vin (www.bordeux.com) etc. is a tourist center, wine tasting bar, and a school under one organization established by the Bordeaux Wine Council. For about 39 euros per person ($50), you can even attend a two-hour workshop as an introduction to understanding, tasting, and buying local wines. For those who want a more in-depth educational experience, the center offers a variety of wine courses in two-, three-, or four-day venues; they also have weeklong programs. Visitors can also simply order wine for tasting at the Maison and enjoy it in the wine bar with its beautiful modern *décor*.

The Bordeaux Wine Council has also produced a wonderful "Smart Bordeaux" app. This handy little app lets you take a photo of a wine label or enter the name of the *château* or brand. *Voilà!* The details about the wine, its origin, classification, critic scores, and food matches pop up on your smart phone for your viewing pleasure. www.bordeaux.com/us/blog/get-smart-bordeaux-wines-newest-mobile-app-s-bordeaux/ A second app called "Bordeaux Wine Trip" allows you to locate wine tours, wine estates, hotel and eating establishments, and more at www.bordeauxwinetrip.com.

In the many wine shops scattered around Bordeaux, wine can be purchased and packaged for hand carry, or boxed to be shipped to your home. L'Intendant is my favorite though. It's located near the Maison du Vin. It carries a fabulous selection of wines, which you'll encounter as you spiral up their magnificent staircase to the thousands and thousands of bottles that seem to stretch into the heavens. (Talk about wine taking you to new heights!)

If, however, you visit Bordeaux in June on the right year, you'll have the added opportunity to attend Vinexpo, the area's premier wine event. Held every other year, more than 50,000 experts and wine lovers converge on Bordeaux for this most prestigious event that's all about wine. The 2014 event twinned Los Angeles with Bordeaux, so there was much hoopla about melding movie magic with wine magic when I visited.

The event features a two-kilometer wine "road" of booths where all manner of wine tasting and information dissemination takes place along the now-beautifully designed Garonne quay (steps from the Bourse). Huge pavilions are dedicated to wine growers and appellations, so there's plenty to see and drink. (Parking is horrendous, however. If you visit, you may want to stay at a hotel in downtown and walk there.)

The Maison du Vin and the Bordeaux Tourism Board offer a *Tasting Pass* to this event for one set price. Or you can enter on an event-by-event price. And of course there's food galore: Bordeaux *charcuterie*, oysters, *foie gras*, cheeses, meets, *canapés*, desserts, and more. A *Vineyard Pass* also gives you access to the wineries themselves. Additionally, the museums and art houses open all around town with wine-themed exhibitions (no surprise there). Street performers and mimes are out to entertain you as you wander. If you like music, there are a number of concert events featuring a variety of performers from all over the planet. You'll thrill at the spectacular light shows projected onto the façades of the ancient buildings. No one does these better than the French. They have the knack for making spectacle with light almost anywhere.

Wine Touring

"[Wine touring] is incomparably the best way to understand wine whether at the simple level of its scenery and culture, or deeper into the subtleties of its terroirs and different philosophies of different producers."

— Hugh Johnson

If you take the opportunity to experience some Bordeaux wine touring—whether by car, bus, or tour group—you'll have a most enlightening experience. You'll sample wines at the source. You'll meet the hardworking vineyard staff that toil year round to produce the lovely vintages. And you'll walk the ancient land that has been producing wine since before the time of Caesar.

Bordeaux has slowly become aware of the public's bottomless desire to visit, sample, and procure these great wines. When I first visited about six years ago, the wine shops were patchy in both Bordeaux and Saint-Émilion. Visits to the wineries were tricky—and many were not very welcoming to the public. I could only find a few touring companies and group opportunities to visit the wineries; it was somewhat confusing and venues were limited.

Today's Bordeaux has been transformed, viticulture-wise, however! On my recent visits, I continue to be flabbergasted by how Bordeaux and its surroundings have opened their wine cellars to the general public. Mass promotion has come to Bordeaux! They now offer dozens of opportunities to access the area, taste the wines, and hobnob with these newly friendly wine pros. Many speak English. And these days they seem to truly value the general public's interest in the wine industry and their wines in particular. Gradually elitism has given way to profitability I suspect.

Many methods are available for learning about wine, sampling Bordeaux products, and visiting these esteemed vineyards. First, I'll talk about taking a walking wine tour of the city of Bordeaux. With a walking wine tour, you'll learn about wine, explore the history of wine making in the Bordeaux region, and sample many of the great vintages; this is all done on foot with a wine guide for under $250 a person or less. Second, I'll explore bus tours via the Bordeaux Office du Tourisme that has multiple wine touring offerings daily; many of these cost only $50 per person and up. They'll give you access to all the major wine areas. Last, I'll detail my experiences with a chauffeured wine escort who ferried me to many of the *Grands Crus* in both the Médoc and Saint-Émilion. This is by far the most expensive option—about $400-$500 per person per day.

Bordeaux City Walking Wine Tour

A good introduction to the Bordeaux wine industry, as well as the city's history, is a walking tour of Bordeaux with a knowledgeable guide. There are many Bordeaux guides who can offer you tours of the city for not only the wine history, but the Bordeaux culinary and lifestyle traditions as well. Names and organizations are available on the Internet and via the Bordeaux Tourism office.

I very much enjoyed my experience with Patrcia McBain's Bordeaux Walking Tours, however. (www.bordeauxwalkingtours.com) Patricia's tours include hands-on activities, tastings and "nibblings," and interactions with the delightful *Bordelais* themselves. (You may even encounter a French chef or two prepping for the day's culinary events.)

Our walking wine tour began at the Three Graces Fountain at the Place de la Bourse. The Bourse buildings were the sight of some of the original *négociant* offices from centuries before. From there, via the high-speed tram, we sped north to the Chartrons District for a visit to the Bordeaux Musée Vin & Négoce (Négociant Museum). This museum is housed in a couple of the original *négociant* warehouses that were used for processing and merchandising Bordeaux wine centuries ago. Without the *négociant* business, Bordeaux would never have become an international wine phenomenon.

This museum shows the evolution of the wine business from the early merchant business of managing, bottling, labeling, and shipping the popular wine all over the world via massive sailing ships. One of my favorite stories about this early wine business is this: The mighty ships arrived in Bordeaux from England and elsewhere filled with rocks; this was done to stabilize the ships and compensate for the weight that would be reallocated to wine barrels on the return trip. Upon arrival, all of these rocks had to be offloaded to make way for the wine. As the wine sailed away to thirsty customers, the rocks were also put to good use. They were repurposed in Bordeaux roads, walkways, and building projects. Talk about recycling!

In the museum wine shop, there are wines for purchase, books about the wine trade, and English-speaking experts who can offer assistance. Our walking tour continued on through the remarkable streets of Bordeaux as we wandered back to the city center and the Maison du Vin for wine tasting. Here we sampled a remarkable set of wines with Patricia expertly detailing their origin throughout the Bordeaux region. *Santé!*

Wine Bus Tour

"Why is it that the wine tasted in the cellar (or even in the region) of its birth has a magic, a vibrancy and vigor that makes it so memorable...The bottles you find yourself have the genie of experience in them."

— Hugh Johnson

I had a delightful experience venturing out into the Médoc countryside with about 25 other travelers. But this time it was via bus, courtesy of the Bordeaux Tourism Office. The Bordeaux Tourism Office/L'Office de Tourisme de Bordeau, www.bordeaux-tourisme. com is located right downtown next to the grand Esplanade des Quinconces (downtown square) and across the street from the Maison du Vin. This busy tourist center offers dozens of tours of Bordeaux on a variety of themes—history, food, wine, etc.

I opted to take one of the half-day bus tours north to the Médoc—for the small sum of 34 euros per person (under $50). These tours are bookable online or in person. At the appointed time, we took our seats on a comfortable bus, and, with an English-speaking guide on the microphone narrating our journey, we drove out to the Médoc north of the city.

Our first stop was one of the Second Growth *Grand Cru*, Château Lascombes. Our skilled Lascombes guide, Benedictte (pictured above next to the wine barrels), showed us the vineyard, the fermentation rooms, the barrel rooms, the grand *château*, and finally the wine store where we were able to purchase some of the fine vintages ($50+).

One of the advantages of bus travel is that travelers can visit some of the high-end vineyards without having to drive out to the Médoc themselves or pay a wine guide to take them. One of the disadvantages of a wine tour via bus is that travelers have a group experience with very little personal time with the wine pros.

Our next stop was Château Saint Ahon, a smaller unclassified winery in the Haut-Médoc with an interesting history. This *château* was first owned by Charles de Montesquieu in the 18th century. Montesquieu was born in the Bordeaux area; he became a famous lawyer and political philosopher during the Enlightenment. He's most well known for his theory of the separation of powers which is now instituted in many constitutions around the world.

Château Saint Ahon is a listed as a "remarkable monument" and serves as the gateway vineyard to the Médoc. Along with the vineyards, the site is a *gîte* (self-catering apartment), has picnic grounds and camping grounds, and has a cute wine boutique. The barrel room was quite picturesque where through the glass windows we could gaze on the barrels while we tasted the most recent vintage.

Personal Wine Touring

"La rosée du petit matin, le château et sa vigne s'éveillent...
L'océan de vignes s'étire...
Respirez vigne terroir...
La suite vous sera dévoilée lors de votre prochaine visite..."
("Early morning dew, the *château* and its vineyard wakes...
The ocean of vines rolls on...breathe vines terroir...
The rest shall be known when you next visit...")

— Pontet-Canet brochure

There's something emotionally intoxicating—and endlessly

CHÂTEAU
PONTET-CANET
GRAND CRU CLASSÉ EN 1855
PAUILLAC

romantic—about the wine industry of Bordeaux. Châteaux Pontet-Canet, like many Bordeaux vineyards, weaves this viticulture mystique into its promotion. Given the struggles that shaped this area since before Caesar, it makes sense that the *châteaux* are capitalizing on their now ethereal place in the evolution of wine.

As I travel through these lush vineyards for private wine tasting, I sense a palpable magnetism that's both dreamy and earthy. It seems to feed the vines and succor the grapes, bringing them to ripe readiness. Then, when midwifed by conjuring vintners working their alchemy, it births pure ecstasy in a glass. As I head out to Saint-Émilion and the Médoc with a personal driver and five *Grands Crus* estates ready for my visit, I sense I'm entering a mystical land. And I wonder: Will I too become part of this extraordinary mystique—at least for a time?

With a personalized tour of any one of these renowned estates, you also can walk the beguiling Bordeaux land that's been home to grapevines for thousands of years. You too can inhale the deep aromas which my French friend Adam says is *l'air du vin*—the air of the wine. You too can divine the secrets of French winemaking. And of course, you too can sip the celestial nectar at the birthplace of the wine itself. It's the experience of a lifetime, in my opinion.

On each of these marvelous wine-tasting adventures, I was accompanied by a personal, English-speaking guide. I enjoyed nearly unfettered access to most all aspects of the wine alchemy process. I walked the vineyards as they were cultivated. Saw new vines sown into the dark soil enriched with river silt. Learned how the old vines—usually no more than 30-40 years on average—are clipped, shaped, and tended, growing perfect bunches of hand-nurtured grapes.

I observed the pickers gently harvesting the ripe fruit, then meticulously separating stem from grape. I inhaled the fermentation aromas from grapes stewing in great vats. Then, I watched as the mix was siphoned into great barrels for storage. I witnessed a little of how the juices are blended to become the great wines released to the world. And yes, I got to taste the wines in all their splendor at the place where they were born.

But these visits were also cultural discoveries—something I hadn't quite expected. They became explorations of the lifestyles of these stalwart, elegant people who proudly make the production of great wines their life's work. As a student of family behavior, I was afforded a personal peak into not only the day-to-day lives of these wine magicians, but into the winemaking heritage of the generations before them. I learned that the drive to make great wine is often a multigenerational conviction. It's a deep value that's distilled through the ages and passed on from generation to generation. I discovered it's not just a work life goal; it is, as the French would say, a *raison d'être*—a reason for living.

I also discovered that the world of wine making perfectly accompanies the French value of living beautifully. This fine art of living well shows up in the manicured rows of wine vines capped by pretty rose bushes. It manifests in interesting sculpture and well-kept *châteaux* or out buildings that provide vistas of well-tended beauty. It appears in the handsome celebrations of mouth-watering cuisine that accompany the fine wines served with panache.

The French simply possess a unique sensibility about blending art, gastronomy, and culture. Hence, many of these fabled Bordeaux estates have fabulous art collections on display as part of the fine-living atmosphere. For many of them, no expense is spared in creating a palatial setting for the fine wines. Many of the estates rotate their art collections or feature special collections year to year. Hence, a visit there becomes not just a one-time wine-tasting adventure. It becomes a look into the psyche of the French people who make the wine. One gains access to their life stories, their deep ancestral commitments, their viticulture successes and failures, and their long-lasting triumph in living beautifully and with dignity.

The stylish, family-run Château Mouton Rothschild, for example, is famous for its original-art labels for its delicious wines. Mouton

Rothschild also has a Museum of Wine in Art located on the premises. Nestled in a former barrel hall, the museum houses rare items of 17th century German gold and silver ware, jugs, cups, and goblets from the treasures of the kings of Naples, plus medieval tapestries, paintings, ivories, glassware, and porcelain from all over the world. It describes itself as "a magical place where so many artists and art forms, cultures and religions bear resounding witness to the eternal and fruitful dialogue between art and wine." Fruitful indeed.

All of these *châteaux* I'm going to detail next are open to the public. However, reservations are required. These are by no means the only opportunities in Bordeaux; if you travel there, you'll find dozens of vineyards awaiting your tasting pleasure. You can go accompanied by a wine guide who can both transport you and escort you through the wineries. You can also make the reservations yourself (or have your concierge do it for you) at the various wineries and hire a driver to take you to the area. You can also join a packaged wine tour that may include a few other people which will most likely include about two hours at each vineyard.

I've provided the website addresses of the estates I visited herein in case you'd like more information. All of the websites have an English version; many have videos, photos, history, and demonstrations on wine making. The wineries include Château Clos Fourtet (Saint-Émilion), Château Lamothe de Haux (Haux), Château Pontet-Canet (Pauillac), Château Gruaud Larose (Saint-Julien), and Château Kirwan (Margaux).

Note: I particularly enjoy driving out to the Médoc and other wine regions by car. The road most used for visiting the Médoc wine *châteaux* is the D2. This windy roadway begins just outside the city of Bordeaux. Then it wends its way through the wine country. It passes through vast fields of vines, near the Gironde River and near many of the *Grands Crus châteaux*. The views are out of this world. The photographic opportunities are priceless. As you meander near the river, there are also many opportunities for picnicking—and even fishing! The same is true of the Saint-Émilion and Entre Deux Mers areas. My advice for wine tasting: hire a car, open your windows, drive slowly, and wander through this wine paradise.

I have two additional comments as we begin our personal wine touring. First, wine drinking should be done in moderation. Second, I rather like Sir Robert Scott Caywood's straightforward attitude toward wine: "Compromises are for relationships, not wine."

Château Clos Fourtet (Saint-Émilion)
www.closfourtet.com

"Nunc est bibendum." (And now we should drink the wine.)

—Clos Fourtet

Historic Saint-Émilion is situated on the Right Bank of the Bordeaux territory. And pretty Château Clos Fourtet nestles within sight of this famous village. It's almost a guardian of the tiny medieval town. In fact, the vines of Château Clos Fourtet literally form a path to Saint-Émilion. And there's good reason for this. Clos Fourtet was originally a medieval fort, Camfourtet ("Camp Fort"), built for one all-important reason: to protect Saint-Émilion from invaders. Underneath and adjacent to the *château* manor house are extensive limestone caves that served as quarries to produce the limestone used to build not only the fort and the *château,* but many of the buildings in Saint-Émilion itself.

When the need for protection faded in the 1800s, Camfourtet was converted into a winery ("clos"). It then passed through various owners, with a name change to Clos Fourtet. The Cuvelier family bought it in 2001 and has tended it with care. Interestingly, some of the encircling walls of the original fort still exist today; Clos Fourtet is one of the few walled wineries in the area. The original weaponry disappeared long ago (though I think I spotted the shadows of some ancient cannon balls next to the wine racks caked in 200-year-old dust). What remains is a handsome *château* that serves as the nerve center of one of the most remarkable red wine producing estates in Saint-Émilion.

Extending outward from the limestone *château* in many directions are tidy, verdant rows of 85% Merlot grapevines, along with 10% Cabernet Sauvignon and 5% Cabernet Franc grapevines. The rich soil sits on a limestone plateau that extends across Saint-Émilion. As the limestone breaks down, it then mixes with clay to produce an excellent *terroir* (climate and soil for grape growing). Like many of the Right Bank vineyards, the acreage is small and hand tended. In the case of Clos Fourtet, about 49 acres (20 hectares) have vines.

Clos Fourtet today is a *Premier Grand Cru Classé B* in the classification of Saint-Émilion wines. Like many of the ancient vineyards in the area, vines were planted in the 16th or 17th centuries, but then they were particularly developed in the mid-18th century. With multiple owners through the centuries, it's now owned by Philippe Cuvelier who also owns Château Poujeaux. Five thousand cases of the Grand Vin Clos Fourtet are produced annually, while 2,500 cases of the second wine, Closerie de Fourtet, are usually produced.

Like many of the wineries in the Bordeaux area, Clos Fourtet is following the biodynamic lead. It uses sustainable, vine-growing methods. Grass is seeded between the rows, for example, to help reduce excess water. The soil between the vines is ploughed, and deleafing is done on the east-facing side at the end of June and on the south-facing side at the end of August to accommodate the path of the sun. Interestingly, vinification takes place in temperature-controlled stainless steel vats using whole-berry fermentation. Then oak is used to age the wine.

What makes Clos Fourtet remarkable to me is that the deep limestone caves—which look to have been carved centuries ago—house the wines in varying stages of barrels and bottles. Less manicured than many of the Left Bank Bordeaux vineyards, these wine caves are raw and real. Descending down into the caves with our wine hostess, I could see the dust and cobwebs clinging to some of the racks. With the candlelit darkness and cool air swirling around my face, I was half expecting one of the three Musketeers to leap out from behind a rack of 1845 Clos Fourtet!

You saw above that some of these bottles are covered in mold and dust. They're part of the ancient reserve that sits next to the newer vintages shrink-wrapped in plastic. These ancient caves of Clos Fourtet are also part of a network of underground caves that link together several *châteaux*, among them Château Beau-Sejour and Château

Canon. Château Clos Fourtet produces some full-bodied wines, with notes of blueberries, currants, smoke, dark chocolate, cinnamon, and even nutmeg. Prices start at $65. I'd highly recommend a visit here, followed by a stroll through old Saint-Émilion.

Château Lamothe de Haux
www.chateau-lamothe.com

"I am proud of these hills overlooking the river…
The region of the Premières Côtes is unsurpassed…
The genie of wine has reigned here since Gallo-Roman times, following the steps of pilgrims on their way to Santiago de Compostela, frolicking through the centuries in the company of the Dukes of Épernon, Toulouse-Lautrec or François Mauriac."

—Château Lamothe de Haux

South of Saint-Émilion is the large Entre-Deux-Mers area. Here, in this sunny expanse filled with vines, stunning vineyards produce a variety of red and white wines of quality. One particular segment called the Côtes de Bordeaux et Cadillac is nestled along the Right Bank of the Garonne River as it travels southward. Among the numerous estates is the picturesque Château Lamothe de Haux.

The *château* foundations date back to the 16th century; the estate has been devoted to winegrowing from the very beginning. It has been in the hands of the same family for four generations since 1956 (when, if memory serves, the original family left Algeria during the conflict). Anne Néel and her children Maria and Damien Chombart manage the 198 acres of vineyards, including neighboring Château Manos purchased in 1991. Later Château Le Giron was added.

The winery has a fine reputation for producing reds and whites at a reasonable price—for under $25. One May, I had the pleasure of taking a walking tour of the estate as well as the underground caverns. Madame Néel escorted us herself. With her faithful dog at her side, she took us down the hillside and around to the massive underground galleries that now serve as cellars for their splendid wines.

Like many of the vineyards in the area, these caves bear the distinct markings of ancient quarries where limestone was cut and hauled up steep embankments for nearby buildings. The massive doors to the caves are so reminiscent of some place the seven dwarves might have called home, I had to take several pictures. Inside, Madame Néel showed us the extensive cave system that houses their wines in both barrels and bottles. The wines are aged up to 24 months in these extensive caves that bear inscriptions, ancient graffiti, and soot from long-gone fires—perhaps made by prehistoric man.

The family even tells a fascinating WWII story about the caves. During the war, German soldiers had occupied the *château*. As the story goes, a savvy French individual was able to use a radio hidden in one of the wine barrels deep in the caves to communicate with the French Resistance. Ultimately, the Germans were expelled—but probably not before they had consumed more than a little of this delicious wine.

Back up top in the sunshine, we enjoyed seeing the grand estate where the family has installed a swimming pool, a private pond (with its own bridge), and a tasting center where the wines are beautifully on display for tasting. The winery offers a delicious sweet wine blend made from Sémillion grapes plus Sauvignon Blanc. It also produces a Cuvee Traditionnelle, Premiere Cuvee, and Côtes de Bordeaux that feature blends of Merlot, Cabernet Sauvignon, and Cabernet France to create delicious reds. Additionally, the winery produces a traditional Clairet (claret) that's basically a more deeply-colored wine similar to a full-bodied rosé. The combined estates produce about 540,000 bottles per year. Château Lamothe de Haux also offers a private bedroom inside the estate for bed-and-breakfast rental. Guests have a private staircase and majestic views of the vineyard. It's a pleasant location from which to tour the southern areas of Bordeaux.

Château Pontet-Canet
www.pontet-canet.com

Château Pontet-Canet, located in the heart of the Pauillac appellation, has an illustrious history as one of the largest vineyards in the Médoc. Jean-François de Pontet, royal governor of the Médoc in the 18th century, combined several plots to form the original Pontet estate. Years later, his descendants bought up neighboring vines in Canet. The name was hyphenated to indicate the vineyard pedigree—and a legend was born. In 1855, Pontet-Canet was included in the famous Médoc *Grands Crus Classés* classification. Sold in 1865 to Herman Cruse, it remained in the Cruse family until 1975 when it was sold to Guy Tesseron, owner of Château Lafon-Rochet in Saint-Estèphe. The estate produces wonderful wine. No wonder: It sits across the road from Château Mouton Rothschild.

Pontet-Canet now has one of the largest productions of any classified growth in the Médoc. Nearly 20,000 cases of its *grand vin* are produced annually, plus another 20,000 cases of its second wine, Les Hauts de Pontet. Our tour of the estate consisted of an initial ride around the 200-acre vineyard. Our escort explained the newest biodynamic wine techniques being used at the vineyard which is under the management of Alfred Tesseron. (Pontet-Canet was also the first Bordeaux wine producer to earn the official *Agence Bio* (AB) organic certification.)

The estate's soil is predominantly gravel and sand sitting on rises of limestone bedrock. This is a fairly inhospitable soil combination that makes it perfect for growing hardy Cabernet Sauvignon grapes—the predominate variety in the vineyard. Like Quintessa in Napa Valley, California, which I have also toured, the estate has instituted a plot-by-plot, biodynamic management system using sustainable farming techniques. This boils down to an "as-little-intervention-as-possible" approach to the vines. Chemical weed killers are banned. The grass is allowed to grow around the base of the vines; this forces the vine roots to dig deeper into the soil to survive. Fertilizers are composed only of organic materials and fed to only the neediest portions of the acreage.

I discovered that old-fashioned horses and carts are used to keep the weeds down, as well as to plow but not compact the soil. These animals apparently also produce an important byproduct for the vines: fresh manure. Feeding the vines takes place only during certain times of the month, according to the fullness of the moon. Vines are cropped carefully. Yields are kept low. The acreage is managed on a section-by-section basis—sometimes even vine-by-vine—allowing a more sophisticated process of combining juice from different plots to create the desired final product. The grape variety distribution is 60% Cabernet Sauvignon, 33% Merlot, 5% Petit Verdot, and 2% Cabernet Franc.

Rose bushes are often planted at the end of a row of vines. Today, they're used mostly cosmetically. In the past however, rose bushes were planted at the end of rows to act as early warning signals for infestation by diseases and insects like aphids. (They hit the roses first.) A vineyard manager who noticed black spots or root rot on the roses sprayed the grape vines before they were damaged. Today's vineyard manager keeps a closer eye on the vines themselves on a daily basis; but the mostly-cosmetic rose bushes remain to enhance the vistas.

The harvesting process at Pontet has been greatly refined over recent decades. The picking crates are now only partially filled, for example, allowing non-crushed grapes to be delivered directly to the sorting table. The sorting is done carefully by hand on the first floor, then dropped by gravity into the fermentation vats which are directly beneath. Each vat is dedicated to one plot. Later, the wine is stored in French oak barrels in a barrel hall or *chai*.

Some of the juice is stored in these new concrete contraptions (shown) that I think look a lot like alien eggs. They're called *nomblots*. These *nomblots* are the creation of Michel Chapoutier of the Rhône Valley who partnered with the Nomblot Company to produce egg-like wine tanks. The concrete *nomblots*, unlike stainless steel vessels, allow

the wine to breathe in a unique way. Since the *nomblot* is porous concrete instead of oak, the wine ages without adding any oak character to the blend as with traditional wooden barrels. The unique shape also enhances a natural stirring effect during fermentation.

You can see that our wine escort is holding up four fingers.

She's indicating that these concrete *nomblots* hold up to four barrels worth of liquid—and produce even more exceptional wine than the old barrel methodology (although Pontet-Canet still uses both). An additional advantage is that Pontet can store even more wine in less space in a *nomblot*.

Note: These concrete eggs are being used by such respected wineries in the U.S. as Quintessa, Harlan Estate, Screaming Eagle, and Viader. I've also discovered that some wine pros believe the upright egg shape is supposed to "concentrate the energy vortex of the celestial energy." I can't attest to the celestial validity of these wine-enhancing claims, but I can agree that Pontet-Canet produces some divine wines!

Additional note: The man standing to the left in the photo is Bruno Delmas, a renowned French wine guide and expert. He happened to join our party as we were touring Pontet-Canet. (Actually we ran into him on the same day at a PREVIOUS vineyard, so I knew we were on the correct wine-tasting trail when he turned up again at Pontet). Though he was not escorting my party *per se*, he very graciously let me pepper him with questions for about two hours about various wine topics. As far as I can tell, he's one of the most knowledgeable wine pros available for hire in the area. I would also add that he does something I've never seen a French guide do: He willingly acts as the group photographer. He cheerfully takes picture after picture of his flock to ensure they capture every precious moment of their experience! His contact info is BD Tours (www.english.bdtours.fr).

Interestingly, Pontet doesn't use computers to monitor the fermentation process. This is done by hand by people working in the cellars 24 hours a day. Later, the liquids from the tanks are meticulously blended and bottled. We had the opportunity to descend into the bowels of the estate to visit the "holiest of holy" Pontet-Canet wine caves where much of the final, prized fine wines are stored. Some of these vintages go back centuries.

Finally, we headed upstairs to the ultra-modern tasting room where we were treated to a professional round of tasting. I can attest to the fact that the classic Pontet-Canet wine is deep ruby-red, sometimes almost black in color. It has a characteristic bouquet of black fruit (especially black currant), licorice, and prune as well as fig, cedar, and sometimes cocoa. It's sold for under $250, depending on vintage. A second tier wine, Les Hauts de Pontet, is sold for around $55 on average.

Tasting wine is much more meaningful when you've been able to tread the very soil where the grapes are grown, then see for yourself how the grapes make the long, meticulous journey from grape to great vintage. By the time we'd arrived in the elegant tasting room, I felt like I could taste 300 years of trial-and-error cultivation in my glass. I like to keep this phrase in mind as I enjoy visits to these wonderful vineyards: "Wine is the son of the sun and the earth but was delivered by hard work." (Paul Claudel, French writer, 1868-1955)

Château Gruaud Larose
www.gruaud-larose.com

The balmy breezes—which sometimes whip into swirling winds—waft regularly across the Médoc. They're filled with a grapey ripeness tinged with Atlantic sea salt but buoyed by the earthy river aromas from the nearby Gironde. With my car window down, these aromas permeated the air—and my head—as we traveled along. With the sun bearing down and a vision of green vines spreading out before me on all sides, I felt physically intoxicated merely by passing through the grapevines. If there was a Garden of Eden, I wondered if this was what it felt like to exist there.

As we turned into the serene Château Gruaud Larose estate, I couldn't have anticipated I'd have a most unexpected encounter with, of all things, a cannon. But this was not just any French cannon, aimed at invading armies or vino-tourists. This was a cannon aimed at lethal rain clouds poised to rain down destruction on delicate grape buds. First, however, a bit of history before I tell the tale.

Joseph Stanislas Gruaud was the proud owner of the Ténac, Sartaignac, and Merle Crus properties in 18th century Bordeaux. He died in 1771 and left the property located in the Saint-Julien area of the Médoc to his friend Monsieur de Larose. Larose added his name to form the current moniker, Gruaud Larose. Inducted into the rarefied list of *Grands Cru Classés du Médoc* in 1855, Gruaud continues today to produce much-admired fine wines under the tutelage of the Merlaut family, the current owners.

The Gruaud Larose winery has stunning views of the Gironde estuary nearby which we drove through to reach it. The Gironde is one of the key players in the creation of this famous vineyard. The land is graveled and mixed with humus, clay, sand, and pebbles left behind when the raging Gironde River overflowed its banks centuries ago. The gravel and pebbles help keep the soil from becoming compacted, thus creating conditions ripe for growing fine vines. This hardy soil, plus the favorable microclimate of sea air, dry winds, and sudden rainfall make for the exquisite *terroir* found at Gruaud.

Some of the Gruaud Larose vines are more than 100 years old. But the majority of the vines, in keeping with common vineyard practice, are around 40 years old. Today, Cabernet Sauvignon grapes dominate Gruaud Larose at 60%, with additional Merlot (30%), Cabernet Franc (7%) and Petit Verdot (3%) grapes adding to the mix. Like Pontet-Canet, Gruaud Larose uses organic compost and has banned insecticides, pesticides, and herbicides in the vineyard.

During the late-spring rains, I soon learned that the vineyard pulls out its secret weapon: The hail cannon. (Even my wine guide hadn't seen one in action!) Luckily, I visited Gruaud on a rainy day that offered us the opportunity to see (and hear) this booming device in action. While standing on the balcony with our Gruaud host, the skies suddenly opened up. Soon, we were pelted with large hailstones. Through my rain-drenched sunglasses, I saw the vineyard staff jump into action since the dreaded hail can annihilate the crop in minutes.

Bam! Gruaud's cannon fired huge blasts of air into the offending clouds, breaking up the mist and obliterating the hail. Yes, I got completely drenched (and momentarily deafened) as I stayed outside to witness this climatic battle. (Everyone else went inside and ogled me from the window. I'm sure they thought I was insane. But it was completely worth the effort. My trench coat, however, still smells vaguely of wine rain. However, since it's the odor of *Grand Cru*, I don't mind.)

Back inside the *château*, damper but probably no wiser, I was ushered by our wine host down to the vat and barrel area. The Gruaud

Larose *chai* is one of the most striking in the Médoc. With its cathedral-like ceilings, it almost feels like a French church—and there certainly was a little worshiping going on as we visited its hallowed halls.

Gruaud is quite sophisticated about its marketing, tour options, and receptions. It offers not only wine tasting but chocolate and wine pairings, harvest workshops, and cooking courses. Prices for these fine wines run anywhere from $100 to thousands, although there are some bottles available for less than $90.

Château Kirwan

www.Château-kirwan.com

"The wine is born in tumult
and grows up in calm autumn, time
for the miracle of vinification."
—Château Kirwan

One of my most memorable experiences in the Médoc was at Château Kirwan (pictured) with Madame Nathalie Schÿler. Madame Schÿler's family has been involved with Bordeaux wines and this *château* in particular for centuries. The story of this beautiful *château* with its storybook façade and elegant grounds perfectly mirrors the historical travails of Bordeaux wine making, therefore I'll explore it in depth.

The Château Kirwan estate sits on a beautiful tract of land on the Cantenac Plateau in Margaux. It was originally named La Terre Noble de Lasalle ("the noble land of La Salle") after the La Salle family who owned it in the 1600s. In 1710, the La Salle family sold the property to the popular English wine *négociant*, Sir John Collingwood. Collingwood's daughter later married a dashing Irish merchant named Mark Kirwan.

Kirwan inherited the estate with Collingwood's passing (in those days, husbands inherited for their wives); the geese artwork around the estate reflects Kirwan's Irish heritage from Galway, Ireland. Kirwan was a member of one of the "Tribes of Galway." These tribes were the 14 merchant families who dominated the commercial and political life of Galway from the 13th to 19th centuries. Irish wine lovers regularly make pilgrimages to Kirwan today as "one of their own."

Mark Kirwan took owning this superb estate seriously. He united the La Salle land with a newly purchased estate called Ganet. He then changed the expanded estate name to Kirwan. Kirwan focused on restoring the *château* while elevating the quality of the wine. He was so successful that his vineyard was one of the handful of estates that Thomas Jefferson visited on his trip through Bordeaux in the late 1700s. Jefferson noted in his records that he was impressed with the wine of "Quirouen," his Americanized spelling for the name of the estate.

In 1789, Château Kirwan was seized during the French Revolution, although Mark Kirwan escaped by virtue of being Irish; he ultimately regained control of the property under Napoleon's rule. He eventually died on his land in 1815. In 1855, Château Kirwan was elevated into the rare realm of the original 1855 Médoc *Grands Crus Classés.*

In 1858, the grand estate was sold to botanist and wealthy philanthropist Camille Godard. Upon Godard's death in 1882, the city of Bordeaux found it had been bequeathed this fabulous estate. Unable to maintain the high quality of wine and run an entire vineyard, however, the city of Bordeaux finally sold the estate at auction in 1904 to the Schÿler family who'd already overseen the estate's trading business for many years. Subsequent decades saw Château Kirwan weather the economic downturn of the 1930s, two world wars, and the deadly spread of phylloxera that nearly wiped out the entire wine region.

Today, the tireless Schÿlers and Château Kirwan have an international reputation for fine wine making and oenotourism. Nathalie runs the property while her brother Yann manages the international *négociant* business.

Nathalie was a wonderful hostess, leisurely walking us through the vineyard, detailing among other things, the arduous process the estate takes to maintain the *Grands Crus* standards. For example, the height and branching pattern of each vine is regulated. Irrigation is not allowed. On this vine at the front of the photo, you can see it has been

carefully trimmed to exactly the regulation number of branches.

The harvest days are also strictly regulated, as is the crushing, vatting, and bottling processes. The 35-hectare vineyard of today's Château Kirwan is the same size as it was when it was awarded Third Growth status in the 1855 *Médoc Classification*. It's planted with 45% Cabernet Sauvignon grapes, as well as 30% Merlot, 15% Cabernet Franc, and 10% Petit Verdot.

Nathalie explained that the grapes are tasted every day to determine the ideal time for harvesting each plot. The fruit is then handpicked and placed in vats batch by batch. The fermentation phase, or *entrée en fermentation*, takes nearly a month (or less), and daily tastings indicate how long to do "pump-overs" to process the grapes during maceration.

Later the wines are barreled, and still much later, the winemaker begins the blending process to combine the juices into bottles. The final bottles are then "racked in candlelight" (moved to other vessels) to make the fabulous Kirwan wines. These noble wines, as Kirwan explains in its literature, are the result of "the wonderful chemistry between the soil, the climate, the vines, and the winemaker's artistry." Nathalie highlights the fact that this is one of the key differences between Bordeaux blended wines and "New World" wines which emphasize the varietal nature of wine (Chardonnay, Merlot, etc.) rather than the sophistication of the blend. In Bordeaux, the land and the weather, as well as the vines and their grapes make up the all-important *terroir* that creates a great Bordeaux wine. Château Kirwan today produces about 16,000 cases annually with about 4,000 cases of its second wine, Les Charmes de Kirwan.

As Nathalie led us around the estate, the *château* was gleaming. It was filled with modern art and the scent of wine. The vat and bottling rooms were run with precision. The vineyards were tended with care, and the high-tech welcome center not only functioned as a wine-tasting locale, but a business office and reception area.

Finally, we made our way to the elegant tasting room. Off to the right, is a beautiful Orangerie (reception hall) that accommodates up to 200 guests for receptions, candlelit dinners, and cocktail parties. Dinners begin with a tour of the estate, plus tasting with *canapés*. The full-service dining choices offer a variety of themed menus designed around specific wines including the Garonne Menu (*foie gras*, salmon, duck, veal, *tarte Tatin*, strawberry salad) and the Margaux Menu (*foie gras*, scallops, veal, steak, chocolate tart, vanilla panacota, violet ice cream). Picnicking on the estate is also available.

Kirwan offers full-day touring such as the Gourmet Day in Margaux which includes other estate tours, lunch, and full guide and transportation services. There's a blending workshop for those who want to create their own wines. And there's a lively workshop for children called "Kirwan for Kids" on Wednesday afternoons; it includes a kid-oriented tour of the vines, the fermentation and bottling processes, plus a snack and collaging as an art project (no wine is offered, of course). They also have weekly offerings of tours and receptions, as well Sunday dinner hostings for Viking River cruise travelers. Médoc helicopter tours are available directly from the estate, courtesy of Kirwan. (As savvy marketers, Château Kirwan leads the way in Médoc accessibility and exciting wine adventures on the property.)

I confess, I came home with several bottles of Château Kirwan which I can report were wrapped by Nathalie herself for carrying in my checked bags. Yes, my checked bags. The bottles arrived home perfectly (despite some air turbulence over Greenland). And yes, they were delicious. Price per bottle: Approx. $75 and up, depending on vintage.

In summary, I enjoyed these five private tours immensely. They were refreshing, informative, and deeply affecting. Naturally, the wines were exquisite, but I think I'll savor the experiences long after the flavor of the wines has faded. I had the unique opportunity to walk the verdant lands where some of the finest wines on the planet are grown, and watch them being bottled and released into an appreciative world.

Did I meet the magic? My dreams would tell you yes. As a therapist who also analyzes dreams with my clients, I would share that sometimes I dream of Bordeaux. I dream of wandering along the vineyards, looking out to the sea, smelling the Gironde, and seeing magnums of rich red wine spilling into fine-cut crystal. Psychologically, the psyche knows no time or place, only *experience*. And so whether I dream of Bordeaux or actually travel there in person, it seems the alchemy lingers with me, awake or asleep.

Shopping

Retail therapy is everywhere in Bordeaux and its environs. Downtown Bordeaux offers modern shops like Galeries Lafayette, Etam, and H&M. There are wine shops galore, and an abundance of *pâtisseries*, *boulangeries*, and *bistros* similar to those you find in Paris. Since this is also a college town, dozens of trendy boutiques and small stores meet the needs of a slim budget. If you're looking for luxury however, stick with the shops in the Golden Triangle: Cours de l'Intendance, Cours Georges Clemenceau, and Allées de Tourny.

Stretching from the aristocratic Place de la Comedie to the student district at the Place de la Victoire, Rue Sainte-Catherine runs through the center of downtown Bordeaux. You can shop for days and not see everything on this long, pleasant street. Not only can you find clothing, shoes, and wine stores on and off Rue Sainte-Catherine, you can buy records and CDs at "Total Heaven" on Rue Candale and designer furniture at Maisons du Monde. Along the riverside and tucked into the squares, you can purchase kitsch and antiques of all sorts. (Note: If you get lost wandering in the twists of the medieval byways like I did once, find your way back to Rue Sainte-Catherine and you'll be fine. It's like Main Street Bordeaux.)

In Bordeaux, and in most of the villages around the area, you'll find these quirky medieval "strip malls" that are tucked into clusters of repurposed buildings. France has gotten very good at turning ancient cottages into adorable shops where sellers of handcrafted food, pre-packed wine, home goods, and clothing do a fast-paced business.

For books, you mustn't miss Librairie Mollat, one of France's largest and best bookshops, located on Rue Vital Carles. (Quirky note: I love going to the English section of French bookstores and finding books like *175 American English Idioms*. They're primers on American slang like "Watch Your Head" and "Yo Dude" that confound French speakers. Scanning them makes me feel less ridiculous when I don't "get" French idiomatic expressions like *donner sa langue au chat* literally translated to "give your tongue to the cat" or "give up guessing.")

Familiar grocery/retail outlets abound including Monoprix and Carrefour. The Carrefour Market Grands Hommes is one of Bordeaux's oldest stores; it's been serving customers since the 19th century. For big mall devotees, Mériadeck is the only covered shopping mall near downtown. Bordeaux-shopping.com is a great resource for locating exactly the store you desire.

Specialty shops include the ever-fabulous chocolate shop Les Chocolats Yves Thuries which features the gourmet creations of Yves Thuries who I mentioned lives in Cordes-sur-Ciel. Of course, there are the gourmet boutiques like Le Comptoir Bordelais and Lafitte Foie Gras that offer delicious Southwest France products like *confits*, *pâtés*, *foie gras*, and various gift packs. Specialty *cadeaux* (gifts) boutiques offer local keepsakes, Bordeaux-logo home goods, and wine-oriented gifts to take home for family and friends—or for you! I often come home with wine-motif towels and wine paraphernalia like corks, bottle openers, magnets, and bar towels. I also love to pick up small artwork, vases, kitchen wear, French baskets, lovely handmade soaps, perfumes, and tapestries.

Remember, when shopping in France, La Poste is your best friend. You'll find a La Poste every few blocks. Over the years, I've never lost one of these orange shipping boxes stuffed with my purchases from France; in fact, they usually beat me home!

Culture & Art

Since the Bordeaux area has been inhabited for centuries, yet remains a cultured, modern city, there's much see and do here. History buffs will find Roman ruins, feudal castles, eccentric villas, fortified churches, and museums. Art lovers will enjoy the splendid galleries downtown or further afield like the Musée des Beaux-Arts of Agen featuring such artists as Odilon Redon, Georges de Sonneville, and René Princeteau (first teacher of Toulouse-Lautrec). The Musée des Beaux-Arts (located about 90 minutes southeast of Bordeaux by car) also features works by Spanish painter Francisco Goya who spent his last days in exile in Bordeaux.

There's plenty of classic architecture to admire, nestled alongside modern Bordeaux buildings in the main downtown area. Every era has produced architectural works of note—and often they exist side by side in ancient splendor with such buildings as the Grand Théâtre de Bordeaux that has been refurbished and techno-lit for modern day appreciation. It sits royally overlooking the Place de la Comédie (where the high-tech tram runs). It was built by Victor Louis in 1780 and was used as the model by Garnier for the Paris Opera House. The magnificent hall features opera and ballet events.

The Musée de Aquitaine can beguile you for hours. It houses a wonderful collection of art, objects, and documents from the history of Bordeaux and the Aquitaine as a whole. It's located in downtown Bordeaux, not far from the Palais des Sports (sports stadium). Linguistic tip: When I first visited Bordeaux and toured the museum, I mentioned it to a couple of locals. They looked at me puzzled. I tried explaining where the museum was in the city. Finally, a look of comprehension passed over their faces. "Oh, you mean The Musée de Aquitaine (pronouncing it something like Ek-EE-Tan)." I, of course, had been pronouncing it in the ripe, round tones of Peter O'Toole as in "El-ea-nor of Awk-wa-ta-a-a-ine." When the French say it, however, it sounds like some brand of tanning gel, "Ek-EE-tan." I stood corrected. (I was tempted to reciprocate with a correction for an English *faux pas* the French constantly make. For some reason, they've dubbed my California home state "Californee"—even on maps! But I saved that for another day. Pick your battles.)

A simple wander around Bordeaux city on foot will afford you chances to visit the Cathedral Saint Andre, a Bordeaux masterpiece which also features regular organ concerts at no charge; the Basilique Saint-Michel which offers a panoramic view from its belfry; and the Place de la Bourse, first built as a royal square, now home to classical buildings with handsome archways and slate roofs.

The luminescent Miroir d'Eau fountain, the innovative water mirror fountain that stretches across the pavement at the foot of the Place de la Bourse, will entertain any time, day or night. You'll find visitors frolicking in the water or striding through the fog that shoots up from the fountain. At night or various times during the day, the Bourse stock exchange buildings will reflect their 18th century elegance in the water mirror.

You can also wander south to the Porte Cailhau, an ancient triumphal arch built on the site of an old city gate celebrating a battle King Charles VIII won in 1495. Or just a short stroll from the Grand Théâtre is the Esplanade des Quinconces. The Esplanade des Quinconces is France's largest square and one of the largest in Europe. It was laid out in the 19th century on the site of the former Château Trompette and is surrounded by trees and anchored by the Monument aux Girondins. This monument, which commemorates the victims of the French Revolution who died on the guillotine during the *terreur*, is an impressive fountain with the allegorical statue of *liberté* on top of the central column. The square is so large it's often used for shows, festivals, and marketing events. When I last visited the square, a classic car show had about 100 classic cars parked for viewing; scores of car buffs were salivating over these well-preserved classics—my husband among them. It was hard to tear him away—even for a glass of *Grand Cru*!

Visitors can also enjoy any number of river events like dinner cruises and boating excursions that are bookable at various tourism locations. One is Gens d'Estuaire/Bordeaux River Cruise. These are the "guys of the estuary" who started a company focusing on all there is to do and see on the Garonne River and the Gironde Estuary. Other larger cruises are available, among them Viking and Viator.

The other cultural experience I find fascinating in France is watching a protest. France takes its hard-won liberties very seriously. I've frequently witnessed marches of all kinds in various cities in France. But I've never seen one advocating for Jesus like a lively group that took over the Place de la Comédie in Bordeaux for an hour (about the same time as the car show). Talk about an action-packed downtown!

Navigating the Area

Bordeaux sits at the center of several routes. You can arrive by plane, boat, river cruise ship, train, car, cycle, or even on foot. Eurostar brings visitors from all over Europe into France, and then you can travel via train, plane, or bus to the Bordeaux area. I've already mentioned that the high-speed TGV can whisk you to Bordeaux from almost anywhere in France, as well as Spain. The international airport has both small carriers (Easy Jet, Ryan Air) and large carriers (British Airways, Air France) buzzing in and out on a daily basis.

I personally have driven in via car and flown in via jet. I love the drive, time permitting, since it's such a picturesque region and the aromas are divine. Some visitors arrive via coach for large group stays; others come in motorhomes or are prepared to camp.

A multitude of maps are available for navigating the area. Even the downtown, though busy, is easy reachable (but there's quite a bit of rush hour traffic). When pressed, you can always walk or take public transportation—or call for *le Taxi* or gem car.

If you choose to drive a rental car, be sure to acquaint yourself with French driving laws. They don't differ a whole lot from other countries (the French drive on the right), but the French signage may be tricky. I quite enjoy driving through the French countryside myself, but I find driving through Bordeaux city to be almost as bad as driving through Paris.

On one visit, my spouse received a French ticket for a stop light infraction when he was heading to the Bordeaux train station to return our rental car. (Not good timing since he'd driven 1,000 miles around France without a problem; but in the last 5 kilometers he got snagged by the speed cameras. Ouch!) Not to worry, however. Via the rental car company, he received a friendly email alerting him that he'd be sent a ticket courtesy of the Bordeaux police. Within days, he received a triumvirate of colorful forms in the mail, instructing him to pay via credit card the grand sum of 90 euros (about $116). He wired the amount with no complications.

Favorites

Bordeaux, *Grands Crus* wine estates, the Médoc, Saint-Émilion, and French cooking classes. The fascinating Bordeaux area offers some exceptional opportunities to explore big-city Bordeaux, the wine-conjuring Médoc, and the medieval hamlet of Saint-Émilion. Travel with me as we explore the modern face of Bordeaux city with its ancient wine history as a backdrop. Join me in climbing the craggy hills of Saint-Émilion sampling treasured wines, and come with me into Lucy's French kitchen as we create some of the most mouth-watering cuisine on the planet. Follow me now on a sumptuous adventure through the wine capital of France.

Bordeaux

As a modern city with a classical face, Bordeaux presents a beautiful image even as you enter her environs. The Pont de Pierre, built in the 1800s, was the only major thoroughfare into the city until the 1960s. And a grand entrance it was—and still is. Driving over this magnificent bridge, you enter the metropolis and typically head uptown parallel to the river waterfront. You'll find an abundance of things to do, delicious places to dine, and many accommodations to lay your head for a night or a fortnight.

In town, vacation stays can vary from luxury hotels to modest B&Bs suitable for any budget. If you choose the nearby countryside, you'll find everything from simple *chambres d'hôtes* to modern hotel accommodations to *château* splendor if you choose one of the famous castles that accept overnight guests. As always, I suggest you check with your local travel agent, consult Trip Advisor, the Michelin Guide France, or other Bordeaux tourism resources. However, these are a few establishment names I can recommend.

The Grand Hôtel de Bordeaux is one of the top properties in downtown Bordeaux. It's centrally located to everything in the city (culture, shopping, restaurants), as well as near all the major transportation. Additionally, the tourism office is within a French block or two. I haven't stayed there but I have dined there. It's elegant, if a little staid. You can't beat the location, though.

The Hôtel Burdigala is a little less grand and further from the city center (about a mile). On my most recent visit to Bordeaux, I stayed at this hotel. Wonderful rooms, decent dining, but a bit far from the center of town. I found the service to be very good, if a little bit starched. Because I was doing a lot of wine touring during my stay there, I seldom dined in the restaurant. I enjoyed the lounge bar which offers reasonable bar food if you're not up for a giant meal. I did have one hilarious encounter at the Burdigala (at least for me), although I'm sure the hotel chalked up my request to being a "crazy American."

Here's the story. I often do a lot of walking when I'm touring an area; I'd actually clocked 12 miles this particular day. I admit my feet were absolutely killing me. I couldn't drag myself from the lobby by the front door where I'd plopped myself to the bar OR the restaurant for a soft drink, though I was dying of thirst. And I had to go out again shortly. Therefore, unlike in most American hotels where they'd serve you a soft drink anywhere, I had to beg the Burdigala staff to bring my companion and me a pair of ice-cold Cokes. After the concierge reluctantly called the restaurant, the food service manager came running out into the lobby at a gallop. She was tugging on her formal jacket that she'd clearly thrown on after being "summoned."

After I requested two soft drinks be brought out to the lobby, she replied. "Madame, you do not prefer a Coke in our bar (about 500 feet away)?"

"No *s'il vous plaît.* Just this once, could you please serve me here in the lobby by the front door? My feet are killing me."

She stared at me as if I'd asked her to fly me to the moon. French service is done in an absolutely prescribed way; any casual behavior like this is frowned upon. She paused a long moment and finally agreed, "Very well madame. We will send out two Coca Colas. *Avec glace?*"

"*Oui,*" I replied. "With ice. And thank you so much."

After a time, the drinks arrived; we gulped them down. Through the bottom of my glass I could see some of the lobby staff ogling the pair of us like we were escaped lunatics. But by that time, I was so tired I didn't care. In all honesty, I try extra hard not be demanding when I travel. But this absolutely had to be done. We got up to leave, and I turned back and noticed the empty glasses on the lobby table. The concierge was eyeing them distastefully as we exited. Despite this etiquette breach on my part, the hotel's service continued to be excellent. (Although I think the Food Service Manager avoided me thereafter!)

Other hotels that get high marks in Bordeaux are the Hôtel de Sèze, the Pullman Bordeaux Lac, and for a modest, no frills hotel that's well situated near everything you'd want to see in Bordeaux, there's the Majestic (although you'll probably have to carry your own bags up the stairs). Other options include the chain hotels like Accor and Etap that provide dependable rooms for a medium budget. One of my favorite things to do however is to stay at a *gîte* in the region. Gîtes de France offers lots of agreeable rentals. Additionally, you can choose a farm holiday where you can stay with a farmer or family for an agricultural-based stay.

And there are wonderful hotels and B&Bs sprinkled all over the Bordeaux wine country that welcome overnight guests. I've noticed some wonderful quasi-resort properties like the Hôtel Relais de Margaux, Château Meyre, and the fabulous Château Cordeillan-Bages that I'm eyeing for my next stay in the Médoc. If you really want the *crème de la crème* of accommodations in rural France, you can seek out the Relais & Châteaux directory (www.relaischateau.com). It lists restaurants as well.

If you want total luxury relaxation, try the Caudalie Vinothérapie spa, just outside Bordeaux. "Where time loses its meaning" is the catch phrase of this exclusive spa located within the grounds of the Château

Smith Haut Lafitte estate. It has a gushing hot springs for you to frolic in, as well as vinotherapy treatments like the Gommage Crushed Cabernet scrub that blends grape pips, honey, brown sugar, and essential oils and the Massage Pulpe Friction that employs grapes to exfoliate and hydrate your skin. The honey and wine wrap is indescribable and uses Merlot grapes (of course). An undeniably French experience is the Vichy shower which showers and massages you while you lie down. (An obvious advantage after a night of wine tasting!) The spa also offers a stunning collection of beauty products related to the noble grape, including grape oils, masks, premier cru creams, facial cleansers, and their famous crushed cabernet scrub in a jar.

Dining opportunities abound in downtown Bordeaux. First class venues like La Tupina or Le Chapon have world-class reputations; reservations are required due to popularity. But everyday food that's a cut above is available at a variety of eateries at affordable prices.

For the top of the Bordeaux gourmand scene, try these: Le Gabriel (One Michelin Star), an exceptional Place de al Bourse restaurant with wonderful views and 18th century sitting rooms where *haute cuisine* is served; Le Chapon Fin (One Michelin Star), a local favorite with a 1900s grotto *décor* and modern cuisine; 7ème Péché (Septième Péché), an intimate eatery that serves elegant, creative, chic cuisine; La Tupina, my favorite "country inn" in downtown Bordeaux where earthy Southwestern France cuisine, as well as roast meat dishes, are done over an open fire in full view of the diners. I go there whenever I can.

Other dining opportunities include Comptoir Cuisine, a small bistro next to the Grand Hôtel with a fine wine selection; Dubern, another highly-rated local bistro; and Gourmand, a gourmet bistro that serves, among other things, *boudin noir* (blood sausage, a favorite of Brits like my husband) and yellow tuna steak with puréed carrots. These are just a few of the many, many eating opportunities in Bordeaux. The curbside places are quite cute like Le Café Napoleon 3 or any of the delightful sidewalk consortiums that will offer you a bite to eat while you watch the Bordeaux world roll by.

Outside Bordeaux city proper, some extraordinary dining can be found. Café Lavinal, a lunch and dinner brasserie of renown is part of the Château Lynch-Bages estate in Pauillac. Lynch-Bages is one of the *Grands Crus Classés* estates that has maximized its outreach by adding a tasting school, cooking school, and the Café Lavinal. Superb food, great wines.

Le Saint-James is the tony restaurant situated in the Le Saint-James Hôtel/Resort. It's a lovely location for a top-notch meal with strong regional elements crafted by Bordeaux local Chef Nicolas Magie. Magie worked with Christian Constant in Paris and is very creative with cuisine. There's a cooking school on the premises as well.

But one of my favorite dining experiences in the area was at Le Saint-Julien. Le Saint-Julien is a darling restaurant located just around the corner from Châteaux Pichon Lalande in Saint Julien-Becheville. I had such a wonderful time lunching here, I could have curled up in a corner of the kitchen for about two days. It all started with the ebullient Chef Claude Broussard who owns the restaurant with his wife. He's definitely a Frenchman oozing charm and culinary finesse. Here's my tale.

We arrived for lunch during a Médoc wine-touring day. It was about five minutes to noon—slightly before our reservation time. We hadn't been to Le Saint-Julien previously, so we inadvertently entered from the patio and sailed past the kitchen. As we passed, I beheld a big burly man puttering around in the kitchen; he had a cropped beard and was wearing a dark t-shirt and jeans. He looked up with surprise, giggled loudly, and then grabbed his chef's coat, all the while talking in rapid-fire French as he moved toward us. (Luckily we were with a friend of his, so we were treated more like family arriving early than pushy tourists.)

After his friend left us (to return later), Chef Broussard began speaking in fractured English. Though his English was spotty, his communication was greatly enhanced by his huge gestures and ready smile. Chef Broussard seated us himself at his best table in the middle of a handsome dining room lined by sandstone walls. The tables were covered in alabaster tablecloths and set with fine china and crystal.

All the while, Chef was talking nonstop, asking us where we were from, what we liked to eat, what we preferred to drink. While we chatted, he swept around behind me to his wine alcove and popped open the wine cooler. Out came a bottle of white Mouton Rothschild's Aile d'Argent which he handily poured into three glasses—two for us and one for himself! He promptly sat down with us and began chatting as he sipped his wine.

"What is this wine?" I blurted as I squinted to see the label.

"Oh, another Mouton Rothschild," he said casually. "They just popped by yesterday and left me several cases of this. Do you like?" He patted my hand as he asked. Then he winked at my companion—whose hand he also patted!

Did I like???

It tasted like liquid gold. I learned later that Aile d'Argent is the estate white wine produced by Mouton Rothschild; it was devised in the 1990s by none other than Baroness Philippine de Rothschild herself. Until recently, she helmed the fabulous Mouton Rothschild estate; sadly, the popular Baroness passed away in August 2014. By

all reports, her oversight of the winery was remarkable. Among her many accomplishments in the last 20 years, she oversaw the completion of a joint venture in Napa Valley, CA with American vintner Robert Mondavi. Most readers will know this collaboration produced the fabulous Opus One estate. However, *this* white wine tasted like nothing I've ever

imbibed; I can say unequivocally that it's the best white wine I've ever tasted. Unfortunately, it's been very difficult to locate, though I finally found it through a U.S. distributor. It's $88 a bottle for the 2010 release. Absolutely nectar on the tongue. (Wine note: Many retailers carry the low-end Mouton white wine labeled Mouton Cadet which sometimes sells for under $15. This is NOT Aile d'Argent. My husband indelicately calls Mouton Cadet "weasel p_ _s" compared to Aile d'Argent. I will more delicately say it's marginally good for a way-down-the-food-chain Mouton Rothschild wine.)

But back to Chef Broussard and Le Saint-Julien. As he was draining the last of his crisp Mouton Rothschild (and pouring me a bit more), he looked at us and asked, "What would you like for lunch? I will cook anything for you…Oh I forgot. I bought blue lobsters this morning for a party of 20 who are coming at 1 pm. But something inside me said, 'There must be someone else special coming—I must buy two more!' They must be for you!"

I replied that I loved lobster. Chef clapped his hands. Then I looked at my companion who I knew preferred the chef's tasting menu. I deferred to my companion who deferred to the Chef. The Chef seemed even more delighted that we wanted him to choose especially for us. We were only too delighted to place ourselves in his hands.

Before he headed back to the kitchen to prepare the most magnificent series of luncheon courses I've ever had, he suddenly turned back and asked, "Madame, is there anything you would NOT like?"

"Snails," I blurted. "Er, *escargot. Non escargot pour moi, s'il vous plait.*"

"*Non escargot,*" he gasped, as if I'd shot him through the heart. Then he teased me by pretending to swoon.

I frowned while mimicking something crawling along the tablecloth. "*Non, Américains ne mangent pas les escargot.*"

Just then my companion piped up, "She may not want any but I will!"

Chef Broussard beamed again and gave me a pat on my arm, "I will bring you something else. It will be superb *mon amie!*" Then he poured a bit more Aile d'Argent. This was just the beginning of several pours of various wines that the jovial Chef Broussard served us throughout our two-hour meal. All the while he kept saying to me, "You must come into my kitchen when you are done eating. I will show you EVERYTHING!"

Soon began a parade of fabulous dishes starting with my non-snail salmon *amuse bouche* and my companion's snail version. This was followed by perfectly steamed white asparagus the size of hot dogs slathered in hollandaise sauce. Soon after came a course of succulent white fish delicately floating on a sauce of cream and lemon served with another fabulous Graves blanc. Next came the main course:

ultra-tender lamb chops served with a glass of Château Lalande.

By the time the main course was cleared, Chef appeared once more to say again that he would show us everything in the kitchen when we were finished eating. He kept clapping his hands like he was a little boy at a picnic. He then asked which cheeses we would prefer. I looked up at him and thought I was going to pass out. I'd had so much rich food and wine (on top of the two *Grands Crus* tastings I'd already enjoyed that day) that I had to stop for a moment. I placed my hand on the sandstone pillar next to me to steady myself as the ceiling began to spin.

"No, Chef. *Pas de fromage!* I will burst!" I pleaded.

He looked crestfallen. Then, he poured more wine as he hugged my shoulder before scooting off to prepare a tiny cheese course. Moments later, he set it before us and insisted we at least nibble a little *fromage* before going on to the first of *two* desserts!

By now, two hours had passed. We were 15 minutes away from our next *Grands Crus* tasting, and the Chef's friend (our escort) had returned to whisk us away. The two conversed in hellishly fast French—too fast for me to keep up. We had to leave *immédiatement*! But Chef whipped out some coffee and *ganache* truffles to send us on our way. We downed our sweets and our caffeine and rose to dash to our next tasting.

As we left, Chef Broussard said how sad he was we would not have time to see his kitchen. I gave him a pat on his chest and replied, "I'll be back someday, I promise. And I'll stay for lunch AND dinner!" He beamed as we waved goodbye.

With that we left—completely satiated with food, wine, and great memories. I would highly recommend this wonderful restaurant if you visit the Médoc. Hopefully Chef Broussard will be in the same good humor when you visit! Be sure to plan for a delightfully long meal.

Saint-Émilion

I visit the renowned wine center of Saint-Émilion each time I'm in the Bordeaux area. It's a captivating medieval enclave surrounded by wine estates. Overlooking the Dordogne valley, this tiny fortified village about 22 miles to the east of Bordeaux city was built in the Middle Ages in the shape of an amphitheater. Its ancient ramparts, monuments, and stone stairways lead to picturesque squares and narrow streets; they're beautifully luminous in daylight or in twilight shadows. Visitors flock here by the droves—and many of these hordes haven't seen similar villages like Saint-Circ-Lapopie or Cordes-sur-Ciel which are also enchanting hill towns. However, Saint-Émilion has one key distinction: It's surrounded by some of the finest vineyards in the world!

It was an 8th century baker-turned-hermit named Émilion who first made a home here. He scratched out a hermit abode from a limestone grotto in the rocky center of what would later become the bustling town of Saint-Émilion. Vines were growing all around the tiny hamlet even then. Soon, a sprightly town sprang up in the rocky crags. During the 12th century, the town was fortified with ramparts, a moat, numerous gates, a City Keep, and a King's Tower, plus inner ramparts built to strengthen the fortifications from intruders.

The medieval town unfortunately became a pawn in the wars between the French and the English from the 13th century to the 16th century, changing ownership several times. By the end of the 16th century, Saint-Émilion was no longer the prosperous center that it had once been. During the French Revolution, nearly all the residents of the town fled; it remained almost completely unoccupied for the next 100 years. In the mid-1800s, the growth of the wine trade and commerce related to it brought a new prosperity to the hamlet. As the reputation for the wines of Saint Émilion grew, so did travel to the town by traders and tourists.

Now a UNESCO World Heritage Site, Saint-Émilion has been invaded once again—but this time by thirsty tourists and wine connoisseurs. Even the intervening six years between when I first visited and when I came again to Saint-Émilion saw an explosion in shops, wine boutiques, restaurants, hotels, and wine bars. Yes, the ramparts and darling streets and cobbled walkways are still there. But they ring now with the constant thud of high heels and tennis shoes.

The dozens of wine stores will ship their wares anywhere in the world—or simply sell them to you to carry back to your domicile. You can tour Saint-Émilion in half a day—unless of course you do a lot of shopping. Parking is available at the entrance of the town or elsewhere along the border streets—but be ready for some steep streets. You'll ultimately find your way to Place du Marché, the main square that's the heart of the busy town. From there, you can wander up and down the two hills, as well as the offshoot streets filled with shops, wine stores, restaurants, churches, monastery remains, towers, and monuments.

If you grow tired of walking, you can hop onto le Train des Grands Vignobles; this tiny white train will chug you into the vineyards for a very pleasant half hour or so—and then offer you a mini-tasting at one of the local *châteaux*. You'll find a number of fascinating museums and art galleries in the town, including the Musée Souterrain de la Poterie, a series of quarries underground filled with 6,000 pieces of pottery from Roman to contemporary times (wear a sweater against the slight chill).

One of my favorite haunts is the exceptional Maison du Vin de Saint-Émilion (wine museum). I love going to this wine museum, since it has not only fabulous wines for sale at a good price, but it offers interesting displays which teach visitors how to identify specific smells that are characteristics of wines. (Yes, you'll finally be able to put your olfactory acumen to the test here!)

Saint-Émilion is not only famous for wine, but it was the home of the original *macaron* cookie (before filling was added). This golden, delicately almond-flavored cookie was first devised in the year 1620 when Ursuline nuns began baking them. Not colored or sandwiched with filling, this is the original old-style *macaron* without frills. Fabulous with tea, coffee, lunch, ice cream, or, of course, wine (especially for dunking).

You can shop in Saint-Émilion on practically every corner. Boutiques carry tapestries, ceramics, sculpture, artwork, handcrafted jewelry, low- and high-end wines, and liquors. And, if you like, you can even buy Saint-Émilion grape vines to plant in your backyard for your own vineyard.

Accommodations in Saint-Émilion come in all sizes and prices. Start with the high-end hotels like the Relais & Châteaux Hostellerie de Plaisance and Au Logis des Remparts in downtown. Then check out ancient out-of-town abodes like Château Camiac and Château de

Sanse, *chambres d'hôtes* that cater to overnight guests. And for the thrifty, you can even camp in the area or park your *caravane* (trailer). But if you really want to try something unique, you can spend a night or two in a wine barrel. Yes, a wine barrel in the heart of the Saint-Émilion vineyards at Coup 2 Foudres. Here, you've got two quirky "wine cask" bedrooms of 20-square-meter living space (about 215 square feet) to choose from. Each has a large bed, kitchenette, and walk-in shower, plus TV and WiFi. Talk about not needing a designated driver! You can climb into your wine cask and never leave.

I've had high-end hotel experiences at places like Au Logis and the Relais & Châteaux; these were very positive experiences since they were right in town. Au Logis is a listed monument and has 20 air-conditioned rooms with unique character.

One of my favorite *chambres d'hôtes* experiences near Saint-Émilion, however, was at Clos de Bertinat. This former wine estate has pleasant rooms, a sumptuous breakfast, and friendly owners. Owner Claude Samuzeau enjoyed showing us his blooming French garden and hosted absolutely superb breakfasts. His lovely wife even brought us a most elegant coffee service accompanied by French chocolate, Saint-Émilion *macarons*, and candelabra.

There's abundant dining in and around Saint-Émilion. Eateries abound up and down the tiny streets of the town, including street *bistros* or famous wine-tasting venues and dining establishments. Favorites are cozy L'Envers du Décor or quirky Le Bistrot du Clocher where you can nosh for 16.50 euros ($21) as a medieval knight stands guard.

If you desire a gourmand's repast, however, I highly recommend Le Clos du Roy. I especially enjoyed a lovely luncheon at Le Clos du Roy served in their elegant dining room on the second floor. Overall, Saint-Émilion has world-class charm in a medieval setting. It's a great place for toasting with friends.

Cooking Classes

One of my favorite adventures in this Bordeaux region brimming with agricultural delights is taking a cooking class. There are dozens of gourmet cooking and wine courses, events, and packaged courses available in the area. My most recent Saint-Émilion-area cooking

course was arranged by Gourmet Touring.

I'd like to share that cooking day with you here. My little group was first escorted to the small town of Castillon-La-Bataille for market day. In Castillon, we were joined by our chef-for-the-day, Lucie Skipwith. (Lucie and her husband Charlie also run a *chambres d'hôtes* out of their home). Lucie proceeded to shepherd us around the Monday morning market where we busily selected ingredients for our day of "cookery" in her very own French kitchen. (Linguistic note: Americans say "cooking;" Brits say "cookery." When I asked Lucie, who's French, about this war of words she just rolled her eyes. Her husband is British like mine and she's used to walking the bilingual tightrope, too. It does take a sense of humor—and patience—from all of us!)

Meandering around a French farmer's market with a real French chef is an eye-opening experience. Lucie brooked no nonsense from anyone behind a pile of produce. She squeezed. She prodded. She sniffed. And she thumped. Only the best ingredients were selected. As she made her choices, she kindly educated me as to why and how she was choosing certain pieces. Unfortunately, I didn't have my recorder going; I assure you, however, that I got a semester's worth of cooking advice during this one morning's shopping experience.

Lucie was preparing us for a phenomenal French cooking experience. Her ambitious menu for us included:

Artichaut Farci et sa Tranche de Foie Gras (stuffed artichoke with foie gras)

Consommé Aux Fruits de la Mer (seafood consommé)

Turnab de Poisson et Langoustines avec Mousseline d'Épinard

(fish fillets with langoustines and spinach mousse)

Petit Maquereau Grille aux Groseilles (grilled mackerel with gooseberries)

Sautés De Pintade au Vin de Porto (guinea fowl with Port)
Petites Aubergines Farcies (stuffed aubergines)
Gigot D'Agneu en Croûte à La Fleur de Thym
(boned leg of lamb with fresh thyme in pastry)
Cassis Au Coulis de Framboises (black currant mousse with raspberry sauce)
Sorbet Dans Leur Petite Tasse en Chocolat avec sa Terrine d'Oranges
(chocolate cups with sorbets and an orange terrine)

Yes, we really did cook all of this. And Madame Lucie did it all in her teeny French kitchen wearing high heels and a dress! (She did pull on a green apron covered in leaping frogs, and she clipped her hair up.

Other than that, she was a force of nature in high heels!)

Building everything from scratch, using exactly what we'd purchased for the day PLUS fresh vegetables and herbs from her very own garden, Lucie guided us through what would become a six-hour day of cooking. I confess I had to sit down several times with a cup of coffee to keep going; Madame Lucie never sat down, however—and she's got at least 10 years on me! Here's a photo of Lucy teaching me how to stuff artichokes with *foie gras.*

Around 7 pm, the six of us (two couples and Lucy and her husband Charlie) all sat down to this magnificent feast in her French dining room. We must have eaten for three hours! Suffice it to say, Madame Lucie was magnificent. I can also share that this was yet another French gastronomic experience I waddled home from AND had the aching feet to show for it. But I would do it again in a heartbeat!

Bordeaux Area in Sum

The Bordeaux region is overflowing with the delights of fine wine, fabulous cuisine, remarkable history, enchanting terrain, and heavenly shopping. If you visit here, plan on at least a week. Even then, it will take you many visits to sample all of its pleasures.

I will say this. If I had to choose a month to stay anywhere in France, it would be here. I say this because Bordeaux has access to nearly everything you could ever desire in France. You can reach Paris by train before lunch. You can scoot down to Spain in a few hours. You can drive or train ride out to the historical Dordogne or Languedoc and see the mighty Carcassonne or the fabulous medieval hill towns of Rocamadour and Périgeux—and be back to Bordeaux the next day or the day after.

Here, in beautiful Bordeaux, you can enjoy the twin delights of modern convenience and ancient history right outside your window. You can sip some of the world's most coveted wine. You can feast on the recipes of Southwestern France enhanced by *haute cuisine* touches. You can savor the beauty of classical France—while you behold the latest in high-tech jets flying overhead.

The past, present, and future are all rolled into one here. Bordeaux, to me, has everything that's beautiful about Southern France. In one place, in one region, with good climate, fine accessibility, and warm, friendly people. If you're lucky enough to go there, it will lift your spirits, educate your palette, and delight your senses. Lastly, I'd like to quote the *Bordeaux Michelin Guide* on why this is such an enchanting area:

"The ancient name of Aquitaine evokes many images; the forests of the Landes and ocean beaches; the wines of Bordeaux and *poule au pot*; Gascon musketeers and bronzed surfers; shepherds in their cloaks in lost valleys; bourgeois bohemians or 'bobos' in espadrilles on the Arcachon Bay; the proud profile of twice-queen Eleanor; the gravelly lyricism of rock band Noir Désir; and the confusing and unique sounds of the Basque language. However hackneyed they might seem, such clichés do express the diversity of this vast territory…If, to sum them all up we had to retain a single image, it would doubtless be that of a certain gentle way of life and a tranquil vitality."

Conclusion

We've come now to the end of our journey through extraordinary Southern France. As you've seen, it's a vast region of varying terrain, differing cultures, region-specific tastes, and unique offerings depending on local values and traditions.

We've roamed the Mediterranean coastline on the Riviera, fueled by the champagne lifestyle of the Cote d'Azur and the sparkling sunshine that inspires genius. We've traveled Provence, enjoying the charms of Provence's delightful cuisine, rosé wines, and traditional values. We've traversed the mighty Languedoc, home to Roman ruins, Carcassonne splendor, and vast tracks of vineyards that grow even as chemtrails fall to earth from jets in the Toulouse sky.

We've meandered with the Dordogne, alongside medieval castles and ecclesiastical enclaves, traversing the hot-air balloon skies and spelunking the prehistoric underground caves, all the while enjoying delectable *foie gras* and Cahors wines. And finally, we've toured beautiful Bordeaux, ripe with world-class wines and steeped in a majestic history that has, in fact, shaped all of France.

It has been a delicious, aromatic, adventurous, magical, and thought-provoking journey. Thank you for taking it with me. If you would like more information about our travels or to see more color photographs of this extraordinary journey, please go to www.meanderingtrailmedia.com or follow us on Twitter @PJAdams10.

Acknowledgments

I'd like to thank a number of individuals who assisted me in writing this book. Among them are Patricia McBain and Hela Soula for their insights on Bordeaux; Tom Leech for his book smarts and mentoring; Peggy and Tom Sullivan for their support when I was flagging; Ashley Regan for her portraiture and willingness to travel with me; Shaun Griffen for her book savvy and editorial wit; Andrea Glass for making sure I dotted each and every "i" and "t" in her always professional style; Rachal Cox for her superb design; Paul Shawcross, journalist, professional photographer, and app designer extraordinaire; and finally, John Birkhead for his keen photography and travel *joie de vivre*.

About the Author

P J Adams is a practicing family therapist, best-selling-author, and former publishing executive working in Southern California. Her previous books include *Intoxicating Paris: Uncorking the Parisian Within*, the self-help book *Daughter Wisdom*, and the psychological thriller *Freud's Revenge*. She enjoys writing, travel, learning French, and discovering new people and places. For more information go to: www.meanderingtrailmedia.com.

44794318R00162

Made in the USA
Lexington, KY
09 September 2015